THE ROUGH GUIDE TO

YOSEMITE

NATIONAL PARK

Forthcoming travel guides include

The Algarve • The Bahamas • Cambodia
Caribbean Islands • Costa Brava
New York Restaurants • Rocky Mountains • Zanzibar

Forthcoming reference guides include

Children's Books • Chronicles: China, England,
India, France • Online Travel • Weather

Rough Guides online

www.roughguides.com

Rough Guide Credits

Text editor: Julie Feiner
Series editor: Mark Ellingham
Production: Rachel Holmes
Cartography: Maxine Repath,
Katie Lloyd-Jones and Ed Wright

Publishing Information

This first edition published May 2002
by Rough Guides Ltd,
62–70 Shorts Gardens, London WC2H 9AH

Distributed by the Penguin Group:

Penguin Books Ltd, 80 Strand, London WC2R ORL
Penguin Putnam, Inc., 375 Hudson Street, New York 10014, USA
Penguin Books Australia Ltd, 487 Maroondah Highway,
PO Box 257, Ringwood, Victoria 3134, Australia
Penguin Books Canada Ltd, 10 Alcorn Avenue,
Toronto, Ontario, Canada M4V 1E4
Penguin Books (NZ) Ltd,
182–190 Wairau Road, Auckland 10, New Zealand

Typeset in Bembo and Helvetica to an original design by Henry Iles.
Printed in Spain by Graphy Cems.

© Rough Guides 2002 288pp, includes index
A catalogue record for this book is available from the British Library.

ISBN 1-85828-886-X

THE ROUGH GUIDE TO

YOSEMITE
NATIONAL PARK

by Paul Whitfield

ROUGH
GUIDES

We set out to do something different when the first Rough Guide was published in 1982. Mark Ellingham, just out of university, was traveling in Greece. He brought along the popular guides of the day, but found they were all lacking in some way. They were either strong on ruins and museums but went on for pages without mentioning a beach or taverna. Or they were so conscious of the need to save money that they lost sight of Greece's cultural and historical significance. Also, none of the books told him anything about Greece's contemporary life – its politics, its culture, its people, and how they lived.

So with no job in prospect, Mark decided to write his own guidebook, one which aimed to provide practical information that was second to none, detailing the best beaches and the hottest clubs and restaurants, while also giving hard-hitting accounts of every sight, both famous and obscure, and providing up-to-the-minute information on contemporary culture. It was a guide that encouraged independent travelers to find the best of Greece, and was a great success, getting shortlisted for the Thomas Cook travel guide award, and encouraging Mark, along with three friends, to expand the series.

The Rough Guide list grew rapidly and the letters flooded in, indicating a much broader readership than had been anticipated, but one which uniformly appreciated the Rough Guide mix of practical detail and humor, irreverence and enthusiasm. Things haven't changed. The same four friends who began the series are still the caretakers of the Rough Guide mission today: to provide the most reliable, up-to-date and entertaining information to independent-minded travelers of all ages, on all budgets.

We now publish more than 200 titles and have offices in London and New York. The travel guides are written and researched by a dedicated team of more than 100 authors, based in Britain, Europe, the USA, and Australia. We have also created a unique series of phrasebooks to accompany the travel series, along with an acclaimed series of music guides, and a best-selling pocket guide to the Internet and World Wide Web. We also publish comprehensive travel information on our website: **www.roughguides.com**

Help us update

We've gone to a lot of trouble to ensure that this Rough Guide is as up to date and accurate as possible. However, things do change and all suggestions, comments, and corrections are much appreciated, and we'll send a copy of the next edition (or any other Rough Guide if you prefer) for the best letters.

Please mark letters "**Rough Guide Yosemite Update**" and send to:

Rough Guides, 62–70 Shorts Gardens, London WC2H 9AH, or Rough Guides, 4th Floor, 345 Hudson St, New York, NY 10014.

Or send email to: mail@roughguides.co.uk
Online updates about this book can be found on Rough Guides' website (see opposite)

Acknowledgments

Thanks go to all those who contributed to this book in any way; sharing hikes and barroom tales, voicing opinions, and helping out with logistics. In particular I'd like to thank Colin Megson who joined me for several weeks exploring the Yosemite backcountry, and Sophie Drieu who shared in some of this. In the park I'd like to thank the Park Service's Johanna Lombard, Karen Hayes from YCS, Nikyra Calcagno from the wilderness center, and Kimberly Cunningham-Summerfield at the visitor center.

A big thank you, too, to the folks at Rough Guides in New York: Martin Dunford for proposing the book in the first place; Andrew Rosenberg for overseeing its various stages; Stephen Timblin for shaping the project early on, and last-minute editing; and particularly Julie Feiner who picked up the reins and guided the book to the last through long days and lost weekends. Also to the Rough Guiders in London for their excellent work: Maxine Repath, Katie-Lloyd Jones, and Ed Wright for the maps; Julia Bovis for general production; Rachel Holmes for typesetting; Michelle Draycott for picture research; Louise Boulton for the cover; Sharon Martins for the color insert; and Russell Walton for proofreading.

Lastly, thanks to Irene Gardiner, who bore with my long absences in Yosemite and sequestered in my study, and was always there to offer advice and support.

CONTENTS

MAP LIST

Map Symbols

▬ ▪ ▪	State boundary	▲	Peak
▬▬	Yosemite National Park boundary	↘	Viewpoint
🛣50	Interstate	⚚	Waterfall
50	US highway	⩟	Spring
41	State highway	⛷	Ski area
⋯⋯⋯	Limited-access road	◉	Accommodation
▬▬	Other road	⛺	Road-accessible campground
H22	Recommended hiking trail	▲	Backcountry campground
⋯⋯⋯	Other trail	✝	Chapel
▬▬	River	✉	Post office
♦	Point of interest	🅃	Toilets
■	Building	★	Shuttle bus stop
♦	Park entrance	🅟	Parking
🏠	Ranger station	⛽	Gas station
ⓘ	Information office	⛳	Golf course
✈	Airport	⬥	Sequoia grove

Introduction

No temple made with hands can compare with the Yosemite. Every rock in its walls seems to glow with life. Some lean back in majestic repose; others, absolutely sheer or nearly so for thousands of feet, advance beyond their companions in thoughtful attitudes, giving welcome to storms and calms alike, seemingly aware, yet heedless, of everything going on about them.

John Muir, *The Yosemite*

More gushing adjectives have been thrown at **YOSEMITE NATIONAL PARK** than at any other part of California. But however excessive the hyperbole may seem, once you've seen the Park's stunning scenery with your own eyes you realize all this praise is actually an understatement.

Simply put, **Yosemite Valley** – only a small part of the park but the one at which most of the verbiage is aimed – is one of the most dramatic pieces of geology found anywhere in the world. Just seven miles long and one mile across at its widest point, the Valley is walled by near-vertical, three-thousand-foot cliffs whose sides are streaked by cascading waterfalls and whose tops, a variety of domes and pinnacles, form a jagged silhouette against the sky. This is where you'll find some of the world's most famous

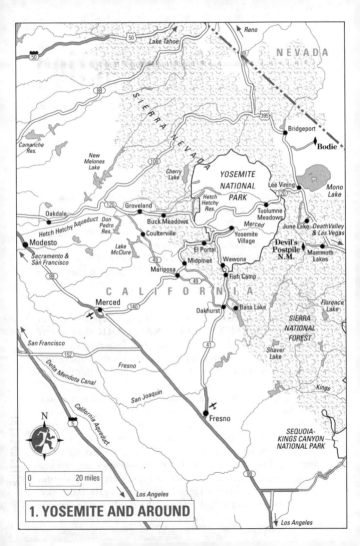

1. YOSEMITE AND AROUND

rocks – Half Dome and rock climbing's holy grail, El Capitan – as well as America's tallest waterfalls, with Yosemite Falls topping the lot. At ground level, too, the sights can be staggeringly impressive. Grassy meadows are framed by oak, cedar, maple, and pine trees, and are home to a variety of wildflowers and wildlife.

Elsewhere in the Park, the crisp alpine setting of **Tuolumne Meadows** (pronounced Too-ol-uh-me), perched close to Yosemite's highest mountains on the Park's eastern border at 8600 feet, offers nature at its most peaceful and elemental. Here you've got easy access to the completely wild backcountry beyond, especially into the **Cathedral Range**, a place much favored by Yosemite's environmental champion, **John Muir**, who was the first to scale the dramatically pointed **Cathedral Peak**.

As if that weren't enough, the spectacle continues, from the glaciated canyons up in the north of the Park, all the way down to the southern reaches near Wawona, where **Mariposa Grove** encompasses one of the most awe-inspiring forests of **giant sequoias** found anywhere.

All of this wondrous scenery is within half a day's drive of

INTRODUCTION

San Francisco and not much further from Los Angeles, so it is understandable that tourists are plentiful. Each year Yosemite has to cope with over three and a half million visitors, most of them intent on visiting Yosemite Valley, which in July and August (and any summer weekend) can get fairly packed. That said, the whole Park is massive enough to endure the crowds, and even places you can get to by car remain relatively serene most of the time.

Because of its size and sheer diversity of landscape, Yosemite National Park can be experienced on a variety of levels: many people just spend a day here doing a quick circuit of the top attractions, either by car or on one of the tours, and walking to the base of Yosemite and Bridalveil falls; others delve deeper over several days; and more than a few return frequently during their lifetime to photograph, explore, observe the wildlife, or just soak up the atmosphere.

GETTING THE BEST OUT OF A SHORT VISIT

With so much to see and do in the Park it's hard to pick favorites; what follows is a brief list of some of the most popular and worthwhile sights and activities.

With **half a day** to play with, aim for the Valley and stroll to the base of Lower Yosemite Falls, hike some or all of the Mist Trail to Vernal Fall, and gaze up at El Capitan from El Cap Meadow.

If you have a **full day**, you could also walk to Mirror Lake, visit the Yosemite Museum and Indian Village, and, if driving, admire the late-afternoon views from Tunnel View on Wawona Road then continue to Glacier Point for sunset and the stars after dark.

On a **two- or three-day** visit, in addition to the above, hike either the Four-Mile Trail, Half Dome Trail, or Upper Yosemite Fall Trail, and make side trips to Tuolumne Meadows and Mariposa Grove near Wawona.

Whatever your interests, be sure to spend some time **hiking**, even if it's just around the Valley floor on one of the nearly-flat, paved trails. If you're willing to hike a few miles and perhaps camp out overnight, you can experience the 99 percent of Yosemite that's untouched by road. It's in this backcountry, too, that the best **wildlife viewing** opportunities occur, but even in the most populous areas it is possible to see deer, coyotes, and even black bears.

When to go

You can visit the Park at any time of year, even in winter when the waterfalls turn to ice and the trails are blocked by snow. Unless you are here for winter activities, choosing the best time to come to Yosemite depends mostly on whether you're here for hiking or viewing waterfalls. Summer is generally dry with occasional thunderstorms; spring and fall are more variable, with Valley temperatures peaking in the seventies. Winter means snow but often with sunny days and highs up into the fifties.

May and June are fairly popular months, particularly in Yosemite Valley where the waterfalls are the big draw. While lowland snows should have melted by this time, throughout May and early June the high country is likely to be off-limits with both Glacier Point Road and Tioga Road still closed by snow. The Park is at its busiest in **July and August** when daytime temperatures in Yosemite Valley and Wawona are regularly in the eighties and nineties, and the rivers and lakes are (just about) warm enough for swimming. This is a good time for hiking since almost all the high-country snow has melted. If you don't mind missing most of the waterfalls, **September and October** are excellent months to visit, with smaller crowds, most Park facilities still in operation, and plenty of hiking in cooler weather and on dry ground. In October, the Valley

CLIMATE CHART			
	PRECIPITATION (INCHES)	MAX (°F)	MIN (°F)
Jan	6.2	49	26
Feb	6.1	55	28
March	5.2	59	31
April	3.0	65	35
May	1.3	73	42
June	0.7	82	48
July	0.4	90	53
Aug	0.3	90	53
Sept	0.9	87	47
Oct	2.1	74	39
Nov	5.5	58	31
Dec	5.6	48	26

and Wawona both put on a decent show of fall colors. **November** is more marginal, with snow storms likely and the high-country roads usually closing early in the month. **December through March** witness cross-country skiing and skating in full swing; tire chains are generally required. By **April**, Wawona and the Valley may well be free of snow, but late storms are not uncommon. With a few lowland exceptions, April is too early for much hiking.

Traveling **outside peak summer** season also offers rewards, with rooms easier to come by and prices markedly lower. Even in winter you can stay in budget tent cabins fitted with heating stoves, and low-country campgrounds remain open.

What to take

Hikers, of course, have special needs (see on p.97), but all visitors should dress in **layers** to be able to peel off or add on clothing as conditions dictate. Sunblock, a hat, and insect repellent are pretty much essential, as is a **flashlight**, since even in Yosemite Valley artificial lighting is kept to a minimum. Shops in Wawona, Tuolumne Meadows, and especially the Valley, stock most things you're likely to need.

Costs

Prices for accommodation, restaurants, tours, and incidentals are fairly high in Yosemite, and those on a brief visit might balk at the $20 entrance fee (though if you arrive by bus, you don't have to pay it). Outside the Park, costs are much the same as you might expect in rural California, though accommodation is still on the pricey side, especially in the peak summer months. In contrast, much of what you'll be doing in Yosemite is **free**. Scenery costs nothing, and many of the most picturesque spots in the Valley are accessible by the free shuttle bus. If you are tackling overnight hikes (for which permits are free) then you can camp in the backcountry for no charge. In addition, the Park Service runs numerous free ranger programs, and much of the evening entertainment comes gratis as well. In winter there's even a complimentary shuttle bus connecting the Valley with the Badger Pass ski area.

THE GUIDE

THE GUIDE

Introducing Yosemite

A t 1169 square miles, Yosemite National Park is about the size of Rhode Island, an irregular oval roughly fifty miles from north to south and almost forty miles east to west. The Park generally slopes upwards from the western foothills at around 2000ft, through the "high country" between 7000ft and 10,000ft, to the eastern boundary at the crest of the Sierra Nevada topped by 13,114ft Mount Lyell. Over 94 percent of Yosemite National Park has been designated as wilderness, land that is off-limits for virtually all commercial activity and only really accessible to hikers using the eight hundred miles of trails which provide access to almost every corner of the Park.

The greatest concentration of sights is in **Yosemite Valley**, a little southeast of the Park's geographic center and very much its dynamic heart. Here you'll find nearly all of the Park's roofed accommodation and restaurants, and more than half its campsites. The Valley is also the hub for hikers' and tour buses that provide access to the rest of the Park.

We've given the area north of the Valley the rough designation **northern Yosemite**, where the big draw is

Tuolumne Meadows, a name given to both a small collection of visitor facilities and the open high-alpine flatlands that surround them. To the west lies **Hetch Hetchy**, something of an outlier, good for tranquil moments among the wildflowers and spring waterfalls.

Stunning views abound throughout Yosemite, but the best of all is in **southern Yosemite**, where a winding road threads its way to breathtaking Glacier Point, on the south rim high above the Valley floor. The southern section of the Park also harbors **Mariposa Grove**, the largest of Yosemite's groves of **giant sequoias**, easily accessed from **Wawona**, a small and fairly relaxed lowland settlement with its own golf course and museum.

Getting to Yosemite

Most people **drive** to Yosemite, which is not surprising considering the Park's well-maintained access roads and some two hundred miles of highway within its boundaries. For much of the year driving in is fine, but you can expect traffic congestion in Yosemite Valley on summer weekends. To circumvent this, drivers are strongly encouraged to leave their cars in nearby towns and then enter Yosemite by **bus**. Most local buses leave from the transport nexus of Merced – eighty miles southwest of Yosemite Valley – which is accessible from further afield using Amtrak **trains** and Greyhound buses. A couple of companies also run direct scheduled bus services and **tours** to Yosemite from San Francisco.

If you **fly**, no matter which of the area's airports you choose, you'll be at a considerable distance from the Park when you arrive.

BY AIR

The nearest major **international airports** to Yosemite are San Francisco International and Los Angeles' LAX, both of which are served by all the major car rental agencies. Using a sequence of buses and trains it is possible to get from either to the Park. **Merced Airport** is the closest airport with regional flights; Skywest flies here from LAX two or three times a day on behalf of United Express. The local YARTS bus service can take you direct from the airport to Yosemite.

The only other airport worth considering is **Fresno**, 95 miles south of Yosemite Valley, which has connections from several regional centers throughout the West. There is no public transportation from here to Yosemite, but car rental is available.

BY CAR

Driving to Yosemite is straightforward, and despite a good deal of recent scaremongering you can still enter the Park in your own vehicle. Of the Park's four entrances, three are from the west and one traverses the Sierra Nevada from the east. The three western approaches are generally open all year (except immediately after snowfall), but the eastern approach (Hwy-120 E) over the Tioga Pass is closed all winter (see "Tioga Road closures" box overleaf). The Park is around 200 miles from San Francisco (just under 4hr), 310 miles from Los Angeles (6hr) and 340 miles from Las Vegas (8hr).

The quickest, most direct route to Yosemite Valley from the west is **Hwy-140**, which runs from Merced through

TIOGA ROAD CLOSURES AND WINTER DRIVING CONDITIONS

For over half the year, the 10,000-foot **Tioga Road** is **closed by snow**. It usually shuts by mid-November and typically reopens again between mid-May and mid-June; for snow conditions and road closures call ☎ 209/372-0200 or consult ⓦ www.nps.gov/yose/now/conditions.

All vehicles entering the Park are required to carry **tire chains** whenever chain controls are in effect, usually from November to April. Rangers probably won't stop you, but the highway patrol occasionally checks compliance. Chains can be rented for around $25 a week from local service stations and auto shops; you might want to shop around as prices vary. It may be more convenient to buy chains rather than have to deal with returning them to the rental place; a basic set costs around $50 from the same outlets. Within the Park there are no chain rental facilities, but they are for sale in stores at inflated prices.

In snowy conditions, signs indicate **restriction levels** on open roads; R1: snow tires or chains; R2: 4WD or chains; R3: chains on all vehicles. Anyone not used to fitting chains should practice beforehand.

With no significant hills, Hwy-140 often stays open when other roads are snowed in, and it is always the first to be plowed. Hwy-120 is the route most likely to have tire-chain restrictions after snowfall.

the small towns of Mariposa, Midpines and El Portal to the Arch Rock Entrance. **Hwy-120 W**, through Groveland, is a slightly shorter but slower route from Stockton and the Bay Area, providing immediate access to Hetch Hetchy. From southern California, **Hwy-41** can be picked up at Fresno, 64 miles south of the Park. Broad and fast as far as Oakhurst, it becomes two narrow twisting lanes for the remaining eighteen miles to the Park's South Entrance, which is close to Wawona and Mariposa Grove.

Hwy-120 E (**Tioga Rd**), which branches off from US-395 close to Lee Vining, climbs steeply out of the Owens Valley, over Tioga Pass, and through Tuolumne Meadows before descending to Yosemite Valley.

For car rental options, see "Directory" on p.213.

BY TRAIN

There is **no direct train service** to Yosemite, though it is possible to get there by combining Amtrak (☎1-800/872-7245, ⓦwww.amtrak.com) and bus services. The nearest train station is in Merced, where several services a day are met by VIA and YARTS buses running straight to Yosemite Valley. You could conceivably visit Yosemite in one long day from San Francisco, but you would only have around three hours in the Park.

The most convenient combination is from San Francisco, where two Amtrak buses (6.55am & 12.30pm) daily connect with trains across the Bay at Emeryville, arriving at Merced (10.28am & 4.05pm) in time to connect with VIA and YARTS buses making the three-hour run to Yosemite Valley.

From Southern California, buses leave Los Angeles' Union Station (1.35am & 10.25am) and connect with trains at Bakersfield, which arrive in Merced (7.45am & 3.47pm) where they meet VIA buses.

Fares are lower if booked a few days in advance. Round-trip to Merced from San Francisco is roughly $56, and about $60 from Los Angeles. Amtrak does sell tickets all the way to Yosemite, but it usually works out cheaper to purchase a ticket to Merced then buy a separate YARTS or VIA ticket to the Park.

GETTING TO YOSEMITE

BY BUS

Bus is the only form of public transportation that will get you right into Yosemite National Park, with year-round scheduled Greyhound services to Merced where you can catch the local VIA or YARTS services to Yosemite. In addition there are YARTS buses into Yosemite from a couple of other gateway towns. Arriving by bus saves you having to pay Park entrance fees.

TOURS AND GUIDED TRIPS TO YOSEMITE

Generally speaking, anything called a sightseeing tour that begins outside the Park involves an unsatisfying race through the Valley. Three organizations buck this trend with niche packages: Green Tortoise and Incredible Adventures offer alternative bus trips for the young in spirit, and the Yosemite Association leads educational field seminars. To read about tours that begin inside the Park, see p.20.

Gray Line's VIA Adventures (ⓣ1-888/727-5287, ⓕ209/384-7441, ⓦwww.via-adventures.com) runs mainstream sightseeing packages. The Merced-based company has a **one-day tour** ($63, kids $45) which takes you on the Valley Floor Tour (see p.21); the **overnight** option (from $150 per person) also offers one or more nights at *Yosemite Lodge*, *Yosemite View Lodge*, or *Cedar Lodge*.

Green Tortoise (ⓣ1-800/867-8647 or 415/956-7500, ⓦwww.greentortoise.com) tours in converted "communal" buses from San Francisco are geared towards active, outdoorsy types who enjoy camping out and pitching-in. Their **weekend trip** (mid-April to mid-Sept; departs 9pm Fri returns

Greyhound

Greyhound (☎ 1-800/229-9424, ⓦ www.greyhound.com) runs buses from all over California to Merced. Slightly cheaper than the train, they're a little slower and less convenient, with few services that directly connect with VIA or YARTS buses. From San Francisco there are at least half a dozen departures daily (4hr), with a similar number from Los Angeles (6-8hr), all calling at various towns along the

7am Mon; $99, plus $31 food fund) heads to the Valley and Mariposa Grove; a slightly more expensive **three-day trip** also allows half a day in Tuolumne Meadows and time around nearby Mono Lake and some hot springs.

Incredible Adventures (☎ 1-800/777-8464 or 415/642-7378, ⓕ 642-7379, ⓦ www.incadventures.com) offers enjoyable minibus tours from San Francisco to Yosemite. The **one-day trip** ($85; 7am–9pm; departs Tues, Thurs & Sat) includes a quick jaunt around the main Yosemite Valley sights and three hours to explore and hike. The more satisfying **three-day camping-based tour** ($185 including most meals; departs Sun & Wed afternoon) includes high-country hiking around Tuolumne and visiting the sequoias.

Yosemite Field Seminars, Yosemite Association, PO Box 230, El Portal, CA 95318 (☎ 209/379-2321, ⓕ 379-2486, ⓦ www.yosemite.org). The Yosemite Association runs small-group "field seminars" from February to October, usually lasting 2–4 days ($200–300) and covering topics such as natural history, birding, hiking, photography and drawing; check their website for a full listing.

way. **Fares** are lowest if booked a few days in advance. Generally you can get a round-trip ticket from San Francisco for about $50; from LA the fare is closer to $60.

YARTS and VIA Yosemite Connection

The Park Service and local authorities set up the Yosemite Area Regional Transportation System, or YARTS, (☎1-877/989-2787 or 209/388-9589, ⓦwww.yarts.com) as a way of encouraging people to leave their vehicles outside the Park. While the service is excellent and quite cheap along the main corridor from Merced, with less frequent buses serving Groveland and Lee Vining, there is no service from Oakhurst or Wawona to the Valley.

The most useful route is along **Hwy-140** from **Merced** through **Mariposa**, **Midpines** and **El Portal** into the Valley. It is run by VIA Yosemite Connection (☎1-888/727-5287 or 209/384-1315, ⓦwww.via-adventures.com) with YARTS and VIA operating on a joint timetable and with identical **fares** – round-trip to Yosemite from Merced is $20, from Mariposa and Midpines $10, and from El Portal just $7. There are always convenient connections to Amtrak trains at Merced, and some buses are timed to coincide with the start of guided tours (see p.20) within the Park. **Timetables** are available on the YARTS website and from visitor centers in the area. There are four departures daily picking up at both the Merced Transpo Center and the Amtrak station and arriving (after brief stops en route at all towns and significant accommodation) in the Valley almost three hours later. They usually drop off at Curry Village and Yosemite Village before the final stop at *Yosemite Lodge*. **Tickets** can be bought on board.

From the **northwest**, YARTS runs a summer-only service on Saturdays and Sundays to and from the Valley, connecting Groveland (9am inbound; 7.25pm outbound; $10 round trip) and Buck Meadows (9.35am; 6.50pm; $8) with the Park's Big Oak Flat Entrance (9.55am; 6.30pm; $6), Crane Flat (10.10am; 6.15pm; $4) and the Yosemite Valley Visitor Center (10.40am; 5.40pm) before continuing on to Valley accommodation areas. Passengers should buy **tickets** locally before arriving at the bus stop. Ticket vending establishments are listed on the YARTS website.

Lastly, from the **eastern Sierra**, YARTS operates a summer-only service to and from the Valley (June and Sept weekends, July & Aug daily). The service connects the *Mammoth Mountain Inn* in **Mammoth Lakes** (7am inbound; 8.50pm outbound; $20 round trip) with the **Lee Vining** *Best Western* (8.10am; 7.40pm; $20), Tuolumne Meadows Store (9am; 6.50pm; $20), Crane Flat (10.20am; 5.30pm; $5), and the Yosemite Valley Visitor Center (10.50am; 5pm). Passengers should buy **tickets** locally.

Arrival, information and maps

Yosemite is always open. **Park entry** – valid for seven days – costs $20 per vehicle (includes all passengers), and $10 for cyclists and hikers. Passengers arriving by bus don't have to pay entry fees, and there are a variety of savings with a number of annual passes (see box overleaf). Pay at the entrance stations as you drive in, or if they're closed, at the Valley visitor center or when you leave.

PARK PASSES

As well as the standard Park entry tickets, you can also buy a **Yosemite Pass** ($40) which allows entry to Yosemite for a year. If your visit is part of wider travels it may be worth investing in the **National Parks Pass** ($50), valid for entry to all US national parks for one year from the date of purchase, or the **Golden Eagle Pass** ($65), valid for a year at all federal fee areas (national parks, national forests, national historic areas, etc). In addition, unlimited access to all national parks is available to US citizens and residents 62 and over who buy the **Golden Age Passport** ($10), and US citizens and residents with permanent disabilities who obtain the **Golden Access Passport** (free). Both passports also give a fifty percent discount on camping fees in national parks.

INFORMATION

On entering the Park, you'll be provided with a free copy of the summer/fall or winter/spring issue of the *Yosemite Guide* newspaper and the current *Yosemite Today* listings insert, both of which are also available from visitor centers. Packed with the latest Park information, including activities and events, they're invaluable, especially when used in conjunction with the free and widely available *Yosemite Magazine* put out annually by Yosemite Concession Services.

General queries about the Park are best directed to the **visitor centers**; those specifically pertaining to hiking are handled by the **wilderness centers**.

For details about banks, postal services, internet access and a whole lot more, see "Directory" on p.212–216.

Visitor centers

At the main **Yosemite Valley visitor center** in Yosemite Village (Map 4, E2; daily: June–Sept 8am–6pm; Oct–May 8am–5pm; ☎209/372-0299; Shuttle stops 5 and 9), you can pick up information and maps, study the latest weather forecast, learn about the ranger programs for that week, and see a number of displays and videos (for further coverage see p.34). The staff here are helpful but often have their hands full.

The three visitor centers outside the Valley are usually less crowded, and therefore better sources of information. The **Information Station** at the **Big Oak Flat Entrance** on Hwy-120 W (see p.53), the **Wawona Information Station** (see p.76), and the **Tuolumne Meadows Visitor Center** (see p.64) all offer similar information to the Valley visitor center and sell books, maps and gifts.

Most of the gateway towns have a visitor center; see the relevant accounts in Chapter 5 for details.

Wilderness centers and ranger stations

While visitor center staff field basic questions about hiking in Yosemite, anyone planning serious treks and overnight backcountry camping trips should direct their inquiries to one of the **wilderness centers**. In addition to issuing wilderness permits and providing information about route planning and backcountry etiquette, they also sell maps and guidebooks, and rent bear-resistant food canisters.

The foremost source of backcountry information is the **Yosemite Valley wilderness center** in Yosemite Village (Map 4, F2; daily: mid-June to Aug 7am–6pm; April to mid-June & Sept to late Oct 8am–5pm, closed in winter;

ARRIVAL, INFORMATION AND MAPS

Ⓣ209/372-0745). In the high country, head for the **Tuolumne Meadows wilderness center**, near Tuolumne Lodge (daily: mid-June to early Sept 7am–6pm; early Sept to mid–Oct 8am–5pm; Ⓣ209/372 0740).

Wilderness permits and more localized information are available from the **ranger stations** inside the **Wawona Information Station** (Thurs–Sun 8.30am–noon & 1–4pm; self-register when closed) and at the **Hetch Hetchy Entrance Station** (mid-April to mid-Oct daily 8am–5pm or later), as well as from the wilderness permit

USEFUL CONTACTS AND WEBSITES

Park resources and reservations

National Park Reservation Service (NPRS) PO Box 1600, Cumberland, MD 21502. Within North America Ⓣ1-800/436-7275, TDD Ⓣ1-888/530-9796; outside North America Ⓣ301/722-1257; Ⓦ reservations.nps.org. Advance campground reservations can be made by mail, on the website, or by phone between 7am and 7pm PST.

Yosemite Concession Services (YCS) 5410 East Home, Fresno, CA 93727; Lodging reservations Ⓣ559/252-4848, TDD Ⓣ559/255-8345; Tour reservations Ⓣ209/372-1240; Ski conditions (Badger Pass) Ⓣ209/372-1000; Ⓦwww.yosemitepark .com. YCS runs virtually all Park lodging, restaurants, tours, activities, and shuttle buses. Reservations can be made up to a year and a day in advance, Mon–Fri 7am–7pm, Sat & Sun 8am–5pm PST.

Yosemite National Park Ⓣ209/372-0200 or TDD Ⓣ209/372-4726 (24-hour hotline), Ⓦwww.nps.gov/yose. Detailed Park Service website and recorded Park information covering just about everything you'll need to know, including weather and

window at the **Big Oak Flat Information Station** (April to mid-Oct daily 8am–5pm; ⊕ 209/379-1967).

Maps

On arrival at any of the Park entrances you'll be given an excellent **map** of the Park, which will satisfy most navigational needs, especially when used along with the maps at the back of this book. For more details of specific areas, consider buying one of the green-and-white concertina-

---

road conditions. A human operator is also available Mon–Fri 9am–noon and 1–5pm PST.

Wilderness Permits and Information Wilderness Permits, PO Box 545, Yosemite, CA 95389 ⊕ 209/372-0740, ⓦ www.nps.gov/yose/wilderness. Park Service contact for obtaining wilderness permits required for overnight stays in the backcountry.

Other sites and organizations

Sierra Club Sierra Club Public Affairs, 85 2nd St, San Francisco, CA 94109. ⊕ 415/977-5500, ⓦ www.sierraclub.org. An outdoor recreation and conservation group founded by John Muir in 1892 and still active on Yosemite-related issues.

Virtual Yosemite ⓦ www.yosemitepark.net/. General resource with FAQs, message board, web cams, links to vacation homes, bookstores and much more.

YosemiteFun.com ⓦ www.yosemitefun.com. One man's comprehensive and irreverent site, with everything from great photos to discussion of local politics.

folded maps published in cooperation with the Yosemite Association, which use an angled projection to clearly show the rock formations and key features. These cover all the main areas – *Yosemite Valley* ($2.50), *Tuolumne Meadows* ($2.50), and *Wawona & the Mariposa Grove* ($2.95) – and are available in almost every shop and hotel in the Park.

Anyone headed into the backcountry should obtain a **topographic map**, the best being the double-sided 1:100,000 *National Geographic Trails Illustrated Yosemite National Park* map (#206; $9) available from visitor centers, which marks trail distances and indicates areas where camping and open fires are prohibited. Keen **hikers**, especially those planning to go off-trail, will want to use detailed USGS "quad" maps ($4), each covering an area roughly eight miles by six miles at a scale of 1:24,000. These are available from stores, ranger stations and visitor centers around the Park, or directly from USGS, Box 25286, Federal Center, Denver, CO 80225 (☏1-888/275-8747, ⓦmapping.usgs.gov).

Park transport and tours

The abundance of public transportation in Yosemite is unusual for a national park. YARTS buses run through the Park to the eastern and western entrances on Hwy-120, free **shuttle buses** travel around the eastern end of the Valley, fee-charging **hikers' buses** fan out from there to Glacier Point and to Tuolumne Meadows where there's another free shuttle (see p.64), and a third free shuttle (see p.76) plies the route between Wawona and Mariposa Grove.

Still, for some of the farther-flung parts, having a **car** is ideal. **Cycling** is also a viable option, and even **hitching is permitted** (though not encouraged).

Yosemite Valley Visitor Shuttle

In the Valley, drivers should park at Curry Village or in the day-use parking area at Yosemite Village, and get around on the free and frequent green-and-white visitor **shuttle buses**. They operate around the eastern section of the Valley floor – shuttle stops are marked on Map 4 – running counterclockwise on a loop that passes through, or close to, all the main points of interest, trailheads and accommodation areas. From May to September visitor shuttles run roughly every ten minutes between 7am and 10pm to most sections of the Valley, with slightly reduced frequency and hours at other times of the year; see *Yosemite Today* for current details.

Other shuttle buses

To stray beyond the Valley, join one of the **hikers' buses** that leaves Yosemite Valley daily in summer, picking up and dropping off at high-country trailheads; one goes to Glacier Point, the other to Tuolumne Meadows. In July and August, you should **reserve a seat** a couple of days in advance through the tour desk at any of the Valley hotels or by calling the Yosemite Lodge Tour Desk (☎209/372-1240). Otherwise, just show up at the lodge a few minutes in advance and buy your ticket there. Unfortunately, there is no public transportation from the Valley to Wawona, though you could ride the Glacier Point Hikers' Bus as far as Chinquapin then hitch from there.

Skiers can take advantage of the free Badger Pass Shuttle Bus, which runs from the Valley and Wawona to the Badger Pass Ski Area.

Glacier Point Hikers' Bus (June–Oct; $15 each way, seniors $12.50, kids $8.50). The Glacier Point Tour (see p.20) also operates as a hikers' bus, treating riders to a full commentary as far as Glacier Point or their chosen trailhead. It runs from the Valley to Glacier Point and back (1hr 10min each way) and is particularly convenient for hikers wanting to hike up the Four-Mile Trail (see p.106) and ride the bus back down, or more likely, bus up and hike down. There are three round-trips daily, leaving Yosemite Lodge at 8.30am, 10am (not in Oct), and 1.30pm, and departing Glacier Point at 10.30am, noon (not in Oct), and 3.30pm.

YARTS buses can also be used to get around the Park, the most useful being the Mammoth and Lee Vining service (see p.11) which provides access to Tioga Road trailheads and Tuolumne Meadows.

Tuolumne Meadows Hikers' Bus (mid-June through the first week of Sept; $14.50 one-way, $23 round-trip, kids half-price, section fares available). The Tuolumne Meadows Tour (see p.21) also operates as a hikers' bus ideal for accessing some of the most stunning scenery in the Park, and the vastest and wildest sections of backcountry. The bus makes a run of just over two hours from the Valley (leaving Curry Village at 8am, then Yosemite Lodge at 8.20am) to Tuolumne Meadows with stops at Crane Flat, White Wolf, Tuolumne Meadows Lodge, and anywhere else you request. The return journey departs at 2pm, leaving around three-and-a-half hours in Tuolumne if done as a daytrip. If you need to be picked up en route, call in advance to make arrangements, then pay the driver when you board.

Badger Pass Shuttle Bus (daily Dec to early April; free) Winter-only service from the Valley (Curry Village, *The Ahwahnee Hotel* and *Yosemite Lodge*) to the Badger Pass Ski Area. There are morning departures at 8.30am and 11am, and return trips at 2pm and 4pm. There is also a free shuttle bus from Wawona to Badger Pass most winter weekends.

Driving

Traffic congestion spoils everyone's fun, particularly in July and August, and over the next few years the number of parking spaces in the Valley will be reduced, making it increasingly difficult to park on busy summer weekends. Visitors are thus encouraged to leave their vehicles in the surrounding towns, and ride buses into the Valley, where you can get around on the free shuttle bus. This makes sense for those staying outside the Park and popping into the Valley each day – there's more time for admiring the scenery, and you don't pay Park entrance fees.

For exploring areas outside the Valley – Tioga Road, Glacier Point Road and Wawona – a car is very handy, and parking is easier to find. Roads within the Park are generally in good condition, but many are winding with unnervingly steep drops to the side; keep your eyes on the road and be alert for other drivers distracted by the scenery. The **maximum speed limit is 45mph** (35mph in the Valley) though often you'll be traveling much slower, perhaps trapped behind a lumbering RV; **be patient** and make sure to pull well off the road to admire the views. In winter and spring watch out for icy patches where the road is shaded by rocks or trees.

Inside the Park, **gas** (for details see "Directory," p.213) is only available at Crane Flat, some fifteen miles away from the Valley, at Wawona, and seasonally at Tuolumne Meadows. Prices are fairly expensive, so fill up before heading to Yosemite.

**For winter driving conditions and information
on tire chains, see the box on p.6.**

Cycling

While roads are narrow and grades are steep in much of the Park, **cycling** remains one of the most enjoyable ways to get around Yosemite Valley, where wide, flat roads are augmented by twelve miles of traffic-free bike paths at its eastern end. Single-speed **rented cruisers** ($5.50 per hour;

GUIDED TOURS

If time is short and you don't mind being herded around, you could join one of the Valley-based **guided tours**, all of which start from Yosemite Lodge, where you can usually buy tickets on the spot at the Tour Desk. In July and August it pays to **buy a ticket** a couple of days in advance either through the tour desk at any of the Valley hotels or by calling the Yosemite Lodge Tour Desk on ☎209/372-1240. An additional tour – the **Big Trees Tram Tour** around the Mariposa Grove – is covered on p.77.

Glacier Point Tour (June–Oct; 4hr; $29.50, seniors $25.50, kids $16.50). Bus tour from the Valley passing by many of its most famous sights and spectacular vistas on the way to Glacier Point, where you'll spend about an hour. Buses depart from Yosemite Lodge at 8.30am, 10am (not in Oct) and 1.30pm daily.

Grand Tour (June–Oct; 8hr; $55, seniors $48, kids, $27.50). Daytour visiting Glacier Point and Wawona, including the Big Trees Tram (see p.77), which leaves Yosemite Lodge at 8.45am and stops for lunch at Wawona where you can eat at the *Wawona Hotel* (additional $6 if bought when you book the tour). Only worthwhile if you are desperate to see as much as possible in one day.

$21 per day) are available from bike stands at Yosemite Lodge (daily, weather permitting 9am–6pm; ☎209/372-1208) and Curry Village (April–Nov daily 8am–6.45pm; ☎209/375-6502). Anyone eighteen or younger must wear a helmet (supplied free to all). Note that there is no mountain bike rental in the Park, and regulations prohibit off-road biking.

Moonlight Tour (May–Sept/Oct when full moon falls; 2hr; $20.50, seniors $18.50, kids $15.50). Essentially the Valley Tour below, done on the nights leading up to full moon, with departures from Yosemite Lodge at either 9.30pm or 10pm. The enchanting silvery views make it worth enduring the somewhat annoying megaphone commentary.

Tuolumne Meadows Tour (July to early Sept; 8hr; $23, kids $11.50). Bus tour featuring all the main Tioga Road viewpoints and sights of interest, allowing three hours for gentle hiking in Tuolumne Meadows. Departs Curry Village at 8am, Yosemite Lodge at 8.20am.

Valley Floor Tour (year-round; 2hr; $20.50, seniors $18.50, kids $15.50, family rates available). A rather dull and predictable 26-mile tour along the Valley roads in an open-air flat-deck tram car (or a bus in bad weather), with a fairly informative commentary. Only worthwhile for extremely rushed visits and for accessing Tunnel View. The tour usually picks up from Curry Village and the *Ahwahnee Hotel*, starting at 9am, then leaves from Yosemite Lodge every half-hour in summer, 2–6 times daily rest of year.

PARK TRANSPORT AND TOURS

Yosemite Valley

n the minds of many visitors, Yosemite National Park is **Yosemite Valley**, a four-square-mile showcase of stupendous scenery. It never fails to impress, no matter how many times you visit, prompting Ralph Waldo Emerson to declare it "the only place that comes up to the brag about it, and exceeds it."

Along the Valley's narrow cleft you'll find the densest concentration of breathtaking cliffs and waterfalls, with the face of **El Capitan** rising majestically over the western entrance to the Valley, and **Half Dome** looking imperiously on a couple of miles to the east. In between, **Yosemite Falls** plunges over the lip of the Valley rim in a double cascade said to comprise the highest fall in the US. Opposite El Cap, **Bridalveil Fall** wafts down to the glossy rocks below, and during the spring snowmelt just about every other cliff spouts a waterfall for a few weeks.

Through it all runs the **Merced River**, which rises in the high country around Merced Lake and expends much of its youthful vigor before entering Yosemite Valley. Here it meanders among meadows where mule deer graze and black bears forage amid black oaks and incense cedars.

Millennia of rockfall from the surrounding cliffs have formed talus slopes at the foot of which people have built

YOSEMITE VALLEY PLAN

Yosemite National Park is poorly set up to cope with more than 3.5 million visitors a year while maintaining its ecological and scenic integrity. While plans to redress this go back to 1980, matters really came to a head in the mid-1990s after rockfalls threatened buildings, and later floodwaters in the Valley wiped out large sections of campgrounds and sluiced away poorly sited lodging. The need to construct buildings away from hazardous areas eventually led to a much more broad-ranging "Final Yosemite Valley Plan," which also calls for removing some Valley roads to allow meadow restoration, extending the Valley shuttle bus system, and, most contentious of all, reducing day-use parking in the Valley and requiring visitors to bus in from outlying parking lots. Though the plan was completed in 2000, political shifts in Washington DC and local lawsuits from opposing interests have left the plan's implementation uncertain.

the infrastructure for year-round habitation over the last century and a half. **Yosemite Village** is effectively Yosemite's capital, home to the main visitor center, wilderness center, the **Yosemite Museum** and **Indian Village**, the **Pioneer Cemetery** and a slew of restaurants and shops. There is accommodation nearby at the ordinary *Yosemite Lodge*, and the extraordinary *Ahwahnee Hotel*. On the southern side of the Valley, **Curry Village** has more places to eat, sleep and shop, and there is handy access to the family-friendly **Nature Center at Happy Isles**.

Because it attracts the bulk of the Park's visitors, the Valley has the busiest **hiking** trails, some gently tracing the river along the Valley floor, but most climbing steeply up

YOSEMITE VALLEY

the walls to the rim of the Valley almost three thousand feet above. Between these two extremes lie the diverse hikes from the popular **Happy Isles trailhead**.

A broad selection of Valley-based hikes are listed from p.98.

Valley highlights: the big cliffs and waterfalls

All visitors are astounded by their first glimpse of Yosemite Valley, with its wealth of magnificent gray granite architecture dominated by defining features **El Capitan** and **Half Dome**. These awe-inspiring monoliths grab you every time you step out of a shop or restaurant, and continue to hold your attention with the shifting angles of sun and moon, ever-changing cloudscapes and, in winter, a heavy blanket of snow. As if this scenery weren't spectacular enough, the Valley is also home to some of the highest **waterfalls** in the country. Nowhere else in the world is there such an array of cascades concentrated in such a small area, though a mild winter can cause many of these falls to dry up as early as July.

Although stunning vistas abound throughout the Valley, one of the most photographed is from **Tunnel View**, just outside the Valley itself and covered on p.68.

SMARTER THAN THE AVERAGE BEAR

You may never encounter a bear anywhere else in California, but spend a couple of days in Yosemite Valley and you may well see one, probably breaking into a car or roaming the campgrounds looking for a free meal. Banging pots and yelling – from a safe distance, of course – will probably drive them off, but dependence on human food leads to several bears being shot each year. Safe food storage is now mandatory in the Park and, as they say, "a fed bear is a dead bear," so do them and yourself a favor by keeping all food and fragrant items – deodorant, sun screen, toothpaste, etc – either inside your room or in the metal bear boxes located in campgrounds and parking lots. Bring a padlock if you're concerned about your things being stolen.

It is important to remember that tents do not deter bears, nor do cars. Yosemite bears have learned to recognize coolers, bags of groceries, food wrappers and even empty soda cans inside vehicles, and once on the scent all the bear needs to do is pop a window by leaning on it or peel back a door with one paw.

You can report bear-related problems to the Bear Management Team on ☏ 209/372-0473.

EL CAPITAN

Map 3, G3

However you approach the Valley, your view will be partially blocked by **El Capitan** (*Tu-tok-a-nu-la*), a vast monolith jutting forward from the adjacent cliffs and looming 3593ft above the Valley floor. One of the largest pieces of exposed granite in the world, "The Captain" is a full 320 acres of gray-tan granite seemingly devoid of vegetation and

EL CAPITAN

so sheer it is no wonder it became the holy grail of rock-climbing worldwide. El Cap's enormous size isn't really apparent until you join the slack-jawed tourists craning their necks and training binoculars and cameras on rock-climbers on the face. Eventually you'll pick out flea-sized specks inching up what appears to be a flawless wall, though closer inspection reveals a pattern of flakes, fissures and small ledges. The most accessible sequence of these comprises what is probably the most famous rock-climbing route in the world, The Nose.

Face on, El Cap looks almost flat, but it really has two principal faces, which meet at The Nose. To the left is **Salathé Wall**, distinguished by a heart-shaped indentation a third of the way up. To the right is the **North American Wall** with its thousand-foot-high patch of dark rock that looks remarkably like a map of North and Central America. Follow it down to the bottom of the dark stain and you'll find El Cap's only significant vegetation, a hundred-foot ponderosa pine rooted in the cracks and hunkered beneath an overhang.

For more about rock climbing, including a brief history of scaling El Capitan and Half Dome, see p.232.

HALF DOME

Map 3, L3

Impressive though El Capitan is, for most people it is **Half Dome** (*Tis-se-yak*) that instantly grabs their attention. A stunning sight topping out at 8842 feet, it rises almost 5000 feet above the Valley floor, smoothly arching from northeast to southwest and cut off on each side. Its two thousand-foot northwest face is only seven degrees off the vertical making it the **sheerest cliff in North America**. According to a member of the 1849 Walker Party (see "History" on pp.219–220) it "looked as though it had been sliced with a knife as one would slice a loaf of bread" and to English naturalist and adventurer Joseph Smeaton Chase, it was a "frightful amputation." It is easy to imagine that the "other half" of the dome was hewn away by a massive glacier, but actually it is faulting in the rock that is primarily responsible for its shape.

To the Ahwahneechee, the weather-streaked cliff is the face of **Tis-se-yak**, a woman who arrived at Mirror Lake with her husband, bowed under the weight of her conical basket. By drinking the lake dry to quench her terrible thirst, she angered her husband who beat her as she fled. When cornered, she turned and flung the basket at him, at which moment they were turned to stone, she as Half Dome with the tears of remorse streaking her face, and he on the opposite side of the Valley as North Dome with Basket Dome to one side. The best view of these three features is from Glacier Point (see p.71).

Ambitious day-hikers (see p.100) wanting to get up close and personal can make it to the shallow saddle of Half Dome's thirteen-acre summit, tackling the final 400 feet by way of a steep steel-cable staircase hooked on to the rock's curving back. The first ascent of this route was made in 1875 by Scottish sailor and Valley blacksmith, **George Anderson**, who spent a week drilling a series of eyebolt holes using homemade drill bits. Daubing his feet in pine pitch and grit to get better footing on the smooth rock, he attached ropes as he went to afford protection on the 45-degree slope. Anderson's pegs and ropes were replaced with cables in 1919 using donations from the Sierra Club and again replaced in the 1930s by the Civilian Conservation Corps. This remained the only way to the summit until climbers forged new routes from 1931 onwards.

HALF DOME

Once at the top, the brave (or foolish) can inch out towards the edge of the projecting lip for a vertiginous look straight down the near-vertical face. While the cables remain all year, the cable supports and wooden slats only stay in place from late May to mid-October, making a winter ascent very difficult (though not impossible). Keep clear of the summit if there are any signs of impending storms; lightning strikes during almost every thunderstorm, which can occur at any time of year.

PEAKS AND DOMES OF THE VALLEY RIM

The immense scale and presence of El Capitan and Half Dome overshadow everything around them, but part of what makes the Valley so striking is its abundance of wildly striking cliffs and spires. Anywhere else these would be star attractions but here they're often relegated to a supporting role. In the words of John Muir, see box opposite, "every attempt to appreciate any one feature is beaten down by the overwhelming influence of all the others."

North side

Moving east from El Capitan, the triple pyramids of the **Three Brothers** – named for the sons of Chief Tenaya who were caught here by the Mariposa Battalion in 1851 – step in symmetry up the Valley wall: **Lower Brother** is presided over by **Middle Brother** which in turn is crowned by the 7779-foot summit **Eagle Peak**.

After a series of less distinguished cliffs you reach a sheer face bisected by Upper Yosemite Fall (see p.32), and to its right the **Lost Arrow Spire**. This thousand-foot column is completely detached from the rock wall at its uppermost two hundred feet, forming a slender pinnacle whose summit

JOHN MUIR

John Muir was one of nature's most eloquent advocates, a champion of all things wild who spent ten years living in Yosemite Valley in the 1870s, and the rest of his life campaigning for its preservation. Born in Scotland in 1838, he grew up in Wisconsin and became a mechanical inventor. At 27, he embarked on his first journey, noting in his diary "All drawbacks overcome ...joyful and free...I chose to become a tramp."

After walking a thousand miles to Florida with little more than a volume of Keats' poems and a plant press for company, he wound up in California in 1868 and asked for "anywhere that is wild." Working in Yosemite Valley as a sheep herder, mill worker and hotel clerk, he spent every waking moment exploring the mountains and waterfalls, traveling light, and usually going to sleep hungry under the stars.

He dubbed the Sierra Nevada the "Range of Light," and spent years developing his theory of how glaciers shaped it. His articles gradually won him academic acceptance, and the general public was soon devouring his journal-based books such as *My First Summer in the Sierra* and *The Yosemite*, which became classics.

Muir was desperate to protect his beloved landscape from the depredations of sheep grazing, timber cutting and homesteading, and through magazine articles and influential contacts goaded Congress into creating Yosemite National Park in 1890. Two years later he set up the **Sierra Club**, an organization whose motto "take only photographs; leave only footprints" has become a model for like-minded groups worldwide. Despite his successes, in 1913 Muir failed to save the Hetch Hetchy valley from being dammed (see box p.55), a blow which hastened his death a year later.

PEAKS AND DOMES OF THE VALLEY RIM

is almost level with the top of the cliff. The pinnacle is only clearly visible in the low-angled morning and afternoon sunlight when it casts a shadow against the cliff behind. Still further east, behind the *Ahwahnee Hotel*, lie the **Royal Arches**, a series of rock arches attached to the cliff face like giant raised eyebrows. In springtime, **Royal Arch Cascade** streaks down the cliff to the left.

Above the Royal Arches the smooth hemisphere of **North Dome** (7525ft) appears to be kept from sliding off the Valley rim by the rocky shoulder of **Washington Column**. Viewed from the south rim, this formation, which is almost detached from the cliff, allegedly resembles George Washington's profile, though few can spot the likeness.

South side

From Washington Column, **Tenaya Canyon** runs toward Tuolumne Meadows, its southeastern side almost entirely formed by the smooth mile-high sheet of rippled granite that sweeps up to the 9926-foot summit of **Cloud's Rest**, the highest peak visible from the Valley.

Moving back downstream, Half Dome is separated from the rest of the Valley cliffs by the Merced River, which cascades down Merced Canyon over Nevada and Vernal falls (see p.33). West of the river, Curry Village hunkers three thousand feet below Glacier Point, the two separated by a smooth, steeply angled quarter-cone of rock known as **Glacier Point Apron**, scene of major rockfalls in the 1990s (see box opposite).

The next major feature is the three-thousand-foot **Sentinel Rock**, a petrified watchtower standing guard over the south side of the Valley. The texture of its fissured, flat face catches the afternoon sun beautifully, especially when viewed from the Four-Mile Trail climbing the Valley wall to its left.

AND THE WALLS CAME TUMBLING DOWN

Yosemite granite is renowned for its robust nature, a quality which accounts for the sheer verticality of the Valley cliffs. But no matter how hardy, the rock is not immune to gravity, and in the past 150 years, over 400 **rockfalls** have been recorded. Evidence is visible both on the Valley floor and on its walls where white patches are left by the detached rock, most of it originating over 2200 feet up, above the scour line of the last glacier to come through the Valley.

One of the largest rockfalls occurred in 1987 at Middle Brother when 1.4 million tons of rock broke loose, leaving a huge pile of talus right to the edge of Northside Drive. Signs still advise drivers not to stop along that section of road. More recently, in 1996, a 500-foot-long slab of granite arch cut loose from cliffs below Glacier Point. After sliding over a ledge, an estimated 80,000 tons of rock went into a 1700-foot freefall before hitting the ground, pulverizing itself and generating a huge blast of wind. The gust peaked at an estimated 270mph and uprooted trees in a large arc, only just missing the Nature Center at Happy Isles. The scattered trees destroyed a nearby footbridge over the Merced River and everything was coated in a two-inch-thick layer of gray dust. One hiker was killed and a dozen more visitors injured. In 1999, a climber was killed and tent cabins in Curry Village were damaged by rock sweeping down Glacier Point Apron.

Records show that only ten people have lost their lives as a result of falling rock in Yosemite, but the physical damage caused by the most recent rockfalls has alerted the Park authorities to the less than prudent building policies of the past and informs much of the thinking behind the Yosemite Valley Plan (see box p.23).

PEAKS AND DOMES OF THE VALLEY RIM

Looming above is **Sentinel Dome**, which casts its eye west past the overlook of **Taft Point** to the magnificent **Cathedral Spires** and **Cathedral Rocks**, directly opposite El Cap. Just around the corner is Bridalveil Fall, and above it, the **Leaning Tower**, a vast slab of overhanging rock.

YOSEMITE FALLS

Map 4, C1. Shuttle stop 6.

At 2425 feet, **Yosemite Falls** (or *Cholok*, "the fall") is widely claimed to be the fifth highest waterfall in the world, and the highest in North America. It is a somewhat spurious assertion since it is actually two falls separated by 675 feet of churning rapids and chutes known as **Middle Cascade**. Nonetheless, the 1430-foot **Upper Yosemite Fall** and the 320-foot **Lower Yosemite Fall** are magnificent, especially in May and early June when runoff from melting snow turns them into a foaming torrent, and a steady breeze blows from the base of the lower fall.

The flow typically dries up by mid-August, leaving a dark stain of algae and lichen to mark the spot. In winter the falls begin to flow again, but just enough to build up a 200 to 300-foot **ice cone** of frozen spray and fallen blocks of ice at the base of the upper fall.

The shuttle bus stops at the beginning of a flat, quarter-mile, wheelchair-accessible asphalt trail along an avenue of incense cedars and ponderosa pines which frame Upper Yosemite Fall. From this angle the upper fall appears to be stacked directly above Lower Yosemite Fall, creating a perfect photo op. At the base of the falls the bridge across Yosemite Creek is always crowded with video camera-wielding tourists, and is a great place to be at full moon in spring and early summer when the spray creates a kind of shimmering **moonbow**.

BRIDALVEIL FALL

Map 3, G5

Perhaps the most sensual waterfall in the Park is the 620ft **Bridalveil Fall**, a slender ribbon at the Valley's western end, which in Ahwahneechee goes by the name of *Pohono* or "spirit of the puffing wind." While Bridalveil seldom completely dries up, it is best seen from April to June when winds blow the cascade outward up to twenty feet away from its base, drawing the spray out into a delicate lacy veil.

The spray-shrouded viewing platform near the base of the fall is at the end of an easy quarter-mile path from a parking lot four miles west of Yosemite Village. The shuttle doesn't go this far west, so unless you visit on the Valley Floor Tour you'll have to drive or come on foot.

OTHER FALLS

Come to the Valley in April or early May and you'll see the 1612-foot **Ribbon Fall** (Map 3, G3), the highest single-drop waterfall in Yosemite (and indeed in North America). It flows down the cliffs to the west of El Capitan and with its small, low-lying catchment is always the first waterfall to dry up each spring. On the south side of the Valley, **Sentinel Fall** (Map 4, C8), cascades off the rim of the Valley beside Sentinel Rock, falling a total of two thousand feet in a series of stairstep drops.

Two of the Park's most striking falls are actually much shorter than these giants, and are guaranteed to still be active in September and October. Sequestered away from the road up the Merced River canyon, they can only be seen on foot from Happy Isles (see Hikes 1–3). It is a relatively easy walk to get a glimpse of the distant 317-foot **Vernal Fall** (Map 3, K4), a curtain of water about eighty feet wide that casts bright rainbows as you walk along the wonderful Mist Trail (see Hike 2). It requires much more commitment to hike steeply upstream as far as the 594-foot **Nevada Fall** (Map 3 L4), but it is worth the effort for a close look at this sweeping cascade that drops for half its height then fans out onto the apron below.

Yosemite Village

Very much the heart of the Valley, **Yosemite Village** is not really a cohesive "village" at all, but a settlement of scattered low shingle-roofed buildings tucked away among the pines and black oaks where mule deer wander freely. Basically a service center for visitors, as well as a home for Park employees, you'll most likely find yourself returning time and again during your visit. The Park's **main visitor center** is here, along with banking facilities, internet access, a post office, shops and several restaurants and cafés, and the **Ahwahnee Hotel** is only half a mile away.

Valley Visitor Center

Map 4, E2. Shuttle stops 5 and 9.

The first stop for most people is the **visitor center** (see p.13 for opening hours and contact numbers), a single-story river-stone building that is basically the hub of the Village. In addition to its facilities, the center provides a quick overview of the Park through fairly pedestrian displays which include material on bears, the Valley Plan (p.23), and the role of fires in maintaining ecological balance, as well as a couple of topographic models – one showing the Valley rock types along with several samples, the other an uninformative relief map of the Park. You can also watch a couple of free short films: the dull orientational *One Day in Yosemite* (runs continuously), and the new 23-minute *Spirit of Yosemite*, which is screened every half-hour in the East Auditorium, immediately behind the visitor center. Despite a somewhat overblown commentary, it is worth seeing for the great images of Yosemite through the different seasons.

Next door to the visitor center is the Ansel Adams Gallery (see p.147 & 210), beyond it the Wilderness Center (see p.13).

Yosemite Museum

Map 4, E2. Shuttle stops 5 and 9.
Daily: June–Aug 8am–5.30pm; Sept–May 9am–4.30pm (closed for lunch noon–1pm); free.

Immediately west of the visitor center is the two-story **Yosemite Museum**, its entrance flanked by a cedar-bark tepee and a hefty nine-foot **slice of a giant sequoia** trunk whose rings are marked with significant dates going back to its sapling days in 923 AD. The museum's small but interesting exhibit of artifacts focuses on Native American heritage, specifically the local Ahwahneechee (a part of the Southern Miwok group) (see box overleaf) and their neighbors, the Mono Lake Paiute, with whom they traded and intermarried. Displays illustrate their way of life and how it changed following their first encounters with whites in the 1850s. One of the few crafts to flourish after contact was **basketwork**: fine examples on display include a superbly detailed 1930s Mono Lake Paiute basket almost three feet in diameter, and its even larger Miwok/Paiute equivalent, painstakingly created by famed basket maker Lucy Telles. Basket-making demonstrations are given by Ahwahneechee practitioners throughout the day.

YOSEMITE VILLAGE

THE AHWAHNEECHEE

The **Ahwahneechee**, a subtribe of the Southern Miwok people, have to some degree occupied Yosemite Valley for three thousand years. While three dozen inhabited sites have been identified here, there were seldom more Ahwahneechee than the few hundred discovered by the Mariposa Battalion when they entered Yosemite Valley in 1851. Many members of the tribe were killed trying to escape capture, and the rest were temporarily bundled off to a reservation in California's Central Valley, before being allowed to filter back to Yosemite. Claims that the Ahwahneechee had signed away their land were never upheld, but the tribe became fragmented and marginalized in the increasingly white Valley. After the formation of the Park Service in 1916, the Indians became a sideshow, providing visitor entertainment disguised as cultural revival, and designer native basket-making flourished.

By the late 1920s the Ahwahneechee had been confined to one large village near the foot of Yosemite Falls; nevertheless, a new Park superintendent sought their virtual eviction. Those whose claims to residency couldn't be denied eventually settled in cramped new cabins constructed west of Camp 4 in the early 1930s. By the 1950s, only those with permanent jobs in the Park could stay, and in 1969 the last remaining residents were rehoused once again and the village was razed. A few Ahwahneechee still live in government housing in the Park, but most live outside, returning primarily for ceremonial occasions.

A couple of **feather-trimmed dance capes** warrant a look, as does the buckskin dress worn by natives in the 1920s and 1930s during tourist demonstrations of basket weaving and dance. Though completely alien to the Miwok tradition, the Plains-style buckskin clothing and feather headdresses fulfilled the expectations of the whites who came to watch. Kids will enjoy displays on Miwok stick and dice games and the opportunity to touch samples of animal fur.

The white man's history in the Park is detailed by hotel **guest registers** from *La Casa Nevada* hotel, which flourished from 1870–1891 near the base of Nevada Fall, and the *Cosmopolitan Saloon and Bath House*.

- -
Just outside the museum (close to shuttle stop #5) there is a small box where you can pick up a leaflet (50¢) for the pleasant **self-guided trail** through **Cook's Meadow**.
- -

Indian Village of Ahwahnee

Map 4, E2. Always open; free.

Wander through the Yosemite Museum (or, when closed, around its western side) to join a self-guided trail through the **Indian Village of Ahwahnee**, a compact reconstruction of a Miwok village built in the 1920s as a venue for native dances on the former site of the largest native village in the Valley. An explanatory booklet available on-site ($1) is rendered somewhat redundant by the numerous signs describing the buildings and the uses of various native plants.

Easily the largest structure, the **ceremonial roundhouse** is almost fifty feet across and crowned with a low-pitched bark roof. While visitors are permitted only to peer into the dark interior through the entrance, the building is still used by the local native community for special occasions. Along with the few traditional bark shelters, there's an early Miwok cabin exhibiting strong Euro-American influence, which illustrates how native builders often had to make do with poor-quality or scavenged materials, building directly on the ground with a central fire pit and smoke hole in the roof.

YOSEMITE VILLAGE

Yosemite Pioneer Cemetery

Map 4, E2. Always open; free.

Anyone familiar with Yosemite's history or simply drawn to graveyards should visit the **Yosemite Pioneer Cemetery**, fifty yards west of the museum. A peaceful, shady spot, it holds some three dozen graves of early white settlers who attempted to farm the Valley. Most of the headstones, dating back to the mid-1800s, are identified by horizontal slabs of rock, some etched with crude or faded writing. Notables include **James Lamon**, who died in 1875 after establishing what is now known as Curry Orchard (an apple orchard which still bears fruit in Curry Village), and Park guardian **Galen Clark** (1814–1910), whose grave is marked by a hunk of granite inscribed with his name and dates. Clark honored Lamon by planting a sequoia beside his grave, then selected half a dozen sequoia saplings for his own resting place. Altogether five sequoias survive, though none are especially large. The main visitor center stocks the detailed *Guide to the Yosemite Cemetery* (see "Books," p.237), for more on the sites.

Ahwahnee Hotel

Map 4, H3. Shuttle stop 3.

Tucked away from the rest of Yosemite Village, a pleasant ten-minute walk (or brief shuttle ride) to the east, the imposing six-story **Ahwahnee Hotel** (☎209/372-1407) warrants a few minutes of your time even if you have no intention of staying or dining here. Designed to blend into its surroundings, the *Ahwahnee* is a harmonious synthesis of a grand European hotel and a backwoods cabin. Now a National Historic Landmark, it was built in 1927 to attract wealthy tourists, something it still does fairly effortlessly. Over the years royalty, heads of state and movie stars have graced the hotel with their presence, including JFK and Queen Elizabeth II.

While the hotel is officially for guests and restaurant patrons only, no one is likely to mind if you pop in to admire the wonderful baronial-style common areas on the ground floor. The finest room is the **Great Lounge**, hung with grand chandeliers, and bookended by matching fireplaces large enough to live in (and blazing in winter). It is decorated with Native American motifs, Miwok basketware, oriental carpets, and old images of the Park on the walls. French doors open on both sides to let in the summer breeze, and the sofas are a perfect place to relax, especially at 5pm when tea and cookies are served for guests to piano accompaniment. If you're interested in rock climbing paraphernalia and old photos of skiing, ski-jumping and tobogganing, you should also take a peek at the **Winter Club** room.

An occasional winter-only **Historic Tour** (Dec–Feb sporadically, 30–60min duration; free) is open to all: check *Yosemite Today* for times or ask at the front desk.

Food and lodging in the Ahwahnee Hotel are covered on p.166 and p.192 respectively.

Curry Village and the eastern Valley

At some point, everyone finds themselves at the eastern end of the Valley, either to hike the **Mist Trail** from the trailhead and nature center at **Happy Isles**, stroll to **Mirror**

Lake or visit the **stables** (see p.150). For many Yosemite visitors this is also "home," as all the main campgrounds are here along with the permanent cabins of *Housekeeping Camp* and the tent cabin complex of **Curry Village**. The main **Southside Drive** (see p.48) runs through the area and is plied by frequent shuttle buses which run year-round to Curry Village and the campgrounds, and from early April to late October also make a loop past Happy Isles and the Mirror Lake trailhead.

LeConte Memorial Lodge

Map 4, G4. Shuttle stop 12. April–Sept Wed–Sun 10am–4pm; free.

From the southern side of Sentinel Bridge, Southside Drive runs along a narrow strip between the foot of the cliffs and the Merced River to *Housekeeping Camp* (see "Accommodation" on p.168). Across the road is the **LeConte Memorial Lodge**, a small rough-hewn granite-block structure where the **Sierra Club** maintains displays on the Club's history, runs a conservation library and has a kids' corner with books and games. There's also a fascinating relief map of the Valley dating back to around 1885, and changing displays on topics relevant to the work of the Sierra Club. Their evening programs (usually Fri–Sun; free) are a little more highbrow than those elsewhere in the Park and might include a slide show or talk by some luminary: check *Yosemite Today* for details.

The lodge itself was built by the Sierra Club in 1903 to commemorate one of its original members, **Joseph LeConte** (1823–1901), an eminent geologist and an early supporter of John Muir. Originally constructed in Camp Curry, where it served as the Valley's first visitor center and marked the northern end of the John Muir Trail, the lodge was rebuilt in its current location in 1919. As the Sierra

Club's Yosemite headquarters, it was managed for a couple of summers in the early 1920s by **Ansel Adams** (see box pp.42–43), who was happy to do anything if it meant he could spend more time in the Valley.

Curry Village

Map 4, I5. Shuttle stops 13, 14, 20 and 21.

After Yosemite Village, the Park's largest concentration of visitor facilities is at **Curry Village**, a rambling area of tent cabins and wooden chalets centered on a small complex of restaurants, shops, pay showers, a post office and an outdoor amphitheater hosting ranger programs and evening shows. There's also a winter ice rink, bike rental, and kiosk which rents rafts for use on the nearby Merced River.

The "village" is the direct descendant of **Camp Curry**, which was started in 1899 by David and Jeannie Curry, who were keen to share their adopted home in the Valley and charged just $12 a week for a "good bed, and a clean napkin every meal." Their first six guests stayed in tents below Glacier Point, but amenities soon improved with a dance hall, tennis courts, croquet lawns, and evening entertainment which culminated in the **Firefall** (see box p.44). Through the Curry's daughter, Mary Curry Tressider, the business stayed in family hands until 1970 but is now run by the Park concessionaire.

The village isn't a place for sightseeing, but you can wander through the aging apple trees of Curry Orchard, planted in the 1860s by the Valley's first year-round white resident, James Lamon. Sadly the orchard now serves as a parking lot for Curry Village.

ANSEL ADAMS

Few photographers have stamped their vision as unforgettably as **Ansel Adams** has done with Yosemite Valley. While he worked all over the American West, Yosemite was Adams' home and the site of his most celebrated works: icons of American landscape photography such as *Clearing Winter Storm*, *Jeffrey Pine*, *Sentinel Dome* and *Moon and Half Dome*.

Born in 1902 into a moderately wealthy San Francisco family, Adams was given his first camera – a Box Brownie – when he was fourteen, on his first trip to Yosemite. Though classically trained as a concert pianist, he claimed that he knew his "destiny" during that first visit to the Park, and soon turned his attention to the mountains, returning every year and taking up a job as custodian of the Sierra Club headquarters.

He first made a mark in 1927 with *Monolith, The Face of Half Dome*, his first successful **visualization**: Adams believed that before pressing the shutter, the photographer should have a clear idea of the final image and think through the entire photographic process, considering how lenses, filters, exposure, development and printing need to be used to achieve that visualization. This approach may seem obvious today, but compared to the hit-and-miss methods of the time, it was little short of revolutionary. Visualization was made easier by applying the **zone system** of exposure calculation, which, though not new, was codified and promoted by Adams as the basis for his teaching.

As Adams fine-tuned his artistic theories through the 1930s, the idea of photography as fine art was still considered novel. Adams was therefore delighted when, in 1940, he was made vice chairman of the newly established **Department of Photography** at New York's Museum of Modern Art (MoMA).

There was still very little money in photography, so Adams continued to take commercial assignments, including shooting menu photos for Yosemite's *Ahwahnee Hotel*. While still demanding the highest standard of reproduction, the artist gradually tempered his perfectionism, and allowed his work to reach a wider audience by appearing on postcards, calendars and posters. By now, he was virtually a household name, and for the first time in his life he began making money to match his status as the grand old man of Western photography. His final triumph came in 1979, when the MoMA put on the huge "Yosemite and the Range of Light" exhibition. That same year, he was asked to make an official portrait of president Jimmy Carter — the first time a photographer had been assigned an official portrait — and was subsequently awarded the nation's highest civilian honor, the Medal of Freedom.

Throughout his life, Adams had another great passion, one that he pursued with the same fervor as photography: **conservation**. Back in 1932, the artist had a direct hand in creating Kings Canyon National Park. Two years later, he became a director of the **Sierra Club**, a position he held until 1971, overseeing several successful environmental campaigns. He never quit campaigning for the cause of conservation, and, after an interview in which he suggested he'd like to drown Ronald Reagan in his own martini, agreed to meet the president to promote the environmental cause.

Since his death in 1984 at age 82, Adams has become even more honored. The mountain that had been widely known as Mount Ansel Adams since 1933 now bears that name officially, and a huge chunk of the High Sierra south of Yosemite National Park is known as the Ansel Adams Wilderness.

ANSEL ADAMS

THE FIREFALL

Hard to believe now, but for decades local hoteliers struggled to lure tourists to the Valley, trying everything from bear feeding to bobsled rides. From the beginning of the twentieth century until the late 1960s, the biggest draw was the **Firefall**, which took place every summer evening (and a couple of times a week in winter) at the end of Camp Curry's evening entertainment program.

Throughout the program, guests gazed up at Glacier Point, 3200 feet above, where a fire made from ten barrow-loads of red fir bark could be seen lighting the night sky. As the show drew to a close, the stentorian voice of camp owner David Curry would boom out "Hello Glacier! Is the fire ready?" The faint reply of "The fire is ready!" could be heard, and at Curry's instruction, "Let the fire fall!" the smoldering pile of embers would be raked over the cliff to create an incandescent thousand-foot cascade that seemed to plunge almost directly onto the guests (but landed harmlessly on a ledge). The Firefall, accompanied by "America the Beautiful" or "The Indian Love Call" on piano, always took place at exactly 9pm, though one night in the early 1960s the proceedings were delayed for half an hour while President Kennedy finished his drink at the *Ahwahnee*.

The event was so popular that spectacle seekers crossed counties, clogged Valley roads, and trampled meadows to stake out the best vantage points. Though the cinders never caused a serious fire, the Firefall was eventually deemed inappropriate for a national park; the last one took place on January 25, 1968. A sense of what it was like can be gleaned from periodic free slide shows; check *Yosemite Today* for times and venues.

Nature Center at Happy Isles

Map 4, L6. Shuttle stop 16. Early May to mid-Sept daily 10am–noon & 1–4pm; free.

Throughout the summer, shuttle buses continue from Curry Village along a car-free loop around the very eastern end of the Valley. First stop is the **Nature Center at Happy Isles**, a modern building amid the pines on the site of a 1927 trout hatchery. It houses the most **family-friendly** set of displays in the Valley, and is the base for the Park's Junior Ranger Program, aimed at kids aged seven to ten (see p.207). Highlights include a section of forest that comes complete with stuffed examples of animals who make Yosemite their home, a hands-on exhibit allowing you to feel how hunks of rough granite get weathered down to sand, and an exhibit on a year in the life of a bear.

At the rear of the Nature Center, be sure to check out the **rockfall exhibit** (unrestricted entry) where a number of explanatory panels highlight the pulverized rock and flattened trees that resulted from the 1996 rockfall (see box p.31).

Towards the Merced River, a couple of bridges lead out to the "**Happy Isles**" themselves, a series of wooded islets first described in 1885 by Yosemite guardian W E Dennison: "No one can visit them without for the while forgetting the grinding strife of this world and being happy." A bit optimistic perhaps, but hanging out at the swimming holes in summer is indeed quite relaxing.

Steps away on the eastern side of the Merced River lies the Valley's most important trailhead. From here the **Mist Trail** (see Hike 2) heads up to Vernal Fall, the **Half Dome Trail** (see Hike 4) continues to the summit of Half Dome, and the **John Muir Trail** (see Hike 47) spurs off to the Tuolumne high country.

Mirror Lake

Map 4, N2. Access from shuttle stop 17.

The lure of Half Dome reflected in the glassy waters of Tenaya Creek makes the mile-long stroll to **Mirror Lake**

(*Ahwiyah*, or "quiet water") one of Yosemite's most popular walks. Really just a wide spot in a stream, Mirror Lake is subject to seasonal variations and is best visited in spring and early summer when it's nearly bursting its banks, particularly in May when the dogwood blooms are at their glorious best. There is little, if any, water left to form a mirror by August or September, but it is pleasant enough just wandering or biking along the broad asphalt path to admire the woods or gaze at the wondrous rock formations all around. The area is now free from the trappings of early entrepreneurial ventures, but a self-guiding trail helps you identify the site of a dance pavilion built out over the water and the location of an icehouse used to store winter-harvested ice for the summer demand.

We've include the walk to Mirror Lake as part of Hike 7, which continues a mile or so beyond the lake and returns along the south side of Tenaya Creek.

Northside and Southside drives

The matchless beauty and variety of Yosemite Valley can't be fully appreciated from the developed areas around Yosemite Village and Curry Village, and you really need to explore either on foot, or along the road system. Two roads make up an eleven-mile one-way loop through the Valley, with the westbound Northside Drive hugging the base of El Capitan and the Three Brothers, and the eastbound Southside Drive running parallel below Bridalveil Fall and

Sentinel Rock. Set aside half a day, allowing time to take photos, have a picnic lunch, or hike the western end of the Valley by following Hike 6.

Around Yosemite Valley and along roads throughout the Park, you'll see wayside markers with a letter and a number: V1–V27 in the Valley, G1–G11 on Glacier Point Road, T1–T39 on Tioga Road, etc. These correspond to entries in the Park Service's *Yosemite Road Guide* (see "Books", p.238), and we've mentioned the nearest marker to points of interest where relevant.

NORTHSIDE DRIVE

Northside Drive heads west from Yosemite Village, initially along a two-way road with the open expanse of **Cook's Meadow** (Map 4, E3) on the left and, on the right, regenerating **black oak woodland** blocking views towards **Lower Yosemite Fall** (V3, see p.32). Opposite the Lower Yosemite Fall shuttle stop (#6) is the entrance to **Yosemite Lodge**, the site of a US cavalry post until 1914, and now home to accommodation, restaurants, a tour desk, and amphitheater for ranger programs. Immediately beyond, you pass the *Camp 4* walk-in campground and the Upper Yosemite Fall trailhead (V5), followed half a mile on by **Rocky Point** (V6), a mountain of boulders left by a major rockfall in 1987 (see box p.31).

Drive on for a mile and a half to reach **Devil's Elbow**, a loop in the Merced River where the bank is being restored after the area was reclaimed from its earlier role as a parking lot. At either end of the restoration area, there are sandy beaches good for swimming once the spring snowmelt abates. Opposite is the **Cathedral Spires Vista** (Map 3, G4), and a short trail leading to the base of El Capitan where climbers begin their multiday ascents.

It is just a few hundred yards further to **El Capitan Bridge** (a possible return route over the Merced River to Yosemite Village) and **El Capitan Meadow** (V8; Map 3, G4), an open field with stupendous views of El Capitan (see p.25), which towers above, and Cathedral Spires across the Valley. Avoid walking on the meadow – it is becoming heavily impacted by thousands of people keen to spy on El Cap climbers.

Another quarter-mile on, the road suddenly dips (V9) as it descends a recessional moraine left by the last glacier to occupy the Valley. The Merced is swift here, as witnessed through a break in the trees framing Bridalveil Fall (V10). The river then slows again at **Valley View** (Map 3, F4), where you're treated to a tremendous long view towards Half Dome.

Highways 120 and 140 now continue out of the Valley, or you can turn left and double back along Southside Drive towards Yosemite Village.

SOUTHSIDE DRIVE

Approaching the Valley along Hwy-120 or Hwy-140 you enter a one-way system at **Pohono Bridge** (Map 3, F4), which crosses the Merced and passes the small **Fern Spring** (V12) on the right. The road soon reaches the edge of **Bridalveil Meadow** and a marker (V13) records the spot where, in May 1903, President Teddy Roosevelt and John Muir camped together and hashed out the conservation measures Muir felt were needed in the Park. Muir (and presumably the surroundings) obviously had some effect, because several of Muir's proposals were enacted over the subsequent years.

At the eastern end of the meadow, Hwy-41 comes in from Wawona. Turn right here for the **Bridalveil Fall** (see p.33) parking lot, or left to continue the circuit. Next stop is **El Capitan Vista** (Map 3, F4), where RVs and buses regularly line the parking bays on both sides of the road for one of the most celebrated views of the big stone. It looks its best early and late in the day when lower-angled light plays on the sheer granite walls and highlights its features.

Cathedral Spires (V15; see p.32) rise up on your right as you drive a mile or so on to a small side road to **Cathedral Beach picnic area** and **Three Brothers Vista** (V16). Another mile on, a side road leads to two more excellent waterside picnic areas, **Yellow Pine** and **Sentinel Beach** (Map 4, A5).

Across the road a sign marks the trailhead for the Four-Mile Trail to Glacier Point (see p.106). In the mid-nineteenth century this was the location of Lower Yosemite Village, home to Camp Ahwahnee and the Valley's original hotel, *Leidig's*, which saw its first tourists in 1856. The hotel is long gone, but the name survives as Leidig's Meadow, reached across a sturdy bridge from the **Swinging Bridge picnic area** (Map 4, B5).

Half a mile on, you get the first really startling view of Yosemite Falls from **Upper Yosemite Fall Vista** (V19; Map 4, D4). Just beyond is the interdenominational **chapel** see *Yosemite Today* for service times or call ☎209/372-4831), erected in 1879 and now the oldest building in the Park still in use. This suitably alpine-looking structure was built close to the base of the Four-Mile Trail, and was later moved three-quarters of a mile to its current site where it is the last remaining building of the old Yosemite Village. This was once the main settlement in the Valley, which lay along the section of road from here to Sentinel Bridge. Several of the other old buildings are in the Pioneer Yosemite History Center in Wawona (see p.74).

A hundred yards on, turn left over Sentinel Bridge to return to Yosemite Village, or continue straight ahead for Curry Village and the eastern Valley.

Northern Yosemite

Only ardent hikers prepared to spend several days in the backcountry get to experience the true remoteness of **northern Yosemite**, whose vast expanse of angular peaks and glaciated valleys stretch beyond the northern Park boundary to the Hoover and Emigrant wildernesses. But between these wilds and the relative civilization of Yosemite Valley lies some of Yosemite's finest scenery, made accessible by **Tioga Road**, which virtually bisects the Park from east to west. Snowbound and unpassable for much of the year, the road climbs up through the densely forested high country to the open grassland of **Tuolumne Meadows**, surrounded by polished granite domes and with a southern horizon delineated by the sawtooth crest of the **Cathedral Range**. Nowhere else in the Park is such fabulous hiking country so close at hand or so easy to reach. Trails run the gamut from a short stroll to the effervescent **Soda Springs** to the two-day journey along a section of the **John Muir Trail** between here and Yosemite Valley.

East of Tuolumne Meadows, Tioga Road becomes the highest road in California when it tops out at the 10,000-foot **Tioga Pass**, the Park's eastern boundary and the center of a historic mining area. To the west of Tuolumne, the best of the Tioga Road scenery is around **Olmsted Point**, where everyone stops to photograph the barren granite walls of Tenaya Canyon, and sparkling **Tenaya Lake**, surrounded by glacier-smoothed domes typically populated by rock climbers.

The only other road-accessible section of northern Yosemite is **Hetch Hetchy**, particularly attractive in spring when three lovely **waterfalls** burst to life among abundant wildflowers.

Big Oak Flat Road and northwestern Yosemite

Considering the quality of road access, the northwestern corner of Yosemite is surprisingly little visited. Plenty of people drive through here on their way from the Bay Area, but few stop for long, except for a quick photo from one of the marked viewpoints or to stroll to the **Merced Grove** of **giant sequoias**. The one major attraction is **Hetch Hetchy**, long controversial for being the only major dam in a national park, and chiefly of interest as a springboard to hikes in the north of the Park.

The Valley to Crane Flat

To get to the northern reaches of Yosemite from the Valley, drive northwest along **Big Oak Flat Road**, which starts climbing as soon as it spurs off Hwy-140 at the Valley's western end. There are great cliff views as the Merced River rapidly drops away to your left; notice how the

Merced River leaves behind the U-shaped Yosemite Valley and takes on the classic V-shape of an unglaciated river canyon.

After two short tunnels, **Elephant Rock View** (B1) reveals a rock vaguely resembling a great granite pachyderm across the canyon. Also visible is The **Old Coulterville Road**, the very first road into Yosemite Valley, built in 1874, which climbs the rock wall to the west. Around a couple of bends, **Cascade Creek** (B2) and less dramatic **Tamarack Creek** drop as dramatic springtime waterfalls right beside the road before joining forces just downstream and plummeting five hundred feet into Merced Canyon as **The Cascades**. Almost half a mile on, **Bridalveil Fall View** (B3) offers an excellent vista of the western half of Yosemite Valley. The longest of the three tunnels on this road runs almost a mile from Bridalveil Fall View to a view of **Merced River Canyon** (B4). **Big Meadow Overlook** (B6), four miles on, affords views of the silted-up lake bed of Big Meadow, once used to grow hay for pack horses, and now an important foraging area for the locally-rare great gray owl. Much of the rolling hillside around here still bears the scars of a major fire that swept through in 1990.

Big Oak Flat Road continues its ascent over the next couple of miles, until leveling off at **Crane Flat** (Map 5, B12), a small meadow where you'll find the Crane Flat Store and gas station and, across the road, the *Crane Flat* campground. Here Tioga Road (Hwy-120 E) heads towards Tuolumne Meadows: our coverage of this stretch continues on p.57.

Merced Grove to Hetch Hetchy Road

Just over three miles east of Crane Flat along Big Oak Flat Road, a small pull-out provides parking for the **Merced Grove** of **giant sequoias** (B10; Map 5, A12), which with only a couple dozen trees is smaller and less spectacular than the Mariposa and Tuolumne groves, but is considerably more peaceful. A broad, sandy **trail** (1hr 30min–2hr round-trip; 3 miles; 600ft ascent on the way back) takes you to five trees heralding the main section of the grove, clustered around the gabled **Merced Grove Cabin** (closed to the public), which was built in 1935 to exhibit the "highest evolution of log cabin construction." Beyond the cabin the grove thins out after one final fifteen-foot-diameter sequoia with a huge hemispherical burl across its entire width.

Continuing east on Big Oak Flat Road, **North Country View** (B11) shows off the Hetch Hetchy reservoir far below, filling the valley behind the dam. A couple of miles past the overlook, the Park's **Big Oak Flat Entrance** (B12) is home to a small **Information Station** (Map 5, A10; Easter–Sept daily 9am–6pm; Oct & Nov Thurs–Mon 9am–5pm; Dec–Easter open occasional weekends only; ☎209/379-1899) and a campground reservations office (April to mid-Oct 8am–5pm). Across the road lies the *Hodgdon Meadow Campground* (see p.184).

A mile west of the Big Oak Flat entrance, Evergreen Road heads north and re-enters the Park on the way to Hetch Hetchy. The approach to the Park along Hwy-120 W is covered on p.81.

HETCH HETCHY

Map 5, C4.
John Muir's passion for Yosemite Valley was matched, if not exceeded, by his desire to preserve the beauty of **Hetch Hetchy**, at one time a near replica of Yosemite Valley, with grassy, oak-filled meadows and soaring granite walls. When Hetch Hetchy came under threat from power and water supply interests in San Francisco in 1901, Muir began a twelve-year losing battle for its preservation (see box over-

leaf). Completed in 1923 and raised to its current level in 1938, the O'Shaughnessy Dam blocked the Tuolumne River, creating the slender, twisting, eight-mile-long Hetch Hetchy reservoir, drowning the meadows under a couple hundred feet of water.

With so much wonderful countryside competing for visitors' attention elsewhere in the Park, it is perhaps not surprising that Hetch Hetchy is little visited. That said, the view up the reservoir from the middle of the dam is stunning, with the bell-shaped dome of **Kolana Rock** dominating on the right and providing an active breeding ground for endangered **peregrine falcons**. Across the water, two beautiful falls drop over a thousand feet from the cliffs on the north side, both of them accessible on relatively easy hikes (see p.108). The voluminous **Wapama Falls** roars away in its dark recess in dramatic contrast to **Tueeulala Falls** (pronounced TWEE-lala), described by Muir as a "silvery scarf burning with irised sun-fire." Both are at their best from April to early June and usually dry up by the end of August.

Long before it was drowned by the reservoir, Hetch Hetchy valley was scoured out by glaciers which ground down the valley of the Tuolumne River, a route later used by Miwok peoples who named the area "Hatchatchie" for a type of grass with edible seeds once common hereabouts. **Wildflowers** are still abundant in the region in spring – look for bright California fuschia, waterfall buttercups, and shooting stars – along with California black oak, incense cedar, ponderosa pine, and big leaf maple.

Relatively warm temperatures and light snow make the Hetch Hetchy area a good place for hikes in early spring, when the waterfalls and wildflowers are at their best.

THE BATTLE FOR HETCH HETCHY

"Dam Hetch Hetchy! As well dam for water-tanks the people's cathedrals and churches, for no holier temple has ever been consecrated by the heart of man."

John Muir, *The Yosemite*

As early as 1867 the burgeoning city of San Francisco, perched at the end of a dry peninsula, began searching for a dependable water supply. In 1900 the US Geological Survey recommended Hetch Hetchy valley as a potential source, where a relatively small dam would hold back a large body of water. San Francisco mayor James Phelan concurred, but Muir and his cohorts, instigating the first environmental letter writing campaign to Congress and obtaining support from most of the country's influential newspapers, initially defeated the proposal.

While Muir was branded "a man entirely without social sense," he labeled his adversaries "temple destroyers, devotees of ravaging commercialism." The environmentalists eventually lost the battle in 1913 when commercial interests persuaded President Wilson to sign the Raker Act, allowing for the construction of the O'Shaughnessy Dam, built between 1914 and 1923. The *New York Times* reported "The American people have been whipped in the Hetch Hetchy fight," no one more so than Muir himself, who died dispirited in 1914.

Though Muir and company failed to stop the dam, their work led to the creation of both the National Park Service and the Sierra Club (see box p.29), the latter a long-time advocate of undamming Hetch Hetchy and returning it to its original state. San Francisco's water supply would at this point barely be affected; the bigger stumbling block would be the loss of power generation – not that there's much of a chance of the proposal being enacted any time soon.

HETCH HETCHY

The only **facilities** at Hetch Hetchy are toilets, drinking water, phones and a backpacker campground (wilderness permit required), which makes a good starting point for treks in the area. Since the reservoir forms part of San Francisco's water supply, swimming and boating are not allowed, and **fishing** is only permitted from the shore if live bait isn't used.

Approaching Hetch Hetchy

The road into Hetch Hetchy (initially Evergreen Rd, then Hetch Hetchy Rd) cuts off Hwy-120 W a mile outside the Big Oak Flat Entrance (Map 5, A10), and twists north through the Stanislaus National Forest for a total of sixteen miles to the O'Shaughnessy Dam. It is generally accessible without chains from mid-April to mid-October. A mile off Hwy-120 W, you pass the **Carlon Picnic Site** where you cross the south fork of the Tuolumne River.

Round a few more bends, the forest opens out at **Ackerson Meadow**, once used for growing hay by an early prospector. Six miles north of Hwy-120 W is the *Dimond O* campground (see p.186); continue a couple of miles to **Mather**, a former sheep ranch and later a stop on the railroad during the construction of the O'Shaughnessy Dam.

Turn right here to enter the Park at the **Hetch Hetchy Entrance** (always open), with a kiosk acting as the **ranger station** (see p.14) where you can pick up wilderness permits.

The Hetch Hetchy Road climbs gently through **Poopenaut Pass** (H2) to reveal a view of the Grand Canyon of the Tuolumne River, the Hetch Hetchy reservoir and dam, and Wapama and Tueeulala falls. From **Poopenaut Valley View** (H3), a mile on, you can see Poopenaut Valley below the dam, where a few cabins remain from the small sheep- and cattle-herding settlement that once thrived there. It is a further three miles to Hetch Hetchy.

Tioga Road to Tenaya Lake

Snow covered for half the year, **Tioga Road** (Hwy-120 E) runs 46 miles from Crane Flat through some of Yosemite's most breathtaking **high-country scenery** to the Park entrance at the 10,000-foot Tioga Pass. It traverses alpine tundra and subalpine forests, cuts through glaciated valleys, and crosses the sublime **Tuolumne Meadows**. All along the route there are trailheads for numerous **hikes** (see pp.109–114) and great places to stop such as **Olmsted Point** with its tremendous views of Half Dome and Cloud's Rest, and chilly **Tenaya Lake** where the brave can go for a swim from sandy **beaches**.

For Tioga Road closures see box p.6.

Tioga Road roughly follows a trading route used by the Mono Lake Paiute, which in 1883 was turned into the Great Sierra Wagon Road by the Great Sierra Consolidated Silver Company to transport machinery and supplies to their mines around Tioga Pass. You can still get a sense of what travel was like in those times by exploring short sections of the old route which spur off to the May Lake trailhead and to *Yosemite Creek* campground.

Facilities along Tioga Road are limited to a handful of campgrounds, and the lodge, restaurant and store at White

Wolf (open mid-June to early Sept), before you get to Tuolumne Meadows. If you're planning to spend a few days out this way, stock up with supplies in the Valley or at the Crane Flat store.

If entering the Park from the east through Lee
Vining, this section will work in reverse order:
those driving from Yosemite Village should first
follow our coverage of Northside Drive (see p.47,
then our account of Big Oak Flat Road (see p.51).

TUOLUMNE GROVE

Map 5, B11. Open all year, but usually snowbound from late Nov to April; free.

The **Tuolumne Grove** of **giant sequoias** can be reached half a mile north of Crane Flat. With just a few dozen trees, it is far less impressive than the Mariposa Grove but is closer to the Valley and has the distinction of being the grove spotted by pioneer Joseph Walker and his party when they first entered Yosemite in 1833.

Access to the grove is along a root-buckled asphalt road that once formed part of the **Old Big Oak Flat Road**, built in 1874, at a time when it took a day and a half of travel to get here from San Francisco. This stretch of the old road is inaccessible to vehicles (including bikes) but sees plenty of foot traffic on the way to the grove. The first sequoia is a mile down the road from the parking lot and marks the start of a mile-long loop trail that passes several more magnificent big trees, a huge **fallen giant** that's gradually crumbling away, and the charred remains of a **tunnel tree** with its car-sized hole.

TAMARACK FLAT TO WHITE WOLF

Three miles east of the Tuolumne Grove parking lot, a drivable but winding and potholed section of the Old Big Oak Flat Road leads three miles southeast to the primitive *Tamarack Flat* campground (see p.185). Immediately past the Tamarack Flat turnoff, **Gin Flat** (T3; Map 5, C11) marks the spot where a bunch of delighted cowboys happened upon a barrel of gin lost off a passing wagon. The next five miles run through a fire-scorched patch of forest, then parallel to the south fork of the Tuolumne River before entering **red fir forest** and passing the grass-fringed **Siesta Lake**, beyond which a side road leads a mile north of Tioga Road to **White Wolf** (Map 5, F7). Surrounded by lush meadow and home to a decent array of facilities (see relevant sections of "Listings"), White Wolf makes a good base for hikes to Lukens and Harden lakes (see pp.110 and 111).

A third of a mile east along Tioga Road, a rough section of the Great Sierra Wagon Road twists and turns for five miles down to the *Yosemite Creek* campground (Map 5, H9).

CLARK RANGE VIEW TO CLOUD'S REST VIEW

Beyond the White Wolf and Yosemite Creek junctions you are into the high country proper; eight thousand feet up, with trails heading off from the road to alpine lakes and craggy peaks. These lofty destinations are visible a couple miles on from the **Clark Range View** (T11), offering extensive views south to the 11,522ft **Mount Clark** with its sharp-ridged back resembling the pointy plates of a giant stegosaurus.

To the east of the viewpoint lies the broad-shouldered gray granite mass of **Mount Hoffman** (10,850ft), the geographical center of the Park. Its angular peak was never

subjected to the ravages of glacial action, and stands in contrast to the smooth slabs of its lower flanks. When Tuolumne
Meadows was two thousand feet under an ice sheet, it was
the surrounding Hoffman Range which divided the flowing
ice into two distinct glaciers, one carving out the Tuolumne
Canyon and Hetch Hetchy, and the other grinding down
the Tenaya Canyon to sculpt Yosemite Valley.

- -
For more on the effects of glaciation see p.227.
- -

Three miles on, Tioga Road crosses Yosemite Creek
(T15; Map 5, H9), which follows the creek seven miles
downstream until it crashes over Yosemite Falls. Four miles
from the crossing, *Porcupine Flat* campground (T17; Map 5,
H10) immediately precedes the 100-yard Sierra Trees
Nature Trail (T18), along which are marked the various
trees whose habitats overlap at this intersection of several
climatic zones.

From here it is half a mile to the **North Dome trailhead** (T19; see Hike 19), a further mile to where a gap in
the trees reveals the magnificent **Half Dome View** (T20),
and a little over another mile to **May Lake Junction**
(T21), where a bumpy two-mile side road leads to the
road-end trailhead for **May Lake** (see Hike 16), a popular,
pleasant hour-plus stroll.

Back on Tioga Road, it's a mile to **Cloud's Rest View**
(T23; Map 6, C6), where you gaze in awe at the vast,
smooth sheet of granite sweeping at 45 degrees from the
base of Tenaya Canyon five thousand feet up to the 9926ft
summit ridge of Cloud's Rest.

OLMSTED POINT TO TENAYA LAKE

Almost two miles east of Cloud's Rest View an expansive vista opens out at **Olmsted Point** (Map 6, D6), named after Frederick Law Olmsted, first chairman of the Yosemite Park Commission and joint architect of New York City's Central Park. Undoubtedly the most outstanding viewpoint from Tioga Road, it offers long views down Tenaya Canyon towards Cloud's Rest and Half Dome, and up the canyon to Tenaya Lake with the sculpted, smooth monoliths of Tuolumne beyond. A quarter-mile trail leads to the top of a nearby dome with even more stupendous views.

Tioga Road hugs the northern shore of mile-long **Tenaya Lake**, named for the native chief who was captured here by the Mariposa Battalion in 1851. The Ahwahneechee knew the lake as *Py-wi-ack*, or "Lake of the Shining Rocks," an apt description as its entire basin exhibits abundant evidence of glacial polish. Arrive in the early morning or evening and it can be a wonderfully peaceful place to appreciate the granite scenery and perhaps dangle a fishing pole.

As it skirts the lake, the road passes **Sunrise Lakes Trailhead**, marking the start of Hikes 14 (see p.108) and 21 (see p.113), then runs beside the sandy **beach** at **Murphy Creek**, before reaching the eastern end and a long strand that's considered the best for **swimming**.

You're now deep into **granite dome** country, which continues for the remaining five miles to Tuolumne Meadows. Overlooking Tenaya Lake on the north side of Tioga Road, you may see climbers tackling the relatively gentle slopes of **Stately Pleasure Dome**. Further on, **Pywiack Dome** rises above the south side of the road with a large pine growing out of its steepest face. **Mendicott Dome** is behind that, and further still is the blunt visage of **Fairview Dome**, the largest of them all. Rounding a bend, the low **Pothole Dome**, to the north, heralds the open expanse of Tuolumne Meadows.

Tuolumne Meadows and Tioga Pass

The alpine area around **Tuolumne Meadows** has a very different feel than that of the Valley, 55 miles (about a ninety-minutes' drive) away. Here at 8575ft, where you seem to be almost level with the tops of the surrounding snow-covered mountains, it is much more open, the light more intense, and temperatures usually fifteen to twenty degrees lower.

By most measures, Tuolumne is far more peaceful than the Valley, but as the main high country congregation point, it often fills up at peak times. Access is easy from the Tioga Pass entrance, and **hikers** find Tuolumne a better starting point than the Valley for the trails that fan out into the surrounding High Sierra wilderness. We've covered a number of hikes in the area starting on p.115.

The meadows themselves are the largest in all of the Sierra; twelve miles long, between a quarter and half a mile wide, and threaded by the meandering Tuolumne River. The distinctive glaciated granite form of **Lembert Dome** (Map 6, I3; see Hike 26) squats at the eastern end of the meadows gazing across the grasslands towards its western twin, **Pothole Dome** (Map 6, G3; see Hike 23), which makes for a great sunset destination.

It is abundantly clear why in 1869 John Muir asserted that "this is the most spacious and delightful high pleasure-ground I have seen." The mountain scenery is particularly striking to the south, where the **Cathedral Range** offers a horizon of slender spires and knife-blade ridges. It is perhaps best seen from **Soda Springs**, where the angled protuberant spire of **Unicorn Peak** (map 6, H4) is indeed most evocative of the mythical beast's horn. To its right is **Cathedral Peak**, a textbook example of a glaciated

"Matterhorn," where glaciers have carved away the rock on all sides leaving a sharp pointed summit.

Snow usually lingers here until the end of June, forcing the **wildflowers** to contend with a short growing season. They respond with a glorious burst of color in July, a wonderful time for a wander.

Soda Springs and Parsons Lodge

Map 6, H3.

If you've only got a short time in Tuolumne, take a stroll across the meadows to **Soda Springs**, one of the area's most popular and rewarding short **hikes**. It is included as part of Hike 24 (see p.115), but can also easily be visited by following a section of the old carriage road which spurs across the meadow three hundred yards east of the visitor center (see overleaf). This takes you straight to the naturally carbonated springs, described in 1863 as "pungent and delightful to the taste," though today the Park Service discourages drinking it, warning of possible surface contamination. By 1885 the area was being homesteaded by the insect collector and so-called "hermit of the Sierra," **Jean Baptiste Lembert**, who ran goats on 160 acres and erected a small enclosure surrounding the springs, of which only the low walls now survive.

The area around the springs became one of the favorite camping spots of John Muir. Noting the devastating effect sheep were having each summer when they were herded up to the meadows from the lowlands for pasture, the avid conservationist, urged on by magazine editor **Robert Underwood Johnson**, campaigned for Tuolumne's protection as part of a newly created Yosemite National Park. Muir wrote two articles for *Century Magazine* outlining his proposal, and in the fall of 1890 Congress passed a bill along the lines that Muir advocated.

Muir's subsequent fight to save Hetch Hetchy (see box, p.55) was supported by high-country guide, Edward Taylor Parsons, who the fledgling Sierra Club honored posthumously by building the rugged but elegantly proportioned **Parsons Memorial Lodge** (mid-July to early Sept daily 11am–3pm or longer; free) right by the springs. Its single room houses displays on local environmental and campaigning issues, and hosts frequent talks and demonstrations (see *Yosemite Today* for details).

The adjacent **McCauley Cabin** was built by the McCauley brothers who bought Lembert's homestead after his death; it was used as a summer residence until 1961, but is now closed to the public.

Tuolumne practicalities

Tuolumne is the sort of place you might base yourself for several days (or even weeks), heading out on long hikes or just strolling the meadows, taking photos, and lying in the sun. Though you won't be pampered while you're here, you can still sleep and eat fairly well. Facilities are scattered along a two-mile stretch of Tioga Road, so visitors without their own vehicle will need to avail themselves of the **Tuolumne Meadows/Olmsted Point Shuttle** (July to first week in Sept daily 7am–6.30pm; free), which runs every half-hour west from *Tuolumne Meadows Lodge* past Tenaya Lake to Olmsted Point and east to the Park entrance at Tioga Pass.

The westernmost building of interest is the **Tuolumne Meadows Visitor Center** (Map 6, H3; mid-June to Sept daily 9am–5pm, later in July and August; ☎209/372-0263), which has moderately interesting displays on alpine wildflowers, local geology and the area's history. The wood and granite building was constructed in 1934 by the Civilian Conservation Corps in a style recalling Yosemite pioneering days and was later used as a work-crew mess hall.

ALTITUDE SICKNESS

While it is unlikely that you will suffer from **altitude sickness**, most people feel some effects (typically shortness of breath) from being at 8600 feet in Tuolumne Meadows, especially if spending the night here after coming up the same day from much lower elevations. Older people and those with heart and lung diseases should consider staying at least one night in the Valley (4000ft) to acclimatize, making sure to avoid fatty foods and alcohol. If you find yourself suffering from headaches, nausea, severe shortness of breath, irritability and general fatigue, the best remedy is to descend.

It is almost a mile east to the **gas station** (June to early Oct daily 8.30am–5pm; 24hr with credit card) and Tuolumne Mountain Shop, which sells outdoor gear and **climbing** paraphernalia, and doubles as the summer home of the Yosemite Mountaineering School (see p.148).

Next door a large white plastic shed houses the fast-food style *Tuolumne Meadows Grill* (see p.196) and the Tuolumne Meadows Store (late May to early Nov daily 8am–7pm), which stocks a reasonable selection of hiking and camping supplies, basic groceries, ice, booze, and firewood, and has a small post office. The huge *Tuolumne Meadows Campground* (see p.185) is tucked behind, with the reservation office a hundred yards or so east of the store and grill. Across the Tuolumne River it's another half-mile past the Lembert Dome parking area to the **wilderness center** (see p.14) and another few hundred yards down a side road to the tent-cabins and hearty meals of *Tuolumne Meadows Lodge* (see p.169 and p.196), where non-guests can also take **showers** (mid-June to Sept daily noon–3.30pm; $2, towel supplied).

Hike or drive a mile down the road beside Lembert

Dome to reach the Tuolumne Meadows Stables (see p.150), which offers **horseback rides** lasting from a couple of hours to several days.

TIOGA PASS AND THE LEE VINING GRADE

East of Tuolumne Meadows the Tuolumne River splits into two forks, the southerly Lyell Fork tracing the floor of Lyell Canyon towards Mount Lyell, while the Dana Fork runs six miles east to Dana Meadows and the Park entrance at Tioga Pass. Tioga Road follows the Dana Fork past a pullout where there's a great view of Cockscomb, Unicorn and Echo peaks silhouetted against the horizon. Mount Gibbs (12,764ft) and the Park's second highest peak, Mount Dana (13,053ft), are both visible a mile further at **Dana–Gibbs View** (T36), from where you can admire their reddish ferriferous tinge, a striking contrast to the ubiquitous gray Yosemite granite.

Just past a stand of lodgepole pines, these mountains appear again as a backdrop to **Dana Meadows**, a quarter-mile wide and studded with erratics deposited by the ancient Tuolumne Glacier, the largest glacier in the Sierra Nevada, which receded twenty thousand years ago. Huge lumps of ice left behind as it receded formed a series of kettle lakes known as **Tioga Tarns**, now an extremely attractive collection of pools in boggy land beside the fledgling Dana Fork.

At the eastern end of Dana Meadows, the road climbs the last few feet to **Tioga Pass** (T39; Map 6, L2), immediately preceded by the trailhead for the hike to Gaylor Lakes (see Hike 33). Over the pass, you drop more than three thousand feet in six miles along the Lee Vining Grade, a steep but fast road which descends the heavily glaciated Lee Vining Canyon, from lodgepole-studded alpine meadows to low sage-covered hills. Beyond lies the small town of **Lee Vining** on the shores of **Mono Lake** (see p.88).

Southern Yosemite

L ying south of the Valley, **southern Yosemite**'s broad swath of sharply peaked mountains extends from the foothills in the west twenty miles to the Sierra crest in the east. This section of the Park is predominantly rugged country, though most visitors only see the thickly forested and more forgiving landscape of its very eastern fringes, accessed along **Wawona Road**. In the 1860s and early 1870s this road was the stagecoach route from the San Joaquin Valley into Yosemite Valley, a harrowing journey typically broken up at the meadowside homestead of **Wawona**. This is still where visitors to the southern part of the Park stay, either at the campground or in the elegant *Wawona Hotel*. Their prime target is the **Mariposa Grove** of **giant sequoias**, by far the largest and most interesting of Yosemite's three groves, a gem which outshines the nine-hole golf course, **Pioneer Yosemite History Center**, and general outdoor pursuits at hand in southern Yosemite.

Partway along Wawona Road, Glacier Point Road cuts east through forests past the winter sports nexus of **Badger Pass Ski Area**, to the Park's **viewpoint** *par excellence* at **Glacier Point**, right on the rim of Yosemite Valley and on level with the face of Half Dome. It is a justly popular spot, especially at sunset when it seems as if half of the

Park's visitors are here hoping to catch the last rays glinting off the distant **Sierra crest**.

South from the Valley: Tunnel View and Yosemite Valley View

Wawona Road (Hwy-41) leaves the Valley loop road near Bridalveil Fall and immediately starts to climb through trees which occasionally open up to allow stunning views of the Valley, the best being from **Tunnel View** (Map 3, E4), a mile and a half up the road. Here, the whole Valley unfolds before you with El Capitan and Sentinel Rock standing as guardians of what lies beyond, most notably Half Dome. The original stagecoach road from Wawona to the Valley (used prior to 1933) runs parallel to and uphill from the current Wawona Road, and can be seen on the trail to **Inspiration Point** (see Hike 8).

Tunnel View immediately precedes 0.8-mile Wawona Tunnel – the longest in the Park – which ends at **Yosemite Valley View**, where Valley-bound visitors get their first glimpse of El Capitan and Half Dome. Above the road is the exfoliated granite form of **Turtleback Dome**, and across the valley are falls known simply as **The Cascades** (Map 3, C4). Although you're not actually much higher here than in the Valley, the vegetation has already changed. Black oaks have been left behind and the ponderosa pines are joined by cinnamon-barked incense cedar, tall, slender Douglas fir, low, scrubby manzanita, and canyon oak.

The next six miles pass through scorched forest to a road junction known as Chinquapin (Map 3, D8), from where Glacier Point Road (see opposite) breaks off to the northeast. South from Chinquapin towards Wawona, a side road soon spurs a mile off to the right to **Yosemite West**, a private development just outside the Park boundary not worth visiting unless you plan to stay at one of the B&Bs (see p.171).

Back on Wawona Road it is an eleven-mile descent to Wawona, almost entirely through evergreens so thick they seldom reveal any views. Just before Wawona you pass the *Wawona Campground*, site of the first Park headquarters from 1891 to 1906, and a small riverside picnic area before reaching Wawona proper, about a mile beyond.

Our coverage of Wawona begins on p.72.

Glacier Point Road

The sixteen-mile-long **Glacier Point Road** (usually open mid-May to late Oct) branches off from Wawona Road and provides the principal access to **Glacier Point**, perhaps the most exalted viewpoint in the whole Park. This is also great hiking country with 7000-foot trailheads saving hikers the grinding haul out of the Valley to get expansive views.

In winter the first seven miles of the road are kept open to provide access to the **Badger Pass Ski Area** (chains sometimes required); the only reason to stop before that is for the view down some 4500 feet to Merced Canyon from a lookout (G1) a couple of miles along.

Badger Pass Ski Area

Map 3, F7. Mid-Dec to early April (weather permitting) daily 9am–4.30pm.

Five miles past the viewpoint is the **Badger Pass Ski Area** (for full coverage see Chapter 9, "Winter activities"), established in 1935 at a time when the National Park Service was eager to attract as many visitors to Yosemite as possible.

GLACIER POINT ROAD

With a handful of short tows, a predominance of beginner and intermediate terrain, and superb cross-country skiing and snowshoe trails, it makes a great family destination.

Bridalveil Creek to Washburn Point

Drive three miles past Badger Pass through forests brimming with red fir to get to the **McGurk Meadow** trailhead (see Hike 35), immediately followed by the *Bridalveil Creek* campground a quarter of a mile south off Glacier Point Road. Bridalveil Creek originates at **Ostrander Lake** (Map 3, K9; see Hike 39) and eventually plummets over Bridalveil Fall before joining the Merced River.

Almost three miles further along Glacier Point Road, you reach **Clark Range View** (G6), where Mount Clark (11,522ft) can be identified by the avalanche trail down its face and into the forest below. To the left is the domed **Mount Starr King** (9092ft), named for the Unitarian pastor who did much to alert America to the wonders of Yosemite through his writings in 1860.

A couple of miles later, **Pothole Meadows** (G7) appears, where in spring and early summer, five-foot-diameter depressions fill with water from the snowmelt.

The sight of **Sentinel Dome** (Map 3, J4) from the G8 marker may tempt you to tackle Hike 37 (see p.125) from a trailhead parking lot just ahead. The trail leads up to the 8122-foot gleaming granite scalp topped by the gnarled and much photographed skeleton of a Jeffrey pine killed off by drought and old age a few years ago. A second trail from the lot (see Hike 36) leads west to **Taft Point** (Map 3, I5) on the Valley rim, where the granite edges have been deeply incised to form the **Taft Point Fissures**. Far fewer people follow this trail, perhaps because of Taft Point's many vertiginous drops, virtually unprotected by barriers.

Glacier Point Road soon launches into a series of steep

descending **switchbacks** marking the last two miles to Glacier Point. Stop halfway along at **Washburn Point** (Map 4, I9) for a striking side view of Half Dome, remarkably slim in profile.

Glacier Point

Map 4, I7.

The most astonishing views of Yosemite Valley are from **Glacier Point**, the top of an almost sheer cliff 3214 precipitous feet above Curry Village, thirty slow and twisting miles away by road. From the lookout, the Valley floor appears in miniature far below and Half Dome fills the scene at eye level, backed by the distant snowcapped summits of the High Sierra.

Right from the early days of tourism in Yosemite, Glacier Point's amalgam of boulders, pines and granite-formed viewpoints was an inescapable lure. The **Four-Mile Trail** from the Valley was one of the earliest to be created, and even before the first road was constructed in 1883, visitors were coming up on mule-back to stay at McCauley's Mountain House. Later the Glacier Point Hotel also accommodated guests in grand style, but revised Park authority policies didn't allow either to be rebuilt after they burned down in 1969.

The hotels may be gone, but 150 years of tourism have left their mark with a network of viewpoints linked by pathways through the scattered pines. To learn something of the forces which created the wondrous landscape, drop in to the **Geology Hut** on the eastern side of Glacier Point, then continue north to the Valley rim to inspect the **Overhanging Rock**, which reaches way out over the void. Postcards found in every Park store depict scenes of performers poised on the end of the rock doing handstands or precarious ballet steps. In one promotional stunt, someone

GLACIER POINT ROAD

even drove a Dodge out onto the end. The rock is supposedly off-limits, though that doesn't seem to deter the foolhardy from wandering out there to be photographed with Half Dome in the background.

Practicalities

Though it is enjoyable to drive up here or ride the shuttle bus from the Valley, the moment of arrival at Glacier Point is much more rewarding if you hike to it on the very steep Four-Mile Trail (see Hike 11). Most people take a couple of photos, raid the **gift store** (June–Oct daily 9am–7pm), grab something from the **snack stand** (June–Oct daily 9am–4pm or later) then leave. But it is worth spending a couple of hours here to hike to the summit of Sentinel Dome then return to watch the lowering sun cast its golden hue over the mountainscape. After dark the crowds will disappear and you'll have time for reflection as the moon casts its silvery glow on the surface of Half Dome. On some evenings the newly remodeled 150-seat granite amphitheater becomes an arena for stargazing (see *Yosemite Today* for details).

Wawona

There's a decidedly relaxed pace at **WAWONA**, located beside the south fork of the Merced River, 27 miles (or an hour's drive) south of Yosemite Village on Hwy-41. At 4000 feet (the same altitude as Yosemite Valley), it is usually warm in the summer, and most people spend their time here strolling the grounds of the *Wawona Hotel*, ambling around the **Pioneer Yosemite History Center**, swimming, or playing golf. While the only essential sight in the area is the superb **Mariposa Grove** of **giant sequoias**, there are also a handful of worthwhile local **hikes** (see pp.129–131) and some great **horseback rides** originating from the Wawona Stables (Map 8, C2; see p.150).

Provided you are prepared for cold, invigorating river water, **swimming** is best done close by the **Swinging Bridge** (Map 8, I4): follow Forest Drive for two miles to the private Camp Wawona, where you branch left for a quarter of a mile along a dirt road, then park and walk five minutes to a deep, crystal-clear pool.

Some history

The meadows of Wawona were originally known as *Pallachun*, or "good place to stop" to Native Americans making their way from the Sierra Nevada foothills to Yosemite Valley. Here they hunted game and gathered acorns and basket-making materials, until their lifestyle was destroyed by the 1851 arrival of gold miners and the Mariposa Battalion (see "History" on p.220). In 1856, 160 acres of the area were homesteaded by 42-year-old Galen Clark who had suffered a severe lung hemorrhage and headed for the hills to live out his last days, but ended up living until he was 96. The area's giant sequoias had been "discovered" as early as 1851, but it wasn't until 1857 that Clark and trail-building entrepreneur Milton Mann thoroughly documented the big trees. Clark called the forest "Mariposa Grove" and renamed his homestead **Big Trees Station**.

Close to the current site of the *Wawona Hotel*, Clark ran a sawmill and blacksmith's shop, and provided for visitors traveling the original carriage road from Mariposa to Yosemite Valley. When Mariposa Grove became part of the Yosemite Grant in 1864, Clark was made guardian. He sold Big Trees Station in 1874 to the Washburn brothers who built the original *Wawona Hotel*, which burned down four years later. In 1879, the existing main building was built, the meadow was fenced for grazing animals, and produce

WAWONA

was grown for hotel guests. Within three years, the area's name had changed again, this time to **Wa-wo-nah**, the local Indian name for the big trees, and the sound of the call of their guardian spirit, the owl.

In the early twentieth century the Washburns' son Clarence persuaded his parents to build a golf course to lure the newly car-mobile visitors. By 1925, planes were landing on the meadow, and there were daily mail and passenger flights until 1932 when the Wawona area was incorporated into Yosemite National Park.

Wawona Hotel

Map 8, C3.

Pretty much everything in Wawona revolves around the **Wawona Hotel**, California's second-oldest hotel (after the *Coronado* in San Diego). Started in 1876 as a small cluster of white-painted, wooden buildings, it was soon joined by the Washburn brothers' main two-story building with its encir-cling broad verandahs and Adirondack chairs. The entire complex is set in expansive grassy grounds with incense cedars and ponderosa pines all about, with a small **swimming pool** for guests only and a **tennis court** ($2 per hour; ball and $2 racquet rentals from the golf shop) open to all. The hotel's **nine-hole golf course**, across the road, is also open to the public (mid-April to Oct; $23.60 for eighteen holes, $14.50 for nine plus $9.50 for club rental; ⊤209/375-6572 to reserve tee time). The fairways sprawl across the meadows, and mule deer are frequent visitors.

Pioneer Yosemite History Center

Map 8, B2. Self-guided walking tour all year, buildings open roughly late June to early Sept Wed–Sun 10am–noon & 2–4pm; free.

Though most of Yosemite's historic buildings have been lost

to fire or simply knocked down, around a dozen have been gathered together at the **Pioneer Yosemite History Center**, two-minutes' walk north of the *Wawona Hotel*. Most were brought here in the early 1960s, and arranged on either side of the **covered bridge**, built over the south fork of the Merced River by Henry Washburn in 1857. Age has taken its toll, and the bridge was recently deemed unsafe and closed to traffic. It is likely to be reopened in 2002 to pedestrians only.

On the bridge's south side, the large **Gray Barn** was used for harnessing-up the carriages and now contains a couple of early stagecoaches, horse-riding paraphernalia and a 1916 toll board – the six-mile journey from Wawona to the Big Trees cost a horse and rider twelve cents. Something of the spirit of the time can be gleaned on ten-minute **stagecoach rides** (late June to early Sept Wed 2–4pm, Thurs–Sun 10am–noon & 2–4pm; $3, kids aged 3–12 $2), which start outside the barn.

The remaining relocated buildings are clustered on the north side of the bridge. Rangers are often on hand here to give **free tours** of these interiors. The stories associated with the buildings are generally more interesting than the architecture itself, which consists mainly of variations on the basic log or pit-sawn-board cabin. Of particular interest are the **Wells Fargo office**, once the hub of telegraph and booking services in Yosemite Valley, and the cabin belonging to **George Anderson**, the Valley blacksmith famous for making the first ascent up Half Dome (see p.27).

Wawona practicalities

There is no convenient public transportation to Wawona from Yosemite Valley or anywhere outside the Park, though you could visit Wawona and the Mariposa Grove on the guided Grand Tour from the Valley (see p.20). Once in

WAWONA

Wawona, make use of the **Wawona–Mariposa Grove Shuttle Bus** (mid-May to early Oct daily 9am–4pm or later; free), which runs frequently from the Wawona Store to the Mariposa Grove parking lot, with an intermediate stop at the South Entrance. It is particularly handy in mid-summer when the Mariposa Grove lot is so full that the access road is closed to cars. The last bus back leaves the grove at 6pm.

Information and wilderness permits are available from the **Wawona Information Station** (Map 8, B3; mid-May to mid-Sept daily 8.30am–4.30pm; ⊤209/375-9501), housed in what was once the studio of landscape painter Thomas Hill. Snacks, camping supplies and a limited range of **groceries** are available from the Wawona Store (Map 8, B3; daily 9am–6pm), and from the Pine Tree Market (Map 8, F1), a mile along Chilnualna Fall Road. The Wawona Store also has a **post office** (Mon–Fri 9am–5pm, Sat 9am–noon), and the Bassett Memorial **Library**, 7971 Chilnualna Fall Rd (Map 8, E1; Mon, Tues, Thurs & Fri 1–5pm, Wed 3–7pm, Sat 10am–2pm), has **internet access**.

Wawona's hotels, campground and restaurant are
all covered in the relevant sections of "Listings."

Wawona doesn't have much in the way of evening entertainment, though there's often a ranger campfire program at the campground (open to all; free) and a few shows a week by Tom Bopp (April–Oct 8.30pm; see *Yosemite Today* for days; free) in the *Wawona Hotel* lounge. A fixture here since 1983, Tom bashes out predominantly vaudeville songs from Yosemite's past on a piano once used to accompany the Firefall at Curry Village (see box p.44), while showing slides pertinent to the piece being played. While some might find it all a bit cheesy, Tom's enthusiasm always carries the evening.

Mariposa Grove

The biggest, most spectacular stand of **giant sequoias** in Yosemite is **Mariposa Grove** (Map 7, F7; snowbound in winter, but open at all times; free), at the end of Mariposa Grove Road, three miles east of the Park's South Entrance on Hwy-41. Eight-foot diameter ponderosa pines and huge cedars are dwarfed by approximately five hundred mature sequoias, some up to three thousand years old, spread over an area roughly two miles by one mile. From the entrance, the sequoias straggle up a hillside gaining 1500 feet from the **Lower Grove**, home to most of the biggest trees, to the **Upper Grove** where there is a greater concentration of sequoias but fewer really enormous specimens.

First explored by Galen Clark in 1856, Mariposa Grove and Yosemite Valley were jointly set aside as the **Yosemite Grant**, the world's first public preserve in 1864. This afforded some protection at a time when sequoias were being cut for lumber and generally mistreated, though tunnels were cut through two of the trees during Clark's subsequent guardianship. Mariposa Grove was finally incorporated into Yosemite National Park in 1916.

Cars are banned from the grove, but anyone with a modest level of fitness should have no trouble exploring some of the two and a half miles of well-maintained **trails** on foot: take your time heading uphill and enjoy the quick stroll back down at the end. If you can't cope with the terrain, join the hour-long, narrated **Big Trees Tram Tour** (June–Oct daily 9am–6pm every 20min; $11, seniors $8.50, kids $5.50) and get towed around a paved road with stops at the major sights. **Tickets** can be bought by the parking lot at the Mariposa Gift Shop (June–Oct daily 9am–6pm), which also sells a limited range of **snacks**.

MARIPOSA GROVE

Try to arrive early or stay late to avoid both the crowds and the commentary from the tram tour which echoes throughout the grove. A winter visit is another possibility, though you'll need snowshoes or cross-country skiing equipment.

The Mariposa Grove parking lot is often full in summer; ride the free shuttle bus from Wawona (see p.76).

Grove highlights

After a century and a half of tourism, Mariposa Grove is presented as something of a sequoia freak show. While it is impressive enough just coming face-to-bark with these giants, throughout the grove unusual trees are singled out for attention: ones which have grown together, split apart, been struck by lightning, or are simply staggeringly large.

In the Lower Grove signs lead to the **Fallen Monarch**, made famous by the widely reproduced 1899 photo of cavalry officers and their horses standing atop the prostrate tree. No one knows when it fell, but it doesn't seem to have deteriorated much in the hundred years since the photo was taken. Following the path beyond the elegant cluster of the **Bachelor and Three Graces**, you arrive at the largest tree in the grove (and the fifth largest in the world), the **Grizzly Giant**, thought to be somewhere between 2700 and 3500 years old. Its lowest branch is said to be thicker than the trunk of any non-sequoia in the grove, a claim that is easy to believe even when viewed from a hundred feet below. Adjacent is the **California Tunnel Tree**, bored out in 1859 for stagecoaches to pass through, but only accessible to pedestrians since the road was realigned in 1932.

It is a ten-minute walk to reach the **Faithful Couple**, two trees that seeded close to one another and appear to be

THE LIFE OF THE GIANT SEQUOIA

Call it what you will – sierra redwood, *sequoiadendron giganteum*, or just big tree – the **giant sequoia** is the earth's most massive living thing. Some of these arboreal monsters weigh in at a whopping one thousand tons, courtesy of a thick trunk that barely tapers from base to crown. They're also among the oldest trees found anywhere, many reaching two, or even three, thousand years of age.

Sequoias are only found in a few dozen isolated groups on the western slopes of California's Sierra Nevada and grow naturally between altitudes of 5000 and 8500 feet. They occupy three main groves in Yosemite (Mariposa, Tuolumne and Merced) but can grow elsewhere too: early residents planted several in Yosemite Valley, some by the chapel and others in the cemetery. None is yet above six feet in diameter, and only time will tell how big they will be once they mature.

The cinnamon-colored bark of young sequoias is easily confused with that of the incense cedar, but as they age, there's no mistaking the thick, spongy outer layer that protects the sapwood from the fires that periodically sweep through the forests. Fire is, in fact, a critical element in the propagation of sequoias. The hen-egg-sized cones, packing thousands of seeds, require intense heat to open them. Few seeds actually sprout because perfect conditions are needed, usually where a fallen tree has left a hole in the canopy, allowing light to fall on rich mineral soil.

Young trees are conical, but as they mature the lower branches drop off to leave a top-heavy crown. A shallow, wide root system keeps them upright, but eventually heavy snowfall or high winds topple aging trees. With its protective bark and tannin-rich timber a giant sequoia may lie where it fell for hundreds of years. John Muir discovered one still largely intact with a 380-year-old silver fir growing out of the depression it had created.

MARIPOSA GROVE

united. Up the hill a bit further, the **Clothespin Tree** is indeed shaped like an old fashioned clothespin with a forty-foot-high inverted V right through its base where it was hollowed out by fire. Continuing uphill you reach a fine stand of trees that marks the beginning of the slightly more open **Upper Grove**, where you'll also come upon the one-room **Mariposa Grove Museum** (June–Oct daily 9am–4.30pm; free), built in 1930 on the site of Galen Clark's original cabin. It contains modest displays and photos of the mighty sequoias, and sells Yosemite- and wood-land-related books and educational materials.

Most visitors don't go much further so you'll have more peace and quiet as you stroll up to the **Telescope Tree**, where you can walk into the fire-hollowed base and peer up the length of the trunk to a tiny disc of sky. A little further on you'll see the **Wawona Tunnel Tree** lying beside the trail where it fell under a heavy load of snow in 1969, after years of struggling to cope with the eight-foot-wide road-way cut through its base in 1881. If you've still got the ener-gy, tackle the half-mile spur trail to **Wawona Point**, at 6810 feet the highest point in the grove, for great panoramic views.

MARIPOSA GROVE

The gateway towns

W hile there is an obvious benefit to staying right in Yosemite – close to everything you want to see and do, with numerous trailheads right on your doorstep – heavy demand for accommodation within the Park drives many visitors to consider staying in one of the small towns along the main access roads. A couple of these are interesting in their own right, primarily because of their gold mining past, but most are regarded as little more than jumping-off points for the Park.

For gateway town locations, see Map 1 in the Introduction; for listings see "Accommodation" from p.171 and "Eating and drinking" from p.197.

From the northwest: Hwy-120 West

The most direct route into Yosemite from the Bay Area follows Hwy-120 W. On this approach, two historic towns make realistic bases for visits into the Park; the more convenient of the two is **Groveland**, located on the highway itself. **Coulterville**, to the south, has more limited facilities.

East of Groveland, Hwy-120 passes a number of tiny communities and a handful of places to stay, then enters Yosemite at the Big Oak Flat Entrance, from where our account continues (in reverse order) on p.51. Immediately before the Big Oak Flat Entrance, Evergreen Road cuts north to Hetch Hetchy.

GROVELAND

Probably the single most appealing town in the vicinity of Yosemite, **GROVELAND**, almost fifty miles from the Valley, straddles the highway for half a mile, its central section retaining the verandahs and wooden sidewalks of its gold mining days. Throw in some good places to stay and eat, a classic old bar called the *Iron Door Saloon*, and a generally relaxed feel, and you can hardly go wrong.

You won't want to spend many daylight hours here, but there is a tiny **museum** (Mon, Wed & Thurs 2–6pm, Tues 1–8pm, Sat 10am–2pm) with changing exhibits of local relevance. The adjacent **library** (same hours; ☎209/962-6144) has free **internet access**.

YARTS **buses** (see p.10) run into the Park on weekends in summer; if you're driving, fairly cheap **gas** can be found a couple miles west of town on Hwy-120.

COULTERVILLE

COULTERVILLE stands a little off the main approaches to the Park on Hwy-49, but you won't regret a brief detour to see the sagging wooden buildings and covered boardwalks of its diminutive center, which date back to the mid-nineteenth century when this was an important gold-rush town. As the gold dwindled, Coulterville transformed itself into a waystation on the original stage route into Yosemite. Some travelers stayed at a hotel that is now the small **Northern Mariposa County History Center** (Feb–Dec Wed–Sun 10am–4pm; donations welcome; ☏209/878-3015), while others – John Muir and Teddy Roosevelt among them – stayed across the road at *Hotel Jeffery* (see p.173). Built in 1851, the hotel remains the centerpiece of town; after a quick tour of the old buildings around it, retire to the long wooden bar of the hotel's *Magnolia Saloon & Grill* (see p.198).

You can obtain tourist information at the small **Coulterville Visitor Center** at 5007 Main St (Thurs–Sun 9am–4.30pm; ☏209/878-3074, ⓦwww.homeofyosemite.com).

From the southwest: Hwy-140

The fastest road into Yosemite, and the one least likely to be closed by snowfall, is Hwy-140, running east from the sleepy Central Valley town of **Merced**, the **transport nexus** for the region. Local buses pass through the gold rush settlement of **Mariposa**, which is lively enough to make a good base with a wide range of accommodation and places to eat. The road from here to the Park runs through the rural hamlets of **Midpines** and **El Portal** and enters at the Park's Arch Rock Entrance.

MERCED

Some eighty miles southwest of Yosemite Valley, **MERCED** is too far from the Park to be considered a good base for exploring, but is very handy for its **transport connections**. Most people pass straight through, but we've detailed some accommodation and restaurants in "Listings" (p.173 and p.199) just in case. If you have some time to kill between connections, pay a visit to the 1875 Italian Renaissance-style courthouse, a gem of a building in the main square that's maintained as the **County Courthouse Museum**, at 21st and N (Wed–Sun 1–4pm; free).

Practicalities

Trains (see p.7) stop at the Amtrak station, 324 W 24th St at K Street, one mile northeast of the center of town: follow K Street off W 16th Street.

Greyhound buses (see p.9) stop downtown at the **Transpo Center**, 710 W 16th St at N Street, which also houses the **California Welcome Center** (Mon–Sat 8am–5pm; ☎209/384-2791, 🖷209/384-2733, 🌐www .yosemite-gateway.org), good for general Yosemite information. The adjacent **Merced CVB**, 690 W 16th St (Mon–Fri 8.30am–5pm; ☎209/384-2793, 🖷209/384-2791, 🌐www.merced-chamber.com), is better for obtaining more local details.

YARTS and VIA buses (see p.10) pick up passengers at the Transpo Center and train station on their way to Yosemite, and there are several **car rental** agencies in town (see "Directory" on p.213).

MARIPOSA

From Merced, it takes about two hours to reach Yosemite Valley along Hwy-140. The only major town along the way is **MARIPOSA**, 45 miles from the Valley, yet another former gold rush town that relies on Yosemite-bound tourism for its keep. Motels are dotted along the highway and its retail core has a number of wayside restaurants and knick-knack/antique shops lodged in old wooden buildings.

The historic heart of town is attractive enough, particularly the **Mariposa County Courthouse**, cnr Jones and 10th streets (tours late May to early Sept Fri 5.30–8.30pm, Sat 10am–8.30pm, Sun 10am–4pm, reservations essential ☎209/966-2456; free), the oldest law enforcement building west of the Mississippi still in continuous use. Also of interest is the **California State Mining and Mineral Museum**, two miles south on Hwy-49 (May–Sept daily 10am–6pm; Oct–April Wed–Mon 10am–4pm; ⓦwww.mariposa.org/calminmuseum; $3.50), which revels in the glory days of the mid-nineteenth century with reconstructions of a mine and stamp mill, plus the largest single gold nugget ever uncovered in California, a thirteen-pound chunk valued at over $1 million.

Practicalities

The very helpful **Mariposa County Visitors Center** at 5158 Hwy-140 (mid-May to mid-Sept Mon–Sat 8am–9pm Sun 10am–6pm; mid-Sept to mid-May Mon–Sat 8am–5pm, Sun closed; ☎209/966-7081, ⓦwww.homeofyosemite.com) provides information about Yosemite and around.

There's a well-stocked **supermarket**, Pioneer Market (daily 8am–9pm), at the eastern end of town, complete with in-store bakery. The **library**, 4978 10th St (Tues &

MARIPOSA

Thurs 10am–7pm, Wed, Fri & Sat 10am–5pm), has free **internet access**.

MIDPINES, EL PORTAL AND INTO THE VALLEY

En route from Mariposa to Yosemite, motels, campgrounds and lodges line the highway. A few are clustered around **MIDPINES**, ten miles east of Mariposa, a scattered settlement with just the Midpines Store and gas station to indicate its center.

From Midpines the road drops down and follows the left bank of the **Merced River** all the way into the Valley. Across the river you can pick out the level terrace where the **Yosemite Valley Railroad** once carried in supplies and tourists from Merced as far as El Portal (see below), and hauled out limestone for cement, barite and logs.

Some seven miles from Midpines, **Savage's Trading Post** marks the point where the south fork of the Merced flows into the main Merced River. Established in 1849 as a conveniently located trading post for Miwok Indians and goldminers, it is now a gift store selling Native American blankets and the like.

Eleven miles on, the last community before Yosemite National Park is **EL PORTAL**, with only the huge *Yosemite View Lodge* motel complex (see p.174) and the El Portal Market grocery visible from the highway.

From El Portal – at 1900 feet – you cross the boundary into Yosemite National Park and start climbing steeply, gaining over two thousand feet along the seven miles to the Valley. Two miles beyond El Portal the **Arch Rock Entrance** (M3) gets its name from overhanging rocks which touch in the middle to form an arch over Yosemite-bound traffic. As the ascent flattens out, the junction with Big Oak Flat Road marks your arrival at Yosemite Valley: coverage continues with "Southside Drive" on p.48.

From the south: Hwy-41

Yosemite visitors arriving from the south will come through the growing town of **Oakhurst**, not a pretty place, but with all the facilities you'll need. The only real alternative is the roadside handful of hotels known as **Fish Camp**, a couple miles from the Park's southern entrance.

OAKHURST

In the last few years, **OAKHURST**, sixteen miles south of Yosemite's South Entrance and fifty miles south of the Valley proper, has become a booming huddle of malls, chain hotels and fast-food joints around the junction of Hwys 41 and 49. The town makes little of its pleasant setting in the Sierra foothills, but the abundance of lodging and restaurants does make it a handy base. There is no useful public transportation to or from Oakhurst, but with your own vehicle you can easily explore the southern section of the Park, and day trips into the Valley are not out of the question.

From Oakhurst, Hwy-41 heads north towards the Park, passing most of the hotels and restaurants and, after half a mile, the **Yosemite Sierra Visitors Bureau**, 40637 Hwy-41 (Mon–Sat 8.30am–5pm, Sun 9am–1pm; ☎559/683-4636, ⓦwww.go2yosemite.net).

FISH CAMP

The tiny grouping of hotels which makes up **Fish Camp** lies fourteen miles north of Oakhurst, and two miles from the Park's South Entrance, making it handy for Wawona and Mariposa Grove. It also has something to entertain the kids

thanks to the Yosemite Mountain Sugar Pine Railroad, usually known as **The Logger**, 56001 Hwy-41 (March–Oct
daily; $12; ⊤559/683-7273, ⊛www.ymsprr.com), an oil-
burning train which plies a two-mile track into the forest
from where hewn timber was once carted.

From the east: Hwy-120 East

Snow typically blocks Hwy 120 E from early November
until late May, but for the rest of the year, this is the most
spectacular approach to the Park. From Death Valley and
southern California, US-395 runs through the dry sage-
brush covered hills of the Owens Valley to Mono Lake and
the small town of Lee Vining. Here Hwy-120 E cuts west
up the Lee Vining grade past a number of good campgrounds to the Park entrance at Tioga Pass, and Tuolumne
Meadows just beyond. Yosemite Valley lies sixty miles on.

Our account of the road from Yosemite
Valley to Tioga Pass is covered from p.57.

LEE VINING AND MONO LAKE

You wouldn't want to drive daily into Yosemite Valley from
LEE VINING, but this small town is just twenty miles
from the eastern reaches of the Park, and sits dramatically
on the edge of a volcanic, desert tableland virtually on the
shores of salty, alkaline **Mono Lake**. Great sandcastle-like
tufa towers and spires rise up from the lake's blue waters,

forming a science-fiction landscape which has been exposed over the past fifty years or so as the city of Los Angeles has drained away the waters that flow into the lake. The towers of tufa were formed underwater, where calcium-bearing freshwater springs well up through the carbonate-rich lake water. As the lake level dropped, the weird formations were gradually revealed, while the lake's aquatic and bird life became endangered. Over the last 25 years, campaigners for Mono Lake's preservation have succeeded in getting Los Angeles to partly restore the water level.

Before striking out for a close look at the lake, stop into the first-rate **Mono Basin Visitor Center**, half a mile north of Lee Vining beside US-395 (May–Oct daily 9am–5.30pm; Nov–April closed Tues & Wed; ☎760/647-3045), which has interesting exhibits about the area and runs a full program of ranger walks. To explore on your own, take US-395 south of Lee Vining and follow the signs to the South Tufa Reserve.

Practicalities

The only useful public transportation is the summer-only YARTS **bus service** (see p.11) linking Mammoth Lakes with Lee Vining, Tuolumne Meadows and Yosemite Valley. Right in the heart of Lee Vining be sure to call in at the **Mono Lake Committee Information Center** (daily 9am–5pm, often until 10pm in July & Aug; ☎760/647-6595, ⓦwww.leevining.com), a general visitor center with an excellent thirty-minute video showcasing the committee's battle for the protection of Mono Lake.

LEE VINING AND MONO LAKE

HIKING AND OTHER OUTDOOR ACTIVITIES

Day hikes

However magnificent the roadside scenery, it is no substitute for striking out on foot along some of the eight hundred miles of **hiking trails** that weave through Yosemite National Park. The solitude and scenic grandeur quickly get their hooks into you, and many people are so captivated by the experience they end up doing far more hiking than they had ever imagined.

Novice hikers may want to join one of the excellent guided day hikes (see box p.95), but it really is very easy to head out on your own along one of the less strenuous walks we've listed. More **experienced hikers** may feel restricted by our day-hiking recommendations and should also flip to Chapter 7, "Backcountry hiking and camping."

The hikes listed in this and the backcountry hiking
chapter have been numbered to more easily locate the
hiking routes on the maps in the back of the book.

Gentle hikes can be undertaken without leaving the Valley floor, but to get away from the crowds you only need to tackle any path with a bit of a slope. Some of the finest and most accessible trails, including the stunning **Mist Trail**

HOW TOUGH IS THE HIKE?

All fifty hikes in this guide have been given a **rating** in one of
four categories:

Easy – generally a walk of up to a couple hours on relatively
smooth surfaces across flat or gently sloping ground.

Moderate – a hike with some gradient but on well-maintained
trails, taking up to several hours.

Strenuous – a hike on fairly steep and occasionally rough
ground, usually consuming most of the day.

Very strenuous – a trek of at least eight hours negotiating
steep terrain on uneven ground.

and the demanding route up **Half Dome**, start from the
Happy Isles trailhead at the eastern end of Yosemite
Valley. In other areas of the Park, **Tuolumne Meadows**
has the greatest concentration of high-country treks,
though there are also plenty along **Tioga Road** and several
more around **Wawona** and **Hetch Hetchy**.

HIKING PRACTICALITIES

Since permits are not required for day hikes, you need only
get yourself to a trailhead and set off. In Yosemite Valley
you can leave your vehicle in one of the day-use parking
lots and ride the free Valley shuttle to the start of the route.
Elsewhere in the Park, either ride the Glacier Point or
Tuolumne Meadows hikers' buses, or drive your own vehicle to the trailhead; you'll usually find enough parking,
along with steel **bear-resistant lockers** in which you
should stash any food and scented toiletries.

Remember to pack out all **trash**, bury **bodily waste** at
least six inches deep and a hundred feet from any water, and
stand quietly aside for **horseback riders**.

HIKING PRACTICALITIES

Staying on track

Every major trailhead and trail junction sprouts a cluster of **stenciled metal signs** stating the distance to prominent landmarks or destinations in each direction. Most trails are easy to follow, and when they cross bare rock you'll see **cairns** (small piles of rocks also known as "ducks") marking the way. In addition, you may also come across a rectangle

---

GUIDED HIKES

If you are uncertain of your ability to navigate, fancy a little commentary, or are just looking for some companionship, the answer might be to join a **guided hike**. As well as their rock climbing instruction and backcountry hikes, the Yosemite Mountaineering School (☎ 209/372-8344, ⓦ www.yosemite-mountaineering.com) runs a series of organized group hikes mostly from April to September. These might include a half-day hike ($45, min three people) such as a Valley Floor loop, or a full-day hike ($70, min four; includes lunch) from Glacier Point along the Panorama Trail to Happy Isles. In addition, the school offers more expensive **customized guided hikes**. They'll tailor the hike to your needs, and combine individuals to form a group to make the price per person cheaper. **Guided overnight hikes** are also available. Typical undertakings include a journey from Tuolumne Meadows to Yosemite Valley, or an ascent of Mount Lyell.

Companies based outside the Park also run guided hikes in Yosemite. One of the best is Yosemite Guides (☎ 1-877/425-3366 or 209/379-2331, ⓦ www.yosemiteguides.com), based at *Yosemite View Lodge* on Hwy-140 (see p.174). They offer full-day hikes ($60–65) along the Valley rim and in the high country, as well as a late afternoon stroll through giant sequoias ($55) and a sunset walk ($55) (both with dinner), and a periodic full moon hike ($45).

HIKING PRACTICALITIES

or letter "T" cut from the bark of trailside trees, remnants of an outdated practice of trailblazing.

It is hard to get lost if you stick to the trail, but that shouldn't stop you from carrying a **compass** and a detailed **topographic map** of the Park. Hikers going off-trail should be equipped with the relevant Quad map (see "Maps" on p.16).

Safety and potential hazards

Safety on the trail is mostly common sense, but in an effort to reduce injuries the Park Service offers considerable precautionary information online (ⓦwww.nps.gov/yose/wilderness/safety). They make no attempt to keep track of hikers in the Park so it always pays to **let someone know where you are going** (and tell them when you get back), especially if hiking alone.

Before setting off, check the **weather forecast** at any of the visitor centers or by calling ☏209/372-0200. While Yosemite's weather is generally stable, sudden summer and fall thunderstorms are quite common, especially in the afternoons. They seldom last long, but it pays to steer clear of exposed places, viewpoints and lone trees which are susceptible to **lightning strikes**, and always carry warm, waterproof clothing; **hypothermia** is a killer.

For all of our hikes we've given an indication of the **normal hiking season**, when the trail is likely to be snowfree, though it pays to check **trail conditions** either through visitor centers or online (ⓦwww.nps.gov/yose/wilderness/trailconditions). Keep in mind that in the high country it can snow as early as October and as late as June.

Hiking in the backcountry is generally far safer than walking city streets, but it helps to be aware of some potential dangers. One of the biggest threats is **water**, particularly during the spring snowmelt period when small streams become raging torrents. Avoid crossing swollen unbridged streams (especially above rapids and falls, which claim lives every year), and stay away from riverbanks, particularly if you've got children in tow.

Animals pose less of a threat, though **mosquitoes** are certainly a nuisance, particularly in June. **Rattlesnakes**, which are fairly common below 5000 feet (and have been seen as high as 10,000 feet), are more of a menace than **bears** which generally make themselves scarce and can easily be driven off with a bit of stamping, clapping and shouting. **Mountain lions** live throughout the Park but are rarely seen. Count yourself lucky if you catch sight of one but minimize the chance of attack by grouping together and trying to appear as large as possible. Don't advance or run away, but retreat slowly and if the lion attacks, fight back.

In the Sierra foothills (up to 5000ft), watch out for **poison oak**, with its oak-like grouping of three green leaves. If the plant's oil gets on your skin it causes burning and itching; wash off as much oil as possible with cold water and apply cortisone creams, which may provide some relief.

What to take

Your most important decision is what to **wear**. Several layers of light clothing work best so that you can bundle up or strip off as required. Shorts and a T-shirt are fine in sunny weather, but cotton is a liability when wet, so bring synthetic materials, such as polyproplene. You'll also need to stay dry; always carry a light waterproof shell.

Apart from the easiest excursions, the hikes listed below are often along rough paths, and you'll be best off wearing **boots with ankle support**. Always take more **food** than you think you are going to need, and on longer hikes, have some means of **water purification**. Also take a map, mosquito repellent, sunscreen, sunglasses, a wide-brimmed hat, and a compass. **Day packs** and other outdoor equipment can be rented from the Mountain Shop in Curry Village (see p.210).

HIKING PRACTICALITIES

CHOOSING A HIKE

Since all the hikes described in the guide are superb, we've resisted the temptation to highlight the "best of the best 50 hikes." Here is a highly subjective list of our favorites in several categories:

Solitude – 31, 39, 44

Company and fellow hikers – 7, 16, 24

Family hike – 7, 26, 41

Early spring – 10, 13, 43

Winter – 5, 6, 9

Waterfalls – 3, 30, 32

Wildlife – 18, 29, 41

Wildflowers – 15, 18, 35

Fabulous views – 4, 19, 21

Alpine scenery – 27, 28, 31

Historic remains – 7, 33, 34

The hikes in each of the following sections are listed in approximate order of increasing difficulty.

HIKES FROM YOSEMITE VALLEY: HAPPY ISLES TRAILHEAD

The hikes in this section start from the Happy Isles trailhead at the eastern end of Yosemite Valley (shuttle stop 16). They all initially follow the Merced River, and each hike builds on the previous one.

🔢 Vernal Fall footbridge

Map 4, L6. Easy; all year.

1.4 miles round trip; 1–2hr; 400ft ascent.

A popular, moderately steep hike over broken asphalt to a perfect pine-framed view up the Merced River to **Vernal Fall**. It follows part of the John Muir Trail (JMT) (see box, p.138), starting just east of the road bridge over the Merced River. Head upstream past a detailed trail distance sign and several breaks in the trees which reveal the churning river and the 370ft **Illilouette Fall** tucked back in Illilouette Canyon. The trail continues to a footbridge over the Merced from where you'll get the best view of Vernal Fall. With the river crashing below it's a dramatic vantage point, usually crowded with people photographing their friends with the falls in the background.

ⓗ Mist Trail to the top of Vernal Fall

Map 4, L6. Moderate; April–Nov.

3 miles round trip; 2–3hr; 1000ft ascent.

If you only do one hike in Yosemite, this should be it. During the spring snowmelt this short walk really packs a punch as it twists up a path so close to **Vernal Fall** that a rainbow often frames the cascading water, and hikers get drenched in spray; bring a raincoat or plan to get wet. Though hardly dangerous, the Mist Trail demands sure footing and a head for heights.

Start by following Hike 1 to the Vernal Fall footbridge, after which the crowds thin appreciably. Continue 150 yards then veer left onto the marked Mist Trail, which starts climbing steadily along a fairly narrow path. Railings protect you from the edge and provide support for the final haul up slippery steps cut into the rock. At the top of the fall you can rest on the smooth slabs beside the deceptively placid **Emerald Pool**. Water flows into the pool over the **Silver Apron**, a thirty-yard-wide shelf of slick rock that looks very tempting as a slide. Though it is quite obviously foolhardy to swim this close to the lip of the fall, people have died doing so.

Either retrace your steps to the trailhead, or return via the JMT, reached along the path leading uphill from near the footbridge just above the Silver Apron.

ⓗ3 Mist Trail to the top of Nevada Fall

Map 4, L6. Strenuous; May–Nov.

7 miles round trip; 5–8hr; 1900ft ascent.

This hike expands on Hike 2, adding an extra 900 feet of ascent, taking in more expansive panoramas of the high country, and culminating in a **close-up view of Nevada Fall**, higher and perhaps even more striking than Vernal Fall.

Follow Hike 2 as far as the Silver Apron, then cross the footbridge immediately above it. Wind your way through the forest to a flat spot which, from 1870 until 1897, was the spray-drenched location of "La Casa Nevada," also known as Snow's Hotel. The path then follows a series of switchbacks climbing up the side of Nevada Fall with the rounded peak of Liberty Cap rearing above. At the junction with the JMT you'll turn right and soon reach the Merced River at the top of Nevada Fall. Peer over the lip at the cascade below, then relax on the smooth gray slabs of rock before returning along the descending JMT. This cuts across the face of a cliff where a low stone wall protects you from the vertiginous drop, then levels off as you're treated to some great views of Half Dome, and across the Valley to Yosemite's northern reaches.

ⓗ4 Half Dome

Map 4, L6. Very strenuous; late May to mid-Oct.

17 miles round trip; 9–12hr; 4800ft ascent.

The summit of **Half Dome** is the most alluring target of ambitious day-hikers, who are rewarded with stupendous views from the broad flat top almost five thousand feet above the Valley floor. Hikers should start at the crack of **dawn**, initially following either Hike 3 to the top of Nevada Fall or following the JMT to the same point; for variety take the other route on the way down. From the junction of the two trails, follow the JMT as it skirts the backcountry campground in **Little Yosemite Valley** and follows Sunrise Creek steeply uphill. Split off the JMT along the **Half Dome Trail** passing the **last water** on the track (half a mile past the junction on the left), then reaching the broad shoulder of Half Dome. From here you'll negotiate a series of steep switchbacks which bring you to the base of **steel cables** and wooden steps lashed to Half Dome's extremely steep curved back, which must be used to reach the summit. The steps are removed in mid-October to discourage winter ascents and reinstalled at the end of May; there's usually a pile of free-use **gloves** at the base of the cables to protect tender hands. Do not approach the summit if there is thunder around (commonly late afternoons from Aug to Oct), as the peak, and the steel cables, attract **lightning bolts**.

Once at the summit, anyone concerned about outdoor credibility will want to edge out to the very lip of the abyss and peer down the sheer 2000ft northwest face. Return the way you came. You have now earned yourself the right to buy an "I climbed Half Dome" T-shirt from the Village Store.

It is possible to do Half Dome as an **overnight hike**, but camping is prohibited on the summit, so you'll have to spend the night at Little Yosemite Valley.

HAPPY ISLES TRAILHEAD

HIKES FROM THE REST OF THE VALLEY

H5 Eastern Valley Loop

Map 4, I5. Shuttle stops 14 and 20. Easy; all year.

2.6-mile loop; 1–2hr; negligible ascent.

This gentle hike weaves through some of the most populated sections of Yosemite, but is surprisingly peaceful as it loops around the eastern end of the Valley past its main features and some attractive riverside scenery.

Starting from the main parking lot at Curry Village, head east along the broad path that runs between tent cabins until you reach the shuttle road. Turn right, and then almost immediately go right again into a parking lot used by overnight hikers. From the lot's eastern corner, a dirt track cuts half a mile through the woods to a swampy area known as The Fen. A boardwalk from here leads you to the Nature Center at Happy Isles beside the Merced River where there is an impressive view of **North Dome** and Washington Column. Cross the Merced on the road bridge and turn left to follow the dogwood-shaded riverbank, gradually veering further left as you approach the Valley stables; there are especially good views of Upper Yosemite Fall along this stretch. At the stables, walk over Clark Bridge then immediately turn right into the **Lower Pines campground** and follow the campground roads to the far northwestern end. Here a narrow path cuts through trees to Stoneman Meadow. Cross over the long boardwalk and continue straight to return to Curry Village.

H6 Western Valley Loop: El Capitan and Bridalveil Fall

Map 3, G4. Easy; all year.
6.5-mile loop; 2hr 30min–3hr 30min; 350ft ascent.

This fairly long but easy and usually peaceful hike visits the meadows and viewpoints at the western end of Yosemite Valley, involving intimate encounters with **El Capitan**, Cathedral Spires, and **Bridalveil Fall**. The trail largely follows the road but is a lot more pleasurable than the equivalent stop-start sightseeing drive, and being shaded makes a good hike on a hot day.

- -

The main features on this walk are discussed
under "Valley highlights" from p.24 and
"Northside and Southside drives" from p.46.

- -

Park near El Capitan Bridge and walk east for a couple hundred yards along a path beside Northside Drive. When you cross over to the north side and into the forest on the trail marked "Bridalveil Fall 4.1," El Capitan's North American Wall will be straight ahead, and you'll soon cross climbers' paths leading to El Cap's base. Continuing west, the trail bridges Ribbon Creek which is dry in late summer but violent in spring when Ribbon Fall (just upstream) is in full flow.

Just past a view of Bridalveil Fall, you'll cross **Pohono Bridge** to the southern side of the Valley following a track that sticks close to the Merced. You are now headed upstream with the river on your left. Don't bother crossing the road to see Fern and Moss springs, and press on to Bridalveil Meadow, keeping close to the road until you meet Wawona Road coming in from the right. After visiting Bridalveil Fall, pick up the wide path that heads east, parallel to Southside Drive. A sign announcing 5.5 miles to Curry Village marks the start of the only significant climb on the walk, which gradually ascends a moraine to reveal great treetop views across to El Cap. It is pleasant up-and-down walking for the next half-hour or so until you reach the "El Capitan 1.4" sign, where you'll turn left and follow a footpath north across Southside Drive. After wandering through young ponderosa pines you'll be back at El Capitan Bridge and your vehicle.

⓱ Mirror Lake and Tenaya Canyon Loop

Map 4, L4. Shuttle stop 17. Easy; all year.
4.2 miles round trip; 2hr; 100ft ascent, 100ft descent.

This undemanding walk calls at **Mirror Lake** (see p.45), one of the Valley's premier sights, then continues into the lower reaches of **Tenaya Canyon**; it is good all year but particularly gorgeous in May and June when the dogwoods are in bloom.

Starting at shuttle stop 17 (easily accessible on foot from Curry Village), follow the traffic-free road to Tenaya Creek Bridge, where you'll return at the end of the hike. The road continues all the way to Mirror Lake, but two hundred yards past the bridge a broad dirt path angles off to the left, offering a quieter, asphalt-free alternative route. The paths meet at the compellingly calm Mirror Lake where you can follow an interpretive trail and, early in the summer when the lake is full, photograph **Half Dome** reflected in its meditative stillness.

Beyond Mirror Lake you'll soon cross an area where a rockfall came down in 1997. About a mile on, the Snow Creek Trail heads up out of Tenaya Canyon to the left; instead bear right and walk over Tenaya Creek on Snow Creek Bridge. Turn right and keep the river on your right as you follow it downstream, until you complete the loop at Tenaya Creek Bridge.

H8 Inspiration Point

Map 3, E5. Moderate; mid-May to Oct.

2.4 miles round trip; 1hr 30min–2hr 30min; 600ft ascent.

This short but taxing hike leads you away from the crowded viewpoint at Tunnel View (see p.68) and takes you to **Inspiration Point**, a spot just as magnificent overlooking the valley, and especially striking in the late afternoon. Switchback steeply through manzanita, oak and conifer woods with plenty of glorious wayside viewpoints, making use of good photo ops to catch your breath.

H9 Columbia Rock

Map 4, B4. Shuttle stop 7. Moderate; all year.

2 miles round trip; 1hr 30min–3hr; 1000ft ascent.

The most easily accessible views on the north side of the Valley are from Columbia Rock, a small promontory part way up the route to the top of Upper Yosemite Fall (see below). The hike starts behind *Camp 4*, and climbs through glades of canyon live oak for about half an hour until the trail gradually bends to the right. Breaks in the trees reveal the Valley far below, but the best vista is saved for **Columbia Rock**, from where Half Dome dominates to the east.

H10 Upper Yosemite Fall

Map 4, B4. Shuttle stop 7. Strenuous; April–Dec.

7 miles round trip; 4–7hr; 2700ft ascent.

This perennially popular, energy-sapping hike climbs steeply to the north rim of the Valley with great views of Upper Yosemite Fall for much of the way, and the opportunity to sit virtually on the edge of the fall and gaze down at the Lilliputian activity below in Yosemite Village. Being on the north side of the Valley, sun beats down on the trail all year,

HIKES FROM THE REST OF THE VALLEY

which keeps it accessible when others are snowbound, but the hike demands an early start in summer; it's best to set off by 7am. If you've got lots of stamina, you can also explore **Yosemite Point**, a mostly level mile from the top of Upper Yosemite Fall, and perhaps Eagle Peak (Map 3, H3), a two-mile hike from the fall with an 1100-foot ascent.

The trail starts far to the west of the base of Yosemite Falls and follows Hike 9 to Columbia Rock. It then descends gradually until you round a corner revealing the full majesty of **Upper Yosemite Fall** straight ahead. During the meltwater period, the power and volume of the water become increasingly apparent as you draw nearer. In the morning light, the cascade casts ever-changing shadows against the rock wall, and you can also pick out **Lost Arrow Spire** standing apart from the cliff face to the right of the fall.

Climbing again, the track gradually pulls out of the trees into the full force of the sun just as the switchbacks get really steep. (This is where you'll wish you'd gotten out of bed an hour earlier). When you get into some shady Jeffrey pines and red firs, a sign points to the top of the fall just a couple hundred yards away.

There are numerous vantage points at the top, but the best is just to the right of the fall (facing downstream) where you can follow a narrow path to a rock shelf below, very close to the top of the fall. In July and August, the low water flows combine with Valley winds to frequently blow the spray back over the shelf.

⑪ Four-Mile Trail to Glacier Point

Map 4, B6. Shuttle stop 7. Strenuous; mid-May to Oct.
4.8 miles one way; 2hr 30min–4hr one way, 5–8hr round trip; 3200ft ascent.

Glacier Point can be reached by car and the hikers' bus, but neither approach is as rewarding as hiking the very popular **Four-Mile Trail**, which climbs the southern wall of the Valley ascending switchbacks the whole way. Originally constructed in 1872, the track was financed by James McCauley, who intended it as a toll route to his hotel at Glacier Point. Remodeled and lengthened since, it now starts from a trailhead parking lot away from the shuttle bus route: from shuttle stop 7 walk west along Northside Drive then take the paved bike and foot path half a mile across the Valley to the trailhead.

Ambitious hikers can combine the Four-Mile Trail with the Panorama Trail (see p.126) for a very strenuous full-day circuit.

The trail surface has been largely neglected, leaving a lot of broken asphalt underfoot. This is now covered in sand, making it fairly slippery; consequently it is safer to hike up than down. The trail starts steeply, but you're in shade for much of the way, and views become ever more expansive as you rapidly gain height. After about an hour, you'll reach the first really fantastic views of Half Dome, Cathedral Rocks, Tenaya Canyon and Washington Column. Further up you're at level with the near-sheer face of **Sentinel Rock**, its fissures cast in relief by the afternoon light. Soon you'll leave the last of the switchbacks behind and skirt some small cliffs with the Valley far below and Yosemite Falls on the far side. After a brief descent, the final forested climb brings you to Glacier Point, and a well-earned ice cream.

HIKES FROM THE REST OF THE VALLEY

HIKES FROM HETCH HETCHY

⒤ Wapama Falls

Map 5, C4. Easy; mid–April to Nov.
5 miles round trip; 2–3hr; 400ft ascent.

This is a relaxing trail in a quiet corner of the Park, following the north shore of Hetch Hetchy reservoir and ideal for accessing the foaming Wapama Falls. Low altitude and a northerly aspect ensure that the path is clear of snow early in the season, which coincides with the falls' best display from late April to June; it generally dries up by August.

Park your vehicle beside the O'Shaughnessy Dam and cross its concrete curve, gazing across the reservoir at the hefty bell-shape of **Kolana Rock**. At the far end of the dam a short tunnel brings you to the trail, which follows mostly level terrain just above the water. The hike is especially nice in the spring, when wildflowers are abundant, and for a few weeks **Tueeulala Falls** plunges down the cliff to the left of the path, its veils of spray wafting onto the path until it dries up in mid-June. At all times keep an eye out for **rattlesnakes** that might be camouflaged in fallen leaves dappled by the shade of live oaks. Further on, **Wapama Falls** drops 1400ft from the valley rim in two steps before pouring over rocks as a braided stream, all best seen from a couple of footbridges on the route.

After you've had your fill of the falls, either head back the way you came, or continue a further five miles to Rancheria Falls (Hike 13).

⒥ Rancheria Falls

Map 5, C4. Moderate; mid-April to Nov.
14.5 miles round trip; 5–8hr; 800ft ascent.

An extension of Hike 12, this hike is similar in character but more arduous, and with a gorgeous springtime reward in the form of **Rancheria Falls**.

From Wapama Falls, the footpath continues up the valley climbing towards the base of **Hetch Hetchy Dome**, eventually reaching a magnificent viewpoint high above the water and directly opposite Kolana Rock. Here you can look back to the dam, and up the lake towards your goal (still an hour and a half ahead) where Rancheria Falls courses down in a jumbled cascade over shelves, ledges and other rocks. Overnighters can camp at the backcountry site beside the falls.

HIKES FROM TIOGA ROAD

⑭ Tenaya Lake circuit

Map 6, E5. Easy; June–Oct.
3 miles round trip; 1hr–1hr 30min; 50ft ascent.

One of the easiest hikes along Tioga Road is this circuit of **Tenaya Lake**, which mostly stays out of the trees and affords open vistas of granite domes the whole way. It starts at the beachside picnic area at the eastern end of Tenaya Lake and loops around the southern side, staying pretty close to the water's edge. In summer, you'll traverse fields of wildflowers, and the views across the water to the climbers' playground of Stately Pleasure Dome are an added highlight. The route rejoins Tioga Road at the major trailhead at Tenaya Lake's western end, from where you can either retrace your steps or complete the lake circuit by hiking along the road. If you time it right, the walk can be shortened by riding the Tuolumne Meadows shuttle along the road section.

⒣⒮ Lukens Lake

Map 5, G8. Easy; June–Oct.

1.6 miles round trip; 1hr; 200ft ascent.

This popular walk is notable for its colorful display of delicate flowers, and also has the added benefit of a beautiful destination in the form of the serene **Lukens Lake**. It is bounded at one end by meadows where lush growth creates a waist-high grassland thick with wildflowers. The path winds through red fir and white pine forest from a trailhead on Tioga Road, but is also accessible directly from *White Wolf* campground along a well-signposted track.

⒣⒰ May Lake

Map 6, D5. Easy; June–Oct.

2.5 miles round trip; 1hr 30min–2hr 30min; 400ft ascent.

This short hike is one of the most popular outside the Valley, chiefly for its destination, the gorgeous crystal-clear May Lake, huddled in the shadow of looming Mount Hoffman, and home to the most accessible of the High Sierra Camps (HSC) (see p.164).

From the trailhead, two miles north of Tioga Road, it is a short but fairly steep hike through woods and open granite-boulder fields with great views down Tenaya Canyon towards Cloud's Rest and the back of Half Dome. As the trail levels out you'll see **May Lake**, reached through the scattered tents of a camping area. Nearby, prime lakeside positions are occupied by the white tent cabins of the HSC, which uses lake water for its supply; swimming is not allowed, but you're free to fish.

Anyone keen to see just why the summit of **Mount Hoffman** was one of John Muir's favorite spots in the Park can continue along a three-mile track to the top.

PAUL WHITFIELD

Gnarled Jeffrey pine, summit of Sentinel Dome

Half Dome and Tenaya Canyon from Glacier Point

Yosemite Falls across the Merced River

Wildflowers in Tuolumne Meadows

Log cabin, Pioneer Yosemite History Center

El Capitan in winter

Mule deer buck

⑪⑰ Polly Dome Lakes

Map 6, E5. Easy; June–Oct.
5 miles round trip; 2–3hr; 500ft ascent.

From a trailhead midway along the north side of Tenaya Lake, this gentle and little used footpath follows **Murphy Creek** through lodgepole pine forest to its source at **Polly Dome Lakes**. Polly Dome itself rises above, and there's good camping all about. Much of the second half of the hike is across rock slabs with abundant evidence of glacial action. The polished surface is punctuated by "percussion marks" where boulders embedded in the base of the glacier have gouged their signature, and the area is littered with erratics.

⑪⑱ Harden Lake

Map 5, F7. Easy; June–Oct.
6 miles round trip; 2–3hr; 270ft ascent.

What this hike lacks in scenic splendor it easily makes up for in the glorious profusion of wildflowers, good from late June to August but especially vibrant in July. Heading north on the gravel service road from White Wolf, follow signs for **Harden Lake**, which bring you alongside a tributary of the middle fork of the Tuolumne River where the banks shimmer with the blue, pink, purple, and white of lilies and lupines. Elsewhere in the area the red and yellow flowers of columbine mix with the delicate pink of Lewis' monkey flower. The lake itself fills a pleasant enough forest clearing, and you've got the walk back to look forward to.

⑪⑲ North Dome from Porcupine Creek

Map 5, I10. Moderate; June–Oct.
9 miles round trip; 4–6hr; 650ft ascent.

HIKES FROM TIOGA ROAD

It is almost all downhill from Tioga Road to the top of North Dome, giving this hike the unusual distinction of approaching a Valley viewpoint from above.

From the Porcupine Creek trailhead, you'll plunge into pine and fir forest broken up by occasional meadows. Follow signs for North Dome and start climbing as the forest begins to open out to reveal expansive vistas. A little over an hour from the start a sign points along a 500-yard spur trail to **Indian Rock**, a slender rock arch that is not much by Utah standards but is an unusual feature in granite. Return to the track and drop steeply along Indian Ridge with Basket Dome off to the left, until you reach **North Dome**. Here, perched high above the Royal Arches and Washington Column, you find yourself face to face with the enormous bulk of Half Dome. Cloud's Rest, too, is prominent, and the daily activity of Curry and Yosemite villages goes on below, with only the distant sounds of shuttle buses to disturb the tranquility.

This can be turned into an overnight hike by camping at the low saddle behind North Dome, though finding water can be a problem once the last of the snow has melted.

H20 Yosemite Falls from Yosemite Creek campground

Map 5, H9. Strenuous; June–Oct.

12 miles; 5–7hr; 700ft ascent.

The top of **Yosemite Falls** is a justly popular hiking destination from Yosemite Valley, but you can cut out much of the ascent on this alternate approach from *Yosemite Creek* campground, five miles off Tioga Road. A longer hike, but on primarily gentle terrain, it follows Yosemite Creek as it cuts its way first through forest, then down small granite canyons choked with rocks.

The footpath starts beside a trail-junction sign by the

campground's entrance, and heads south, slowly descending through woods until reaching a section where Yosemite Creek is confined between high banks; take a few minutes to watch smooth sheets of water break up over cascades then calm themselves in deep blue pools. Broad sandy areas alternate with thicker forest and offer a few potential camp-sites along the way as you cross Blue Jay Creek and eventu-ally pass a trail junction for Eagle Peak. Half a mile on you'll encounter exhausted hikers ascending the Upper Yosemite Fall trail. Join them for the final couple hundred yards to the falls, best viewed from a wonderful viewpoint (see Hike 10). There are potential side trips to Yosemite Point and Eagle Peak before returning the way you came.

H21 Cloud's Rest from Tenaya Lake

Map 6, E5. Strenuous; June–Oct.
14.5 miles round trip; 7–10hr; 1800ft ascent.

The easiest and most popular approach to **Cloud's Rest** is from Tenaya Lake; it is still a strenuous undertaking but involves only a third of the ascent you'd have to negotiate if starting in the Valley.

From the trailhead at the western end of Tenaya Lake you first cross a small creek and then turn south through meadows before beginning to climb to the rim of **Tenaya Canyon**. Follow Cloud's Rest signs past a junction that leads to the Sunrise HSC, and drop down to a little meadow near the foot of Sunrise Peak. The small creek at the lowest point is your last chance for water. Ascend until you pass another trail junc-tion, then continue through white pine as the knife-edge peak of Cloud's Rest comes into view. At the base of the summit ridge a poorly signed path marked by cairns on bare rock rises to the top. Alternatively follow the horse trail that skirts the ridge on the southern side, then join a better-marked track from the western end of the ridge. Either way, be sure to watch your footing around the summit. The views from Cloud's Rest, the highest peak visible from Yosemite Valley, are breathtaking; Half Dome dominates to the west, the Cathedral Range bristles to the east, and below you a wave of smooth granite sweeps down to the base of Tenaya Canyon.

⑫ El Capitan from Tamarack Flat

Map 5, D12. Strenuous; June–Oct.
16.5 miles round trip; 7–10hr; 1240ft ascent.

While the summit of **El Capitan** is the goal of some of Yosemite's most spectacular and intense rock climbs, it is also accessible by trail from Tamarack Flat, three miles off Tioga Road. Begin hiking along a disused section of the Old Big Oak Flat Road at the eastern end of *Tamarack Flat* campground, crossing Cascade Creek after a couple of miles. Continue downhill for another half mile or so to a point where a log jam forces you left onto a narrower path which climbs steadily for almost three miles, following a ridge to the diminutive Ribbon Meadow. There are potential campsites where you cross Ribbon Creek, just before the rim of El Capitan Gully gives you your first really good Valley views. El Cap dominates the scene ahead, its sheer face topping out not with a plateau but with a surprisingly steep slope rising back from the lip to a domed summit. The trail skirts the top and continues east along the Valley rim, with just a few cairns marking the way down to the lip. Watch your footing as you head to the edge for tremendous views up the Valley towards Tenaya Canyon and Half Dome, and across to the face of Sentinel Rock and the knife-blade ridge of Mount Clark. Return the way you came.

HIKES FROM TUOLUMNE MEADOWS

H23 Pothole Dome

Map 6, G3. Easy; June–Oct.
0.5 miles round trip; 40min–1hr; 200ft ascent.

This short but fairly steep walk ascends **Pothole Dome**, which marks the western limit of Tuolumne Meadows. The relatively small dome commands great views of the Meadows, Cathedral Range and virtually all of the High Sierra, seen to best effect in the hour before sunset. A ten-minute walk around the base of the dome is followed by a short, stiff scramble up bare granite. The more-or-less level summit is a lesson in glaciation. The rock here is **porphyritic granite**, its fine granular structure embedded with feldspar crystals an inch or two long. As glaciers ground over the rock, it was planed smooth leaving a beautiful mosaic which shimmers in the low light. Notice, too, the glacial erratics deposited on the summit, now elegantly juxtaposed with stunted pines.

H24 Soda Springs and Parsons Lodge

Map 6, H3. Easy; June–Oct.
4-mile loop; 2hr; negligible ascent.

This is an easy meander around some of Tuolumne Meadows' best and most accessible features. Start from the visitor center and walk about 300 yards east along Tioga Road before turning left on a track across the meadow which was once part of the original Tioga Road. While it is a pleasant walk at any time, in June and July the wildflower display along here is superb – look out for penstemon, shooting stars, yellow goldenrod and white pussytoes. On the meadows' far side, you cross the Tuolumne River beside a small path leading up to **Soda Springs** and **Parsons Lodge** (see p.63). From here, take the wide path following signs for Tuolumne Meadows stables and the Lembert Dome parking lot; it is essentially a nature trail, lined with panels explaining flora, fauna, glaciation and a little history. An alternative route from Soda Springs picks up a narrow unmarked riverside trail winding upstream past beautiful small rapids and pools. The two routes meet close to the base of Lembert Dome from where you can walk to the visitor center along the road, or ride the shuttle bus, saving a two-mile walk.

⒣㉕ Dog Lake

Map 6, I3. Easy; June–Oct.
3.2 miles round trip; 1hr 30min–2hr 30min; 600ft ascent.
This relatively easy there-and-back hike ends at the small, attractive **Dog Lake**, where you might linger for a picnic lunch, an afternoon with a book, or maybe a swim.

From the Lembert Dome parking area follow a trail through trees across a flat patch of polished granite then keep heading right at a series of trail junctions. The climb then turns steep, but only for a mile or so, until you fork left for an easy stroll to Dog Lake. (The right fork goes to the summit of Lembert Dome.) Find a spot to relax amid the lodgepole pines and small patches of meadow, or continue right around the lake for good views back to the Cathedral Range.

The "Dog Lake" and "Lembert Dome" hikes
can easily be combined into one hike
(4.5 miles; 2hr 30min–4hr; 900ft ascent).

🄷㉖ Lembert Dome

Map 6, I3. Moderate; June–Oct.
3.7 miles round trip; 2–3hr; 850ft ascent.
As the most prominent feature on the Meadows' perimeter, **Lembert Dome** has an immediate lure – the expansive views from the summit, with interesting glacial features found there adding to its attraction.

Follow Hike 25 as far as the trail junction where the Dog Lake path bears left. At this point head right, initially steeply but with the gradient easing until you reach the northeast corner of Lembert Dome. Here a series of cairns marks the fairly steep route across bare rock to the summit. After exploring the exposed stunted pines, glacial erratics and long views across Tuolumne Meadows and up Lyell Canyon, return to the trail and turn right for the descent to Tioga Road. Cross the road to the wilderness center where you can pick up a track running west and back to your starting point.

🄷㉗ Elizabeth Lake

Map 6, I3. Moderate; June–Oct.
4.8 miles round trip; 3–5hr; 900ft ascent.
One of the more popular day hikes around Tuolumne Meadows, this trail culminates where the idyllic Elizabeth Lake nestles in a hollow scooped out by an ancient glacier, surrounded by pine trees.

The trailhead is at the back of the *Tuolumne Meadows* campground, most easily found using a free campground map from the kiosk near the entrance. The trail soon crosses the John Muir Trail and climbs steadily through forest, steeply at first and then more gradually alongside Unicorn Creek. Shortly after the track bridges Unicorn Creek you arrive at the glistening waters of **Elizabeth Lake**, perhaps not quite as exquisite as Cathedral Lakes (Hike 28), but still

HIKES FROM TUOLUMNE MEADOWS

a gorgeous spot surrounded by steep craggy mountains and ringed by paths which provide access to spots ideal for fishing, a picnic, or, for the brave, a swim.

Anyone with an interest in scrambling (see p.149) might enjoy an assault on the needle summit of Unicorn Peak, a round trip of about three hours from Elizabeth Lake (if you're reasonably fit). Just use a little common sense and keep heading uphill until you can go no further. From the top there are great views of Cockscomb, Cathedral Peak, Echo Peak and the end of Matthes Crest.

H28 Cathedral Lakes

Map 6, H3. Moderate; June–Oct.
8 miles round trip; 4–6hr; 1000ft ascent.

A candidate for the best Tuolumne day hike, this route follows several miles of the JMT as far as Cathedral Lakes, a pair of gorgeous tarns in open alpine country with long views to a serrated skyline.

From the trailhead just west of the Tuolumne Meadows visitor center, the footpath climbs moderately steeply through lodgepole forest and small meadows. The blunt end of Cathedral Peak seen from this early section of the trail is barely recognizable as the same spiky two-pronged mountain you'll see further on. Its aspect changes as you continue through rolling woods to a junction at three miles. Here, a half-mile side trail leads to **Lower Cathedral Lake**, a divine spot lodged in a cirque now partly filled with lush meadows and split by a ridge of hard rock polished smooth by ancient glaciers. Looking back the way you came, the twin spires of **Cathedral Peak** catch the afternoon light beautifully and, on still days, may be reflected in the lake's waters.

Return to the JMT, turn right and continue for half a mile to reach **Upper Cathedral Lake** at 9585ft. Here, there's a more open feel though you are still ringed by mountains: the truncated ridge of Tressider Peak to the south, Echo Peaks rising up to the east, and Cathedral Peak always drawing your eye to the northeast.

Camping is prohibited at Lower Cathedral Lake, but there are plenty of lovely spots available around Upper Cathedral Lake.

🅗29 Lyell Canyon

Map 6, I3. Moderate; June–Oct.
11 miles round trip; 4–5hr; 100ft ascent.

This long but gentle and virtually level walk follows the John Muir and Pacific Crest trails (see box p.138) through the somewhat mis-titled **Lyell Canyon**, a quarter-mile-wide valley flanked by wooded slopes rising a couple thousand feet on either side. There's no real destination, so if you don't fancy hiking the full eleven miles, just go as far as you please then retrace your steps.

Pick up the JMT at the eastern end of the *Tuolumne Meadows* campground where you immediately start following the **Lyell Fork** of the Tuolumne River, climbing very slightly as you pull out of the forest and into more open country. The river courses hurriedly amid fields thick with

---

The John Muir Trail runs for twelve miles through Lyell Canyon (Hike 29) to the 11,000ft Donohue Pass, where it leaves the Park. Robust hikers can make it from Tuolumne to Donohue Pass and back in a day, climbing 2000 feet in the last three miles, through some stunning alpine scenery with views of the Park's highest mountain, Mount Lyell, and its attendant glacier.

---

wildflowers in early summer but by September is reduced to a steady trickle through grasses burned golden by the high-country sun. Swimming in the river is particularly nice (if cold) in late summer, and anytime of year there is decent wildlife spotting for anyone with patience. The broad-shouldered Mammoth Peak is initially almost directly ahead, and as the trail swings to the south you get distant views to some of Yosemite's highest peaks; in fact, the further you go, the better the mountain scenery.

H30 Glen Aulin

Map 6, I3. Strenuous; June–Oct
11 miles round trip; 6–8hr; 600ft ascent on the return.

This there-and-back hike to Glen Aulin is one of Tuolumne's finest, following the Tuolumne River all the way as it cascades its way to a beautifully situated High Sierra Camp and campground.

From the trailhead at Lembert Dome, hike along the broad, flat path to Soda Springs then follow signs for Glen Aulin along a good track that's made less pleasant by the evidence of all the horse traffic headed for the HSC. With lodgepole pines all about, the trail begins to dip slowly, the trees often pulling back to reveal fabulous views of the surrounding mountains. The river, too, is wonderfully picturesque all the way. Frenetic during the snowmelt in early summer, the water courses down the canyon over house-sized boulders, slithers over slickrock and eases into deep, bottle-green pools lined with polished river stones. By autumn the torrent subsides, making the pools between the cataracts calm enough for bathing. The classic photo stop is at **Tuolumne Falls**, the most vertical drop along this stretch, and there are more cascades as you continue further downstream with the descending trail switchbacking to **White Cascade** and the HSC. Press on a few hundred yards downstream to **Glen Aulin** itself where shallows provide access to a deep pool below a marvelously sculpted rock chute. Here you can rest a while before embarking on the long uphill hike back.

㉛ Young Lakes

Map 6, I3. Strenuous; June–Oct.
13.5 miles round trip; 7–10hr; 1500ft ascent.
At the end of this hike, the three beautiful **Young Lakes** make a suitable reward for your efforts, as do the spectacular vistas of the Cathedral Range en route.

From the Lembert Dome parking area follow signs for Dog Lake (Hike 25) for the first mile and a half. At a trail junction, follow the Young Lakes sign to some wide open meadows bordered to the east by Mount Dana and Mount Gibbs. After a long and steady climb over a forest ridge and past a granite dome you emerge on a hillside studded with stunted trees and backed by the gap-toothed Ragged Ridge. Here you get a grandstand view back across Tuolumne Meadows to the whole of the **Cathedral Range**. Nowhere else do you get such an incredible panorama for relatively little effort. Mount Lyell and its acolytes stand above everything else at the left and scanning right you can pick out Unicorn Peak, Echo Peak, Cathedral Peak, Fairview Dome and the distant Mount Hoffman.

After a short ascent you descend for a while and then climb again up forested moraine to the first of the lakes, with barren rocky ridges all around. Take a break beside the water's edge before exploring higher up (using informal and unsigned trails) where two smaller lakes nestle in marshy meadows. Though an excellent day hike, Young Lakes also makes a great backpacking destination with ideal lakeside camping.

⑫ Waterwheel Falls

Map 6, I3. Very strenuous; June–Oct.

17.5 miles round trip; 8–12hr; 2100ft ascent on the return.

This hike is an extension of Hike 30, continuing past Glen Aulin, following the Tuolumne River as far as Waterwheel Falls.

Beyond Glen Aulin you're into a two-mile-long almost unbroken series of cascades officially called **California Fall**, **LeConte Fall** and Waterwheel Falls. In reality, each fall tumbles into another with little to distinguish where one ends and another begins. As the footpath winds down alongside, you get occasional views before **Waterwheel Falls** themselves, where a couple of midstream rocks on a smooth chute throw the snowmelt torrent up twenty feet into the air like a pair of paddle-wheels. Though accessible throughout summer and autumn, the falls are at their best in June and early July.

HIKES EAST OF TUOLUMNE MEADOWS

⑬ Gaylor Lakes and the Great Sierra Mine

Map 6, L2. Moderate; June–Oct.

3 miles round trip; 2–3hr; 500ft ascent.

A couple of pretty alpine lakes in open country above the treeline and the opportunity to explore some meager silver mine workings make this a particularly rewarding short walk. The lakes can be fished, but there is no camping in this area.

From the trailhead right beside the Tioga Pass entrance station, the track is initially quite steep, and unless you're accustomed to being at 10,000ft you'll quickly become breathless. At the crest of a blunt ridge there are views back to the scattered pools in Dana Meadows, and north beyond

Granite Lake to the Sierra crest. The footpath then drops down into the shallow **Gaylor Lakes** basin, almost entirely filled by the lower Gaylor Lake. Bear right around the lake and start climbing gently towards the upper of Gaylor Lakes, with Gaylor Peak on your right. After skirting the left side of this lake, climb a ridge to reach the ruins of a stone cabin, virtually all that remains of the **Great Sierra Mine**. A hundred yards on, just on the Park boundary, you'll find a couple more dilapidated stone huts and the vertical shaft that briefly sustained the mine.

ⓗ34 Mono Pass

Map 6, L3. Moderate; June–Oct.
8 miles round trip; 4–6hr; 1000ft ascent.

Some old miner's cabins, delightful alpine tarns, and mountain scenery geologically distinct from most of the Park make this an interesting day hike. There are opportunities for camping in Inyo National Forest just over **Mono Pass**, an area with a beautiful high-country meadow right on the Sierra crest, overlooked not by granite but by the iron-rich red rocks of Mount Gibbs and Mount Lewis which lured late-nineteenth-century miners here.

The hike starts six miles east of the Tuolumne Meadows store, and climbs steadily pretty much all the way, alternately passing through meadows and lodgepole forest. After three miles you'll reach the treeline and the break out into open country before closing in on the 10,600-foot Mono Pass. Several small lakes mark the pass and make a pleasant lunch spot. Mine hounds should retrace their steps for a couple hundred yards and head south for ten minutes along an unmarked path. This drops briefly then climbs over a ridge to reach what remains of the **Golden Crown Mine**, just five primitive and strikingly weathered but well-preserved cabins.

HIKES FROM GLACIER POINT ROAD

Ⓗ35 McGurk Meadow

Map 3, H7. Easy; mid-May to Oct.
1.6 miles round trip; 1hr; 150ft ascent.

McGurk Meadow makes a peaceful destination for this stroll through lodgepole pine forest. The trail starts almost opposite the entrance to *Bridalveil Creek* campground, and visitors staying there can walk straight from their site. Otherwise, park a couple hundred yards east of the trailhead at a small turnout, then head into the forest. Descend gently until you notice a tumbledown summer sheepherders cabin. Wildflower-filled McGurk Meadow is just beyond.

Ⓗ36 Taft Point and the Fissures

Map 3, J4. Easy; mid-May to Oct.
2.2 miles round trip; 1hr; 250ft ascent.

For such an easily accessible and wonderfully scenic spot overlooking the Valley, Taft Point is surprisingly little visited; all the more reason to hike this trail.

From the Sentinel Dome parking area the dusty and undulating path heads west across a meadow, descending all the while. As you enter a patch of forest you cross a small creek where wildflowers flourish in the damp margins, then descend more steeply until you emerge from the trees just before Taft Point: the **fissures** are just to the right, the prow of **Taft Point** itself just beyond. Unlike crowded Glacier Point with its walkways and barriers, Taft Point has just a flimsy railing in one spot to protect you from the vertiginous drops all around. A hundred yards to the right, the granite edges have been deeply incised to form the **Taft Point Fissures**, narrow thirty-foot slices carved out of the Valley rim where you can stand astride a gap with hundreds of feet of air between your legs.

You can't see Half Dome from Taft Point, but that is more than compensated for by the view of the monstrous face of El Capitan, the staircase of the Three Brothers, and the slender white streak of Upper Yosemite Fall.

The "Taft Point" and "Sentinel Dome" hikes can be easily combined to make an appealing loop (5 miles, 2–3hr; 600ft ascent) using a couple of miles of the Pohono Trail.

Ⓗ³⁷ Sentinel Dome

Map 3, J4. Easy; mid-May to Oct.
2.2 miles round trip; 1hr; 250ft ascent.

The most popular hike for Glacier Point visitors is to the gleaming granite scalp of **Sentinel Dome**; the Valley floor isn't visible from the summit, but just about everything else is. Sentinel Dome is directly accessible from the Glacier Point parking lot, but most people set off from a trailhead two miles back along Glacier Point Road. From here, the track crosses sandy ground with little shade; bring plenty of water. Sentinel Dome becomes visible on the left and the trail gradually curls around towards it, following waymarkers and getting progressively steeper. The final push to the summit takes you up the east side, the lowest angled (but still steep) approach.

Now you're a thousand feet higher than Glacier Point and views extend to the Park boundary in almost every direction. The summit is crowned by a gnarled and much-photographed skeleton of a Jeffrey pine which still bore cones until the mid-1970s when a multiyear drought finally killed it off. Its former grandeur can be seen in a widely reproduced Ansel Adams image.

H38 Panorama Trail

Map 3, J4. Moderate; mid-May to Oct.
9 miles one way; 6–8hr; 800ft ascent, 4000ft descent.

One of Yosemite's oldest routes, the **Panorama Trail** passes the top of the otherwise inaccessible **Illilouette Fall**, skirting above the Panorama Cliff with its views down towards Glacier Point Apron and Happy Isles.

The Panorama Trail links Glacier Point with the top of Nevada Fall, and can either be tackled as a there-and-back trek from Glacier Point, or combined (as we've done here) with the John Muir Trail to make a one-way hike from Glacier Point to the Happy Isles trailhead in the Valley. Either ride the Glacier Point Hikers' Bus to Glacier Point, or go for a strenuous day hiking up the Four-Mile Trail (Hike 11) and down the Panorama Trail.

Just south of the gift and snack store at Glacier Point, a large sign announces the start of the several hiking routes. Follow directions for the Panorama Trail and start a two-mile-long descent to Illilouette Creek. Forest burned in 1987 provides little shade, but has regrown a hardy understory of chinquapin (with its distinctive chestnut-like fruit) that provides ideal cover for California blue grouse. Beyond the junction with the trail to Mono Meadow, switchback down into the forest, keeping an eye out for a short path on the left which leads to one of the only places with a good view of Illilouette Fall. The route soon crosses Illilouette Creek near some cascades and rock chutes just above the fall. It is a perfect spot for a break, but camping is not allowed.

Climbing steeply away from the fall, the track passes the unsigned but fairly obvious Panorama Point and continues up until **Nevada Fall** comes into view. After a trail junction you descend on switchbacks to meet the JMT. Before turning left to head down to the Valley, it's worth detouring right a quarter of a mile to the top of Nevada Fall.

H39 Ostrander Lake

Map 3, I7. Strenuous; mid-May to Oct.
12.6 miles round trip; 5–7hr; 1600ft ascent.

Best known as a winter cross-country skiing destination, **Ostrander Lake** makes an equally good summer goal, either as a day hike or to camp near the waterside Ostrander Lake Ski Hut, which is managed by the Sierra Club. Originally known as Pohono Lake, Ostrander Lake feeds Bridalveil Creek, which enters the Valley as Bridalveil Fall (or Pohono). Whatever you call it, it is a fine spot nestled in a hollow with the rocky exfoliating scarp of Horse Ridge on the far side.

From the trailhead on Glacier Point Road, about a mile east of *Bridalveil Creek* campground, the footpath is initially flat as it winds through lodgepole forest burned in 1987 and where the saplings are already over six feet high. After three miles the trail begins a steady climb which continues until just before the lake. Occasionally you emerge from the forest onto the bare rock slopes that run down from Horizon Ridge, the route waymarked by small cairns. As you crest the ridge, breaks in the trees allow views of Half Dome, the Clark Range and Mount Starr King, before a final descent brings you to the lake and rustic **Ostrander Lake Ski Hut**.

- -

The Ostrander Lake Trail can also be accessed from the southern end of *Bridalveil Creek* campground: head towards the horse camp and just before you cross Bridalveil Creek turn right. After about a mile and a half a trail veers left to link up with the Ostrander Lake Trail.

- -

⑭⓪ Pohono Trail

Map 3, J4. Strenuous; May–Oct.
13.8 miles one way; 5–8hr; 2800ft ascent.

The **Pohono Trail** ties together all the viewpoints along the south rim of the Valley, emerging from the forest periodically for magnificent vistas, each one significantly different from the last. Often tackled as part of a longer backpacking trip, the Pohono Trail can be done in a day, either combining it with the Four-Mile Trail to form a very strenuous loop or using the Glacier Point Hikers' Bus for one leg of the journey. Neither the starting nor finishing points are close to where you're likely to be staying, so transport considerations are paramount.

From Glacier Point, signs guide you onto the Pohono Trail, which initially ascends through forest then skirts the north side of Sentinel Dome, seen on the left. Occasionally views can be glimpsed through the trees, but none prepare you for **Taft Point** and its fissured fringes (see Hike 36). For the next couple of miles you drop down to **Bridalveil Creek**, a good spot to take a break, bathe and refill water bottles. Late in the season many creeks dry up, so this may be your last decent supply. Climbing out of the watershed, ignore the trail cutting south to *Bridalveil Creek* campground, and continue back to the Valley rim at **Dewey Point**, distinguished by several isolated rocky viewpoints accessible with a little easy scrambling. The end of the trail at Wawona Tunnel is visible below and to the left, still over four miles away. Press on to nearby **Crocker Point**, where you can look directly across to the top of El Cap, and down on Bridalveil Fall. **Stanford Point**, another half-mile on, offers a slightly different perspective before you begin the final forested descent. The last viewpoint is **Inspiration Point** (see Hike 8) from where it is a mile down to the Tunnel View parking area.

HIKES FROM WAWONA AND MARIPOSA GROVE

ⓗ41 Wawona Meadow Loop

Map 8, C3. Easy; March–Dec.
3.5 mile loop; 1–2hr; 200ft ascent.

The easiest of the walks around Wawona, this circuit of **Wawona Meadow** is mainly of interest for the plethora of wildflowers which bursts forth in April, May and June. Popular as it is, you'll be sharing the trail with cyclists, horses and even Wawona dog walkers.

From the *Wawona Hotel*, cross Wawona Road and follow the paved footpath through the golf course to a small parking area. The road straight ahead is the Chowchilla Mountain Road, first pushed through to Wawona in 1856 as a toll trail from Mariposa to Yosemite Valley. Four years later, Galen Clark developed it into a stage road to lure coaches to his hotel at Clark's Station (now Wawona).

Don't follow Chowchilla Mountain Road, but instead turn left and follow the loop trail with the Wawona golf course on the left. This soon gives way to meadows as the route follows a fire road through ponderosa pine and incense cedar. Keep an eye out for wildlife, especially mule deer who favor the forest margin.

After almost circumnavigating the meadow, the trail meets Wawona Road, which you'll cross to return to the *Wawona Hotel*.

ⓗ42 Mariposa Grove to Wawona

Map 7, F7. Easy; April–Nov.
6.5 miles one way; 2–3hr; 2000ft descent.

This downhill-all-the-way track from Mariposa Grove to the *Wawona Hotel* isn't especially spectacular by Yosemite standards, but it is still a pleasant forest walk and warrants a mention here to complete a convenient loop. Ride the free shuttle bus from Wawona to **Mariposa Grove** and spend as much of the day as you like exploring the paths among the sequoias. When you've seen enough, hike the trail back to the hotel for a well-earned cocktail on the verandah, and dinner.

In Mariposa Grove take the Outer Loop Trail until, after 0.7 miles, a left fork is signed to Wawona. Continue steadily downhill through trees allowing sylvan views of Wawona Dome and the Wawona basin. After an hour or so you come to a small roadside parking bay and, at a trail junction 200 yards beyond, take the left fork and follow it along a broad undulating ridge used by horses. Keep going straight to reach the hotel.

ⓗ⁴³ Chilnualna Fall

Map 7, E4. Moderate; April–Nov.

8.2 miles round trip; 4–6hr; 2200ft ascent.

South-facing and at low elevation, the Chilnualna Fall Trail is perfect in early spring and fall. Though it gets quite hot on summer days, you can cool off in deep pools along Chilnualna Creek.

The route starts 1.8 miles along Chilnualna Fall Road, with the first few hundred yards ascending among granite boulders alongside roaring cascades, where the water continues to carve out channels and hollows in the rock. Moving west away from the river you continue ascending through manzanita, deer brush and bear clover, and return briefly to the river before again looping west to a point with long views down to Wawona and across the valley to Mariposa Grove. All along the way, wildflowers bloom throughout spring and early summer. Finally the trail rejoins the creek at the top of **Chilnualna Fall**, an intimidating spot where snowmelt gathered in the high country thunders down into the narrow chasm below your feet. Catch it in early spring when the spray clings onto the walls in an organ pipe accumulation of icicles.

Take a break here, but don't turn back yet. Instead, continue upstream to yet more tumbling cataracts; use caution where the spray coats the slick riverside rock, making it very slippery. Return the way you came.

(H44) Alder Creek

Map 7, C4. Moderate; April–Nov.
12 miles round trip; 5–7hr; 1700ft ascent.

Alder Creek Trail faces south and is mostly at low elevation, so it sheds its layer of snow early in the season making it perfect for springtime hikers, especially those keen to catch the first of the wildflowers. At any time of year it is a lovely but little-used path gradually climbing a forested ridge to a **sixty-foot fall on Alder Creek**.

The route starts on Chilnualna Fall Road and follows a former railbed used for extracting timber from the area's enormous trees. This is initially fairly open country with long views to distant ridges, but as the trail ascends the forest gradually hems you in. After almost three miles the track meets a side path down to Wawona Road, but the Alder Creek Trail continues uphill, crosses into the Alder Creek watershed and finally reaches the falls themselves. This is a great place to relax, and makes a good camping spot if you're thinking of exploring the area further.

HIKES FROM WAWONA AND MARIPOSA GROVE

Backcountry hiking and camping

T here's no denying the appeal of spending the night under open skies, with the last rays of sun glinting off the granite domes and a pearlescent alpenglow silhouetting the tall pines. Add in a hearty meal after a day of hiking past thunderous waterfalls and you have a recipe for a magical experience. By camping out you'll open up the majority of Yosemite's **backcountry**, essentially anywhere more than a mile from a road. With over eight hundred miles of trails to explore, we've only scratched the surface, and what follows is just a handful of the most popular overnight hikes and some general pointers.

Much of the backcountry is pristine, with very little evidence of human impact. The exceptions are **Little Yosemite Valley** (Map 3, M4) at the top of Merced Canyon, which sees almost a quarter of all wilderness travelers, and the five **High Sierra Camps** (HSCs; see p.164), semi-permanent clusters of frame tents designed to cater to those who don't feel like lugging a tent and cooking gear. All six places have adjacent primitive campgrounds (free) with pit toilets, bear boxes and a water source.

See box on p.95 for guided overnight hikes.

When hiking you can often leave your **vehicle** right at the trailhead. Hikers setting off from the Valley, or using one of the hikers' buses to get to the start of the trail, must park their vehicles in the **backpackers' parking area** between Curry Village and Happy Isles. In Tuolumne Meadows, backpackers need to park beside the wilderness center, and should note that vehicles are not allowed to remain overnight at Tioga Road trailheads (including Tuolumne Meadows) from mid-October until the following spring when the road reopens, effectively ruling out overnight hikes starting here at that time.

Backcountry hikers should also read the introduction and practicalities detailed in Chapter 6, "Day hikes".

BACKCOUNTRY INFORMATION AND PRACTICALITIES

Backcountry information is best gleaned from one of the **wilderness centers** (see p.13), particularly those in Yosemite Valley and Tuolumne Meadows, which are both close to numerous trailheads. They'll help sort out your wilderness permit and fill you in on backcountry safety and etiquette.

Wilderness permits

Anyone planning to spend the night in the backcountry (including at the High Sierra Camps) must obtain a **wilderness permit**, either in advance or in person (see box overleaf). Each trailhead has a **daily quota**, with sixty

RESERVING WILDERNESS PERMITS

Large groups, people with inflexible schedules, and anyone hiking at busy times should **reserve wilderness permits in advance** ($5 per person) from 24 weeks to two days ahead of your trip. Book either by phone (☎209/372-0740), via the website (ⓦwww.nps.gov/yose/wilderness), or by writing to Wilderness Permits, PO Box 545, Yosemite, CA 95389, stating your name, address, daytime phone, the number in your party, method of travel (foot, ski, horse, etc), start and finish dates, entry and exit trailheads, and main destination, along with possible alternate dates and trailheads. Checks should be made payable to the Yosemite Association, and credit card bookings must include the number and expiration date.

On the spot permits are available free of charge in person from any of the wilderness centers or information stations (see p.13); you are expected (though not obliged) to get your permit from the station nearest to your trailhead. At busy times, line up outside one of these places early in the day.

In winter (Nov–April), when demand is at its lowest, there is no need to reserve in advance: free wilderness permits are self-issued at trailheads.

percent of permits available in advance and the rest available on a first-come, first-served basis on the day of or the day before your first planned hiking day. During the busiest period, from mid-July to the end of August, you should reserve well in advance for hikes from all trailheads. Most summer weekends are busy enough to justify making **reservations** for those hikes beginning at popular trailheads such as: Happy Isles and Upper Yosemite Fall in Yosemite Valley; May Lake along Tioga Road; Sunrise Lakes at the western end of Tenaya Lake; and Cathedral Lakes and Lyell Fork at Tuolumne Meadows. Outside these times it is usually easy enough to obtain a permit by showing up the day before you plan to begin hiking. Remember that quotas are trail-head based, and you may find that you can start from a slightly different spot and still do largely the hike you wanted to.

Camping equipment and clothing is for sale in the Valley (and to a lesser extent in Tuolumne Meadows), but prices are higher and it pays to come already fully stocked. The Yosemite Mountaineering School **rents** overnight packs, sleeping bags and pads, gaiters, snowshoes and more.

Selecting a campsite

In Yosemite's backcountry, you are free to camp wherever you wish, subject to a few limitations which we've covered below. In the most well used areas – Little Yosemite Valley and beside the five High Sierra Camps (see p.164) – you are encouraged to camp in existing **primitive camp-grounds**, each with fire rings to contain your campfire and some form of water source (which may need to be treated).

Away from these areas you can pitch your tent almost anywhere, though **you can't camp** within four miles of any settlement (principally Yosemite Valley, Tuolumne Meadows, Hetch Hetchy, Glacier Point, and Wawona), less than one mile from any road, or within a quarter of a mile of the Yosemite Valley rim. In addition, **you must select a site** at least a hundred feet from any watercourse, away from fragile vegetation, and out of sight of hikers on nearby trails.

Hikers' passage into and out of the backcountry is eased by the existence of drive-in **backpacker campgrounds** (no reservations necessary; $5) in Yosemite Valley, Tuolumne Meadows and Hetch Hetchy. Here, hikers with valid wilderness permits have a place to camp for their last night before a trip and a place to stay when turning up late in the day after several days hiking.

Campfires, cooking and bear-resistant food canisters

No special permits are required to light **campfires** in the backcountry, but to preserve Yosemite's delicate ecology and limit pollution you should try to manage without a fire, or at least build a small warming one rather than a large bonfire. Where they exist, fire rings should be used; burn only dead and downed wood. There are never all-out fire bans, but fires are not allowed above 9600 feet where trees grow slowly and suitable wood is scarce.

For cooking, it makes sense to take a **portable stove**. **Fuel** is available for most types of stoves, though anyone planning on using gasoline should remember that there is none available in the Valley. Coleman fuel works well and is widely available in Park stores. Those with Trangia stoves should bring denatured alcohol (aka methylated spirits) from outside the Park, where it is usually sold in hardware stores.

Bear awareness

Yosemite Valley **bears** (see box p.25) may be smart, but their backcountry cousins are no less adept at obtaining food from hikers. They're too timid to ambush humans, but unless you're happy to go hungry, it is essential to correctly store your provisions overnight. The only places with in-situ bear boxes are the campsites at Little Yosemite Valley and beside the High Sierra Camps.

The "counterbalance" food-hanging technique is now considered merely a delaying tactic and is outlawed above 9600 feet where suitable trees are almost impossible to find. Instead, rangers strongly encourage using a **bear-resistant food canister**, a three-pound plastic cylinder which fits in your backpack and can contain enough food for three–five days. They can be rented from stores, wilderness centers and information stations (see "Directory" on p.212) for $3 with a $75 deposit per trip (no matter how long). When you are done, simply drop off the canister at any of the rental locations. You can also buy canisters ($75) from sports shops in the Valley.

Water, personal hygiene and waste disposal

In the backcountry there is no safe **drinking water**, so hikers must be prepared to filter, chemically purify or boil anything obtained from lakes and rivers. Use a giardia-rated filter, an iodine-based purifier, or boil water for three to five minutes. During the spring snowmelt there is no shortage of supply, but as the summer wears on creeks dry up and you should plan your hike with this in mind. That said, even creeks which aren't flowing often have stagnant pools that will satisfy your needs when necessary.

Except when using the pit **toilets** at Lower Yosemite Valley and the High Sierra Camps you're expected to protect water quality by burying human waste. It should be deposited more than six inches deep in mineral soil (not in sand or among rocks), at least a hundred feet from watercourses; portable plastic shovels are available from the wilderness centers for $2. When **washing**, be sure to carry water well away from the watercourse; even so-called "biodegradable" soaps pollute the water.

WILDERNESS PERMITS, BACKCOUNTRY INFORMATION AND PRACTICALITIES

All other waste – packaging materials, food scraps, etc – should be carried out. Do not burn trash: **pack out what you pack in**.

THE JOHN MUIR AND PACIFIC CREST TRAILS

Yosemite is traversed by two of the best-known **long-distance trails** in the western United States: the John Muir and Pacific Crest trails. The 211-mile **John Muir Trail** is usually tackled north to south, starting at the Happy Isles trailhead in Yosemite Valley and winding up to Tuolumne Meadows before turning south along Lyell Canyon. The JMT leaves Yosemite at Donohue Pass and continues through Kings Canyon National Park to finish on the 14,496-foot summit of Mount Whitney, the highest peak in the contiguous 48 states. Most hikers cover eight to twelve miles a day, making it a three-week trek, best done in July and August. They carry everything on their backs, though every few days there is an opportunity to buy food or pick up supplies they've sent ahead.

The **Pacific Crest Trail** is a much more serious undertaking running 2650 miles from Mexico to Canada through all the major western ranges and following the JMT through southern Yosemite then striking through the north of the Park. Every year a few dozen people tackle the entire trail in one season (about five months), starting at the Mexican border in early spring and hiking north so that they arrive in Canada just before winter sets in. PCT hikers can often be found at the Tuolumne Store in early July, ripping into the food parcels they've had shipped to the post office here.

For more information contact the Pacific Crest Trail Association, 5325 Elkhorn Blvd, PMB# 256, Sacramento, CA 95842-2526 (℡ 916/ 349-2109, ℻ 349-1268, ⊛ www.pcta.org).

OVERNIGHT HIKES

The following hikes have been numbered so they may be easily located on the maps at the back of the book.

H45 Pohono Trail–Panorama Trail Combo

Map 3, E5. Mid-June to Oct.

23 miles one way; 2 days; 3600ft ascent, 4000ft descent.

This hike combines the **Pohono Trail** (Hike 40, here tackled in reverse) and the **Panorama Trail** (Hike 38) to take in a full west-to-east span of Yosemite Valley from the south rim. It is not entirely a wilderness experience – the two trails meet at Glacier Point – but this does have the advantage of assuring hikers access to food, potable water and flush toilets along the way. Be aware, however, that there is **no camping** within four miles of Glacier Point. A good strategy is to start by catching the Glacier Point Hikers' Bus as far as the Pohono trailhead at Tunnel View, then camp early before the Glacier Point exclusion zone (perhaps at Bridalveil Creek). The second day is long, passing through Glacier Point for supplies before hitting the Panorama Trail, possibly camping a short distance off the route at Little Yosemite Valley. Day three can then be spent exploring and descending along the Mist Trail or JMT. By pacing yourself this way you'll always be camping near water, a significant consideration in late summer.

H46 North rim of Yosemite Valley

Map 5, D13. Late May–Oct.

30 miles one way; 2–3 days; 5700ft ascent, 6700ft descent.

The summit of El Capitan, Eagle Peak, the top of Yosemite Falls and North Dome can all be linked together in one lengthy traverse of the Valley's north rim. Though possible throughout the summer and fall, timing is everything: too early and you'll have to cope with patches of snow; too late and most streams will have dried up. July and August are the most suitable months.

The best bet is to start at the trailhead on Big Oak Flat Road two hundred yards uphill from the Foresta turnoff: in season you can catch the Tuolumne Meadows Hikers' Bus. The route then crosses a couple of minor streams then meets a disused section of Old Big Oak Flat Road (see Hike 22) and follows it downhill for a little over half a mile. Logs across the road mark the resumption of the track which climbs to the top of **El Capitan** then undulates along the Valley rim with a short spur trail to the summit of **Eagle Peak**. A short descent brings you to the top of **Upper Yosemite Fall** where there are numerous camping spots located a quarter-mile back from the rim.

The way ahead climbs out of the valley cut by Yosemite Creek to reach **Yosemite Point**, then veers away from the Valley rim to sidle around the head of Indian Canyon. Follow signs for **North Dome** and make a short detour to its summit. You then double back and head south again for the steep descent down Snow Creek which eventually brings you past Mirror Lake and back to the Valley settlements.

🟣 John Muir Trail: Yosemite Valley to Tuolumne Meadows

Map 6, B9. June–Oct.

20 miles one way; 2–3 days; 6100ft ascent, 1500ft descent.

Several routes from Yosemite Valley lead to Tuolumne Meadows, but one of the best, and certainly the most popular, follows the **John Muir Trail**: reserve a permit early. In two fairly easy days you'll be rewarded with some of the finest hiking available, with views to match. The track starts at the Happy Isles trailhead and follows the Merced River to Nevada Fall, mostly keeping away from the river and switchbacking up the canyon wall before traversing along the head of the fall. The major features of this region are discussed in Hikes 1–3 which follow the Mist Trail, parallel to the JMT.

From Nevada Fall, the JMT skirts around Liberty Cap to reach the ever-popular primitive campground at **Little Yosemite Valley**. Soon after, the JMT becomes more peaceful as most hikers leave it to head for the summit of Half Dome. The JMT now follows Sunrise Creek, climbing fairly steeply to crest a ridge revealing your first startling views of the Cathedral Range. A short descent brings you to the **Sunrise HSC** and a primitive campground, set by a meadow overlooked by Merced Peak and with a striking view of Mount Clark to the south.

Edging around the meadow, the route continues into mixed country of forests and meadows to the shallow saddle of **Cathedral Pass** and a virtually unsurpassed view of the wildly ragged ridge of the **Cathedral Range**, showing off Cathedral Peak, Echo Peak and the sinuous Matthes Crest. The trail then heads to the beautiful **Upper Cathedral Lake**, from where it follows Hike 28 (in reverse) to the Cathedral Lakes trailhead. Immediately before the trailhead, turn right and follow the JMT parallel to Tioga Road for the last two miles to Tuolumne Meadows.

H48 Merced Lake HSC

Map 6, B9. June–Oct.
27 miles round trip; 2–3 days; 3300ft ascent.

Though **Little Yosemite Valley** is one of the Park's gems, few bother to explore its three miles of glacier-sculpted two-thousand-foot walls, lush meadows, and feathery

OVERNIGHT HIKES

waterfalls. It is too far from the Happy Isles trailhead to allow full exploration in one day, so is best tackled by spending a night or two at **Merced Lake**, either camping or at the High Sierra Camp. Tack on an extra night at the *Little Yosemite Valley* campground and you could also summit Half Dome.

From Happy Isles follow Hikes 1–4 as far as the *Little Yosemite Valley* campground. Here you leave the Half Dome and JMT hikers and follow the right bank of the Merced River as it winds its way across mostly level ground around the massive lump of **Bunnell Point**. The river here slithers over **Bunnell Cascade**, one of many falls, gorges and slides along this active part of the Merced. The meadows of **Echo Valley**, just beyond, herald the liveliest stretch of the river, a mile-long tumbling torrent where springtime eddies have hollowed out great bathing spots. Merced Lake lies a bit further, along with the campground and HSC.

⑭⑨ Grand Canyon of the Tuolumne River

Map 6, I3. June–Oct.
28 miles one way; 2–3 days; 4000ft ascent, 4800ft descent.

The **Grand Canyon of the Tuolumne River** is probably the most-used overnight backpack route north of Tioga Road, but you'll see far fewer fellow hikers here than in the popular areas between Yosemite Valley and Tuolumne Meadows. It is unlike other hikes in the Park, following a single river for over twenty miles as it cuts deep into a granite canyon, alternately erupting into wild cascades, then easing to deep bottle-green pools. Vegetation changes from stunted lodgepole pines to lowland forests then back to alpine up the relentless four-thousand-foot climb out to White Wolf.

The hike is best divided into three sections with nights spent at Glen Aulin and Pate Valley. With the trail wedged between river and cliff for much of the way, there are few other legal places to camp, though the authorities have a grudging acceptance of the use of "heavily impacted" sites where hikers have obviously camped before.

From Tuolumne Meadows the first five miles follow Hike 30 to the **Glen Aulin HSC** and campground; good sunbathing and swimming possibilities abound a quarter of a mile downstream. Beyond the Glen Aulin camp you're on ground covered by Hike 32 as far as **Waterwheel Falls**. Just beyond that is the confluence of the Tuolumne River and Return Creek, an attractive shaded spot with an impacted camping area. You now climb away from the river for a couple of hours as it negotiates **Muir Gorge**.

It is then a steep descent to Register Creek where a pleasant waterfall makes a good place to recover. Ten minutes after Register Creek you cross Rodgers Creek and rejoin the Tuolumne at a collection of attractive impacted camping spots.

Here, down below five thousand feet, the canyon traps the heat of summer, allowing black oak to predominate and encouraging **rattlesnakes** to sunbathe: keep your eyes peeled. The trail levels out beside languid pools as you approach **Pate Valley** and a legal camping spot ideal for recuperating before tomorrow's big ascent.

A mile after crossing the Tuolumne you start uphill on a series of switchbacks. Towards the end of summer there's no flowing water along the way, though several streams have stagnant pools that can be pressed into service when you're thirsty: fill up whenever possible. About halfway up you cross the biggest stream, **Morrison Creek**, then five minutes beyond arrive at a camping spot with nice views down to Hetch Hetchy and **Kolana Rock**. After a final series of switchbacks the terrain eases and, after a couple of trail junctions, hits **Harden Lake**, a pleasant waterside camping area. From here it is three miles to **White Wolf**, described in reverse in Hike 18.

OVERNIGHT HIKES

Ⓗ50 The High Sierra Camp Loop

Map 6, I3. June–Oct, camps open late June to early Sept.
47 miles; 6 days; 8000ft total ascent and descent.

The most civilized way to spend time in Yosemite's backcountry is to make a **loop of the five High Sierra Camps** (see box p.164), all situated at least seven thousand feet up and linked by a wonderful high-country circuit that passes through some of the very finest landscapes the Park has to offer. If you are unlucky with the HSC lottery (or simply prefer to rough-it a bit more, the campgrounds beside each camp make convenient and beautifully sited alternatives. All have toilets and most have potable water. Locations are spaced just five to ten miles apart (eight on average) making it an easy circuit, especially if you're not carrying camping gear.

Most people start in Tuolumne Meadows and make a counterclockwise loop, perhaps spending the first night at *Tuolumne Meadows Lodge*. The first stop is the **Glen Aulin HSC**, reached along a dramatic stretch of the Tuolumne River by following Hike 30. From there, the route doubles back slightly to join a trail heading southwest, eventually depositing you at the **May Lake HSC**, exquisitely sited by the lakeshore with Mount Hoffman reflected in its waters. Follow the day-hikers down to a parking area, then cross the road to descend through forest to Tioga Road. From here, turn left to get to the Sunrise trailhead at the western end of Tenaya Lake. You now pick up Hike 21 as far as Sunrise Lakes junction; turn left to get to the **Sunrise HSC**, also with a nice lakeside location.

From Sunrise Lakes, follow the JMT half a mile north, then turn right and swing south for eight miles to Echo Valley where you meet Hike 48 for the delightful final two miles to the **Merced Lake HSC**. For many the next day is the toughest, only eight miles but with a 3000-foot elevation gain to the **Vogelsang HSC**, perched high in alpine country with gorgeous tarns and barren mountains all around. There's a choice of routes: the shorter, steeper and more popular trail along Fletcher Creek to the west, and the quieter and more scenic **Lewis Creek** to the east. From Vogelsang it is a relatively easy amble down through forests and meadows beside **Fletcher Creek** to meet a section of the JMT for the final mile or so into Tuolumne Meadows.

Summer activities

W hile hiking is by far Yosemite's most popular summer activity, it is by no means the only one. Anyone seeking more adventure can go **scrambling** up the more accessible peaks or experience technical **rock climbing** with the Yosemite Mountaineering School. The majority of visitors, though, are content with less daring pastimes: **horseback riding**, **rafting**, **fishing** and **swimming**.

It is also great fun **cycling** around the Valley floor, something we've covered under "Getting around" on p.20, and Wawona even has a **golf** course (see p.74).

ROCK CLIMBING AND SCRAMBLING

Yosemite Valley and Tuolumne Meadows are renowned for their excellent granite walls and domes, and fine weather – a combination that has attracted rock climbers from all over the world. Given the exceptional natural beauty of the surroundings, it's hard to imagine a finer place to learn the fundamentals of rock climbing. For something of the history and spirit of the Park's rock climbing scene, see "Contexts," p.232.

Even for the most sluggish couch potato, it is hard to visit Yosemite without becoming fascinated by the antics of

PHOTOGRAPHING YOSEMITE

It's hard to resist getting infected by the spirit of Ansel Adams (see box p.42), who spent more than half a century creating a splendid visual record of Yosemite, and **photography** is almost certain to be a main aspect of your visit. When taking photos, remember that it's usually best to do so in the early morning and late afternoon when the low light casts shadows that give a greater sense of depth. And, don't put your camera away when the weather turns nasty – some of the best shots of Yosemite are taken during (or just after) storms or with snow or mist all around.

If you would like detailed guidance, think about joining one of the ninety-minute **free photo walks** that take place in Yosemite Valley, at Glacier Point, Wawona and occasionally in Tuolumne Meadows. They're frequent in summer but are also offered in the Valley throughout the year, either by the Ansel Adams Gallery or by Yosemite Concession Services: see *Yosemite Today* for times.

Ordinary print film is available at just about every shop in the Park but for specialized **photographic supplies**, visit the Ansel Adams Gallery (Map 4, F2; ☎559/271-7960, ⓦwww.anseladams.com), which stocks slide, black-and-white and pro film, filters and a small selection of cameras, along with works by the celebrated photographer. The gallery also runs a series of workshops; check their website for details.

rock climbers, particularly in Yosemite Valley where the sound of climbers calling out to one another is often heard around the base of the cliffs. Some of the most accessible areas in the Valley for **watching climbers** in action are: Swan Slab (Map 4, B3), just north of *Yosemite Lodge*; Church Bowl (Map 4, G2), between Yosemite Village and the *Ahwahnee Hotel*; and El Cap Meadow (see p.48).

ROCK CLIMBING AND SCRAMBLING

The main rock climbing **season** runs from April to October, with most of the action concentrated in the Valley in April, May, June and October. When it gets too hot, most climbers migrate to the cooler Tuolumne Meadows, which sees the majority of the climbing from July to September. A good source of general information about climbing in the Park can be found at Ⓦ www.nps.gov/yose/wilderness/climbing.htm.

Formal training is conducted by the **Yosemite Mountaineering School** (April to mid-Nov Ⓣ 209/372-8344, Ⓦ www.yosemitepark.com), based at the Curry Village Mountain Shop in Yosemite Valley in spring and fall. From late June to August, they decamp to the Tuolumne Meadows Sport Shop, located in the gas station near the Tuolumne Meadows Store. Individual and group **climbing courses** are offered, and beginners should sign up for the seven-hour Go Climb a Rock! course ($170 for one person; $90 each for two; $70 each for three or more), which includes climbing basics and some rappelling up to 60ft. For those with some experience, greater ambition is satisfied on courses like Leading/Multi-Pitch Climbing (8hr; $220/$120/$100) and the two-day **Big Wall Climbing** ($240 each for two; $200 each for three). Also worth looking into are the **summer snow climbing** courses, covering safe travel through snow country, avalanche avoidance, and the use of ropes and ice axes on steep snow and ice.

All classes are a minimum of six hours, involve only a short hike in, and require you to bring food, water and sunscreen. Climbing **equipment** is provided except for climbing shoes, which can be rented ($6 a day). Reservations are highly recommended.

ROCK CLIMBING AND SCRAMBLING

Scrambling

Anyone who likes to get off trail but lacks the skill or inclination to go rock climbing should consider **scrambling**, essentially low-grade rock climbing on terrain where you feel tolerably comfortable without a rope. All you need is a head for heights, a pair of strong boots, and the ability to read a detailed topographical map. It's also a good idea to discuss your proposed route with a ranger before you start.

With so many exposed ridges and dramatic peaks in Yosemite, it is beyond the scope of this book to cover scrambling in detail, but an obvious starting point is Tuolumne's **Cathedral Range**. Here, in 1869, John Muir scaled Cathedral Peak solo and with no technical equipment, and never commented on any difficulties encountered. Even by modern climbing standards, most people would want a rope to scale the final summit block, but scramblers can easily reach the spectacular saddle between the true summit and its attendant Eichorn Pinnacle. Cast your eyes along the horizon from here and numerous other possibilities present themselves: Unicorn Peak from Elizabeth Lake, Echo Peaks, some of the less technical sections of Matthes Crest, and much more.

HORSEBACK RIDING

Unless you're bringing horses into Yosemite, **horseback riding** is limited to trips from the Park's three stables. For beginner-oriented short rides you can usually just show up, but reservations are recommended for longer excursions. All riders need to be at least seven years old, over 44 inches high and weigh less than 225 pounds, and should wear long pants and closed-toed shoes.

Though slated for closure sometime after 2003, the most extensive facilities are currently at **Yosemite Valley Stables** (Map 4, K4: April–Oct, ☎209/372-8348, ✉vstables@dncinc.com), which offers two-hour rides into Tenaya Canyon up to Mirror Lake (8am, 10am, 1pm & 3pm; $40); four-hour rides along the John Muir Trail with views of Vernal and Nevada falls (8am & 1pm; $55); and all-day rides to Half Dome (7.30am; $80).

In the summer months, splendid scenic riding can be done from the **Tuolumne Meadows Stables** (Map 6, I3; July to early Sept; ☎209/372-8427). They offer two-hour rides around Tuolumne Meadows (8am, 10am, 1pm & 3pm; $40); four-hour rides along the Tuolumne River (8am & 1pm; $55); and all-day outings to Waterwheel Falls and elsewhere (8am; $80).

In the south of the Park **Wawona Stables** (Map 8, C2; May to early Sept; ☎209/375-6502) offers perhaps the least scenic horseback excursions, including two-hour rides around the Pioneer Center and Wawona Meadow (8am, 10am, 1pm & 3pm; $40); four-hour rides to Chilnualna Fall (8am; $55); and all-day rides around the Deer Canyon Loop (8am; $80).

Horseback rides are also available just outside the Park's South Entrance at Fish Camp with Yosemite Trails Pack Station (☎559/683-7611, ✉larryk@sierratel.com).

High Sierra saddle trips

An excellent way to spend several days in the high country is to join one of the High Sierra **saddle trips**, four-to-six-day journeys with professional guides and packers who look after your horse and tend to the mules which carry the gear. They're based at Tuolumne Meadows Stables and

HORSEBACK RIDING

make a loop of the High Sierra Camps (see box p.164) with all accommodation and meals included in the price: $620 for four days, $720 for five days, and $975 for the full six days. These generally run from July to early September; for full details contact Yosemite Valley Stables. Customized guide excursions can also be arranged.

Going it alone

The Park Service makes considerable provision for people bringing horse and pack animals into the Park. You're allowed on most of the Park's trails, and there are stock camps at Wawona, Tuolumne Meadows, Bridalveil Creek and Hetch Hetchy (one night maximum), with each site ($20) accommodating six people and six head of stock. Sites can be reserved as much as five months in advance using the campsite reservation system (see p.181. Rules and regulations can be found, along with a list of trails closed to stock traffic, at Ⓦwww.nps.gov/yose/wilderness/stock.htm.

RAFTING AND CANOEING

While commercial whitewater rafting isn't permitted in Yosemite National Park, there's still plenty of **low-key boating activity**, chiefly on the relatively calm waters of the Merced River in Yosemite Valley. At Curry Village you can **rent** rafts (usually June to mid-July; $12.75; Ⓣ209/372-8341) which hold up to six adults. Make a day of it by taking lunch then getting onto the river at Sentinel Bridge from where you float three miles down to El Capitan; ride the free transport back to Curry Village.

    There are no other boat rental facilities in the Park, but if you bring your own you are free to use the Merced River between Stoneman Bridge and Sentinel Beach (daily 10am–6pm) and the south fork of the Merced in Wawona

RAFTING AND CANOEING

from Swinging Bridge down to the *Wawona* campground (daily 10am–6pm). In the high country the only feasible venue is Tenaya Lake, which lends itself to exploration by kayak or canoe, though it is exposed to windy conditions.

Top class whitewater rafting takes place from April to late June on the Merced River (Class III–IV) and the Tuolumne River (Class III–IV+) downstream from the Park. Contact ARTA River Trips (Ⓣ 1-800/962-2782 or 209/962-7873, Ⓦ www.arta.org) or Ahwahnee Whitewater (Ⓣ 1-800/359-9790 or 209/533-1401, Ⓦ www.ahwahnee.com).

FISHING

Yosemite isn't really a fishing destination. None of the rivers and lakes are stocked (though many once were), and over half of Yosemite's lakes have no fish at all. That said, there is some pretty decent trout fishing along the 58 permanent streams, notably at lower elevations such as along the Merced River in Yosemite Valley and on the Tuolumne River above the Hetch Hetchy reservoir. The Merced offers enjoyable fishing all summer and into the winter where the descendants of hatchery-raised brown and rainbow trout are the main attraction.

To fish, anyone over sixteen needs a California sport fishing **license** ($11 for a two-day permit), which must be visibly attached to your upper body. These are sold at the Tuolumne Meadows Store, the Wawona Store, and the Sport Shop in Yosemite Village, which has the best supply of **fishing gear**. It is openseason year-round on lakes and reservoirs, and the stream- and river-fishing season (late April to mid-Nov) excludes Frog Creek and Lake Eleanor, which open mid-June.

Bag limits vary with location, and you should check with the Park Service rangers, but along the popular Happy Isles to Pohono Bridge stretch of the Merced you can only fish with artificial lures or flies with barbless hooks, and it is catch and release only for rainbow trout. A bag of five brown trout is permitted.

For instruction, novices should attend the ninety-minute "How to Catch a Fish in Yosemite" **interpretive talk** (see *Yosemite Today* for details); keen fishermen might consider engaging the services of Yosemite Guides (☎1-877/425-3366 or 209/379-2331, ⓦwww.yosemiteguides.com), who run personalized fly-fishing trips. A full day costs $200 for the first person and $50 each for up to two more, and includes tackle and lunch.

SWIMMING

Your enthusiasm for **swimming** in Yosemite will be dictated largely by your pain threshold: the Park's rivers, streams and lakes are generally icy-cold. Even in the middle of summer the languid waters of the two most popular swimming venues – the Merced River in Yosemite Valley and the south fork of the Merced in Wawona – could hardly be called warm. Still, when the sun is beating down and temperatures are in the nineties, half a day at one of the riverside beaches becomes very alluring. Be aware, though, that currents can be deceptively swift and submerged logs can be a hazard. There are delightful swimming holes and sandy beaches at the eastern end of **Yosemite Valley**, particularly near the stables, beside *Housekeeping Camp*, and downstream at Sentinel Beach. **Wawona**'s branch of the Merced has good swimming by the campground and beautiful swimming holes by the Swinging Bridge a couple of miles up Forest Drive from the *Wawona Hotel*.

Away from these low-lying areas, Yosemite is filled with chilly mountain streams that can be dangerously turbulent from April to June, but which later form deep pools just perfect for washing away the sweat of tired hikers. The most popular locale for high-country swimming is eight thousand feet up at frigid **Tenaya Lake**, with exquisite views of granite domes as you swim (briefly) from a couple of easily accessed sandy beaches. Always keep away from tempting pools above waterfalls.

There are also public outdoor **swimming pools** (mid-May to mid–Sept; guests free, others $2) at Yosemite Lodge, Curry Village and the *Wawona Hotel*.

SWIMMING

Winter activities

From sometime in November until about mid-April, much of Yosemite is cloaked in a mantle of snow and looks even more magical than it does the rest of the year. Anywhere over 5500 feet has an almost continuous coating during these months, but even in lowland areas like the Valley, pines and cedars are frequently bowed with the weight of snow, waterfalls glisten with icicles, and Half Dome is topped by a thick white cap.

If your vehicle is equipped with tire chains, you can experience the Valley, Wawona and a limited number of other areas from the road, but to fully appreciate Yosemite at its seasonal best, you'll need to indulge in some **winter activities**. Much of the action at this time takes place at the **Badger Pass Ski Area** (see box overleaf), but ice skaters glide around the popular outdoor rink in Curry Village, and snowshoe and cross-country ski enthusiasts have virtually the whole Park at their disposal.

CROSS-COUNTRY SKIING AND SNOWSHOEING

Perhaps the best way to get a true impression of Yosemite in winter is to head out **cross-country skiing** into the back-country. Almost the entire Park is open to skiers, though most activity is concentrated around areas with easy access

BADGER PASS

The **Badger Pass Ski Area**, a forty-minute drive from the Valley on the road to Glacier Point (Map 3, F7; generally mid-Dec to early April daily 9am–4.30pm; snow conditions on ☎ 209/372-1000, information desk on ☎ 209/372-8430), is both Yosemite's only **downhill ski area** and the Park's gateway to subalpine cross-country activities, specifically **cross-country skiing** and **snowshoeing**, with ninety miles of marked trails and 25 miles of machine-groomed track fanning out into the backcountry.

In winter, Glacier Point Road is kept open only as far as Badger Pass, which is accessible by a free **shuttle** that leaves Yosemite Lodge daily at 8.30am and 11am, and departs Badger Pass at 2pm and 4.30pm. Once there, you'll find gear rental, a tuning shop and some fairly basic **restaurants** and snack bars – the *Sundeck BBQ*, *Skier's Grill*, and *Snowflake Room* – that'll keep you supplied with sandwiches, salads and drinks without breaking the bank.

The best source of advance **information** is the Badger Pass

to facilities in winter, particularly **Badger Pass** (see box above) with its gear rental, lessons and guided trips.

Complete **beginners** should take either the two-hour introductory **lesson** (daily 10.15am & 2pm; $19.50), or the Learn to Ski Package (daily 10.15am & 2pm; $40) which additionally includes gear rental and an extra two-hour group lesson. Intermediate (daily 10.15am & 2pm; $19.50) and advanced (daily 2pm; $19.50) lessons are available as well, as is tuition in **telemark** skiing (Wed, Sat & Sun 10.15am & 2pm; $30, $40 including rentals), and **skate** skiing (daily 10.15am & 2pm; $28, $38 including rentals). One-hour **private lessons** cost $28 for the first person and $15 each for up to three others.

website (Ⓦ www.badgerpass.com), which includes full details of facilities, rental prices and lessons, along with links to snow conditions and **special deals**. The most useful of these is probably the Yosemite Winter Passport (Jan to mid-March; $20) that buys an all-day lift ticket for Badger Pass, a session at the Curry Village ice rink (including skate rental), and a Valley Floor tour. The pass must be reserved in advance, is available only to those staying at Yosemite Concession Services lodging any night from Sunday to Thursday, and is valid the day after your stay. Savings can also be made with **accommodation packages** such as the Go For The Snow ski package (Jan to mid March Sun–Thurs; $135) that includes one night's lodging at *Yosemite Lodge* and two Yosemite Winter Passports.

People traveling with **children** will appreciate the Badger Pups Den (9am–4.30pm; $4 an hour, $25 a day), a day-care for three-to-nine-year-olds that only requires you to provide and eat lunch with your kids. Those aged four to six can take one-hour Badger Pups ski lessons ($10), and get all-day gear rental for $8.

You're free to follow the groomed trails that meander through the forests around Badger Pass, but experienced skiers might want to join a **guided day tour** such as the Ski Tour (Tues, Thurs, Sat & Sun 10.15am–4pm; $40, $50 including rentals; min three), designed to improve your off-track skills. The ski school also organizes a number of **multi-day trips**, including an overnight snow camping trip ($150; min three) that teaches basic snow travel and winter camping skills.

One of the most popular **trails** is the intermediate-grade 21-mile round trip to Glacier Point along Glacier Point Road. At Glacier Point the summertime snack and gift store is converted into the **Glacier Point Ski Hut**, with dormitory accommodation and hearty meals provided for

CROSS-COUNTRY SKIING AND SNOWSHOEING

WINTER WILDERNESS CAMPING

Winter backcountry regulations are essentially the same as for summer. You still need a wilderness permit (advance reservations not needed) and those leaving Yosemite Valley must reach the Valley Rim before camping. The Tuolumne Grove of giant sequoias is still off limits, but in winter (Dec to mid-April) you can **camp in Mariposa Grove** as long as you are uphill from the Clothespin Tree. Be aware that although bears do spend long periods sleeping, they don't hibernate and can be after your food at any time.

those on the guided Glacier Point Overnight Ski Trip (Sun, Mon & Wed nights $150; Fri & Sat nights $180; min five; a similar midweek package exists for novices). Bring or rent a sleeping bag and wake up to a winter sunrise over Half Dome.

Skiers (and snowshoers; see below) wanting to overnight in the backcountry can also stay at the stone **Ostrander Lake Ski Hut**, nine miles southeast of Badger Pass (Map 3, K9; open mid-Dec to mid-April; $20 per person per night; ☏ 209/379-2317). Cooking facilities are provided, but bring food, water-purifying equipment and a sleeping bag.

Elsewhere in the Park, most of the cross–country action happens at **Crane Flat** (Map 5, B12) and **Mariposa Grove** (Map 7, F7), each of which has marked trails for all levels of ability ranging from a half-mile loop to sixteen-mile backcountry epics. Maps are available from visitor centers and information stations.

Snowshoeing

Snowshoeing isn't much harder than walking, and is another convenient and fun way to explore the backcountry. Anywhere that's open to cross-country skiers is potential snowshoeing territory; just don't walk in the tracks the skiers have carefully grooved. Snowshoes can be rented ($14.25 all day, $9.75 half day) at **Badger Pass** (see box p.156), where Park Service naturalists also lead frequent two-hour **snowshoe walks** (free), teaching about snow dynamics and plant and wildlife adaptations to winter. On the three or four evenings leading up to full moon (if clear) there are free two-hour Full Moon Snowshoe Walks (Feb–April 6.30pm) as well: sign up at the Yosemite Lodge Tour Desk.

In the rest of the Park, hiking trails (see chapters 6 and 7) are obvious candidates for those sufficiently skilled, but most snowshoers head for the winter trails at Crane Flat and Mariposa Grove. For anything ambitious you'll need winter camping equipment, the main exception being the Ostrander Ski Hut (see p.127).

DOWNHILL SKIING AND SNOWBOARDING

Yosemite's only tows for **downhill skiing** are those at family-friendly **Badger Pass** (see box p.156), which is seldom crowded, and has runs best suited for beginners and intermediate skiers. The **vertical drop** is a modest 800 feet, with five lifts feeding nine runs.

Lift tickets cost $28 a day on weekends, $25 during the week, and there's a one-ride ticket for $5. There are slight discounts for both half-day (12.30–4.30pm) and kids tickets (12 and under), while seniors (65 and up) get free passes on weekdays and pay full-price on weekends. **Equipment rental** costs $20 for downhill skis, boots, and poles; $30 for snowboarding gear.

The Yosemite Ski School has been providing high-quality ski instruction for over seventy years. Novices should take the **Guaranteed Learn to Ski Package** (daily 10.15am;

Mon–Fri $40, Sat & Sun $49), with two two-hour group lessons plus ski rental and beginners' lift ticket; those looking to improve their technique will want the **Refresher Lesson Package** (daily 10.15am–2pm; Mon–Fri $40, Sat & Sun $49) with a two-hour lesson, gear rental and a full-day lift ticket. In addition there are one-hour **private lessons** (daily 9am–12.30pm) costing $47 for one person, $69 for two, $88 for three and $105 for four.

With its gentle terrain Badger Pass is equally good for learning to snowboard, with either a **Learn to Snowboard Package** ($59), including lesson, board rental and beginner hill lift ticket, or a two-hour lesson (daily 10.15am & 2pm; $23 for one, $40 for two).

ICE SKATING AND SLEDDING

Though plenty of enthusiasts ski and snowshoe around the Valley, the most popular winter activity here is **ice skating** at the open-air rink at Curry Village (typically mid-Nov to late March; ☏209/372-8341). Two-and-a-half-hour sessions cost $5 (kids $4.50; skate rental $2) and run daily at 3.30pm & 7pm, with additional sessions at 8.30am and noon on weekends. Comforts include a warming hut, fire pit, and snack service.

Sledding is permitted at the snow play area at the *Crane Flat* campground, along with tobogganing and inner-tubing. There are no rentals, so bring your own toys.

LISTINGS

Accommodation

O n most trips to Yosemite, **accommodation** will be the biggest expense, and procuring it can easily become a huge headache unless you reserve well in advance, especially on summer weekends and holidays. Even in spring and fall, visitors find themselves paying more than they had hoped or accepting accommodation below their standards; indeed, canvas tents in the Park cost what you would pay for a reasonable motel elsewhere. The best advice is to plan as early as possible, or resign yourself to being flexible.

PRICE CODES

All accommodation prices have been coded according to the **least expensive double room** in each establishment **inclusive of local taxes** during high season. For campgrounds, and hostels that offer individual beds or bunks, we have given the per person price (including tax) along with a code for any private rooms.

- ❶ up to $40
- ❷ $40–55
- ❸ $55–70
- ❹ $70–90
- ❺ $90–110
- ❻ $110–140
- ❼ $140–170
- ❽ $170–200
- ❾ $200+

HIGH SIERRA CAMPS

Hikers who fancy carrying a light load and ending the day with a shower, bed and a full meal might consider staying at one of the five **High Sierra Camps**, spectacularly sited complexes of tent cabins about a day's walk apart in the Tuolumne back-country. Located at Glen Aulin (Map 6, G2), May Lake (Map 6, D4), Sunrise (Map 6, F6), Merced Lake (Map 6, G8) and Vogelsang (Map 6, I6), each camp sleeps thirty to sixty people in four- to six-bed dormitory-style tents. All you need to bring are sheets or a sleep sack, a towel and personal items.

Unfortunately, the season is short (late June to early Sept) and the demand is high, so you have to enter a **lottery** to stay in the HSCs. Applications are made between October 15 and November 30 using a form obtainable from ☏ 559/253-5674 (Mon–Fri 8am–5pm, Sat & Sun 8am–3pm) or Yosemite Reservations, 5410 E Home Ave, Fresno, CA 93727. Applicants are notified by the end of March, and cancellations become available on April 1; check ⓦ www.yosemitepark.com click on "Accommodations & Reservations." The front desk at *Tuolumne Lodge* also keeps a list of vacancies for the next three days.

The cost is $109 per night (including tax; kids $70) for a bed, three-course dinner, a big family-style breakfast and hot showers (except at Vogelsang where showers are not available). Tents are usually single-sex, though members of a party can be accommodated in the same tent. **Dinner** may also be available to nonguest hikers who reserve in advance ($32.25; ☏ 559/252-4848).

Most people prefer to stay **in the Park**, with the scenic splendor close at hand, and we have included all of the accommodation options within Yosemite here. Still, as you'd expect, there's a greater range of options and lower prices **outside the Park** along the western approach highways and in the gateway towns (see Chapter 5), and many of these are covered here as well.

We've divided the accommodation into two main sections, with hotels, motels, lodges and B&Bs grouped together, and campgrounds and RV parks in a subsequent section. Visitors looking for low cost "indoor" accommodation should also check under "Campgrounds and RV Parks" as several of the listed options also rent out budget cabins.

Within the Park, most of the lowland hotels and lodges (and even some of the campgrounds) stay **open all year**, though snow restricts access to high-country lodges such as those at Tuolumne Meadows and White Wolf.

HOTELS, MOTELS, LODGES AND B&BS

Virtually all noncamping accommodation **in the Park** is managed by Yosemite Concession Services, 5410 E Home Ave, Fresno, CA 93727 (Mon–Fri 7am–7pm, Sat & Sun 8am–5pm; ⓣ 559/252-4848, ⓦ www.yosemitepark.com), which takes reservations up to a year and a day in advance. The most basic and cheapest lodging is at *Curry Village*, *Housekeeping Camp*, *White Wolf* and *Tuolumne Meadows*, where most guests are housed in either canvas-walled tent cabins, or three-sided concrete "cabins." Standard hotel- and motel-style rooms predominate at the *Wawona Hotel* and *Yosemite Lodge*, and for those who want to splurge, there are gorgeous rooms and suites at the exemplary *Ahwahnee Hotel*.

Near Wawona, *The Redwoods* vacation home rentals are the only non-YCS accommodation in the Park, and a dozen or so B&Bs can be found at **Yosemite West**, a small enclave just outside the Park boundary accessible only from inside the Park off Wawona Road. This is also the closest accommodation to the Badger Pass Ski Area.

Outside the Park numerous motels and B&Bs line all three highways from the west, and many more pack the surrounding towns of Groveland, Coulterville, Merced, Mariposa and Oakhurst. In the east, only Lee Vining has much in the way of accommodation with a few motels. The budget-conscious should also be aware of the excellent *Yosemite Bug* **hostel** ten miles east of Mariposa.

Yosemite is popular year round, but most places offer **reduced prices** outside the summer season. In the Park, *Curry Village*, *Housekeeping Camp*, *Wawona Hotel* and *Yosemite Lodge* all have a so-called "Value Season" (typically early Nov to mid-March), when you'll save $5–10 on standard prices, perhaps a little more midweek. Outside the Park, savings tend to be greater with most places dropping at least one price code.

It is also worth looking out for discount **lodging packages** on the YCS website, which frequently offers off-season long-weekend or midweek deals.

IN THE VALLEY

Ahwahnee Hotel

Map 4, H3. Open all year; reserve with YCS; front desk ⊤209/372-1407; shuttle stop 3. Undoubtedly the finest place to stay in Yosemite, the 1927 *Ahwahnee Hotel* is set a short distance from Yosemite Village among the trees and meadows below the Royal Arches. Rooms are decorated in keeping with the hotel's Native American motif and equipped with top quality furnishings and bedding along with TV, phone, and in many cases a wondrous view. Despite rates that start at $400, reservations must be made months in advance. For the same price you might prefer one of the two dozen guest cottages with a rustic feel and all the expected facilities and, in some, a fireplace. The hotel's top floor has been converted into four gorgeous suites that feel like you're staying in someone's very luxurious home, and so they should for $700–1000 a night. There's also a superb restaurant and a separate bar (see p.192), and numerous other facilities including a seasonal tennis court, a heated outdoor pool, free coffee and pastries in the morning, and free tea and cookies with piano accompaniment at 5pm daily in the Great Room. Special weekend deals are listed on the YCS website. **9**

For more on the *Ahwahnee* and its public areas see p.38–39.

Curry Village

Map 4, I5. Open all year; reserve with YCS; Shuttle stops 14, 15, 21 and 22.

Largest of all the accommodation areas in the Park, Curry Village dates back to 1899 when it was opened as the budget Camp Curry (see p.41). Because it still caters largely to families, it is seldom peaceful; nonetheless, it is handy for its several restaurants, shops, swimming pool, ice rink, bike and raft rental and more. There are no self-catering facilities, though there is the 1904 Camp Curry Lounge, complete with a river-stone fireplace.

Most people stay in canvas-walled tent cabins that sleep two, three or five. All come with beds and an electric light, and some have a propane heater for winter use. One step up are the carpeted four-person cabins with a table and heater. Other options include: larger and vastly more appealing rustic cabins with bath and a small deck in a quiet area; sixteen standard rooms fashioned from what was originally the 1904 dance hall; and a few specialty cottages all decorated to a higher standard. None of the accommodation options here have a phone or TV. Cottages **7**, rooms **6**, cabins with bath **5**, cabins without bath **4**, tent cabins **3**

HOTELS, MOTELS, LODGES AND B&BS

Housekeeping Camp

Map 4, G4. Open April to late Oct only; reserve with YCS; shuttle stop 13.

Loved by many, *Housekeeping Camp* is a cluster of strangely primitive "cabins" located among the pines by a bend in the Merced River where there's a convenient beach. Sort of like camping without a tent, you get three concrete walls, a concrete floor, a white plastic roof and one side which opens through canvas curtains onto a cook-out area with outdoor seating. Each cabin has a double bed, two fold-down bunks (bring your own bedding), a table and electricity supply, and an outdoor grill pit. There's access to toilets, free showers, pay laundry, and an on-site grocery store; gas stoves can be rented for cooking, and all food must be stored in the bear-proof boxes dotted around. ❷

Yosemite Lodge

Map 4, C3. Open all year; reserve with YCS; shuttle stop 8.

Often filled with tour groups, this sprawling site with more than 250 rooms occupies the Valley's middle ground. Accommodation is motel-style; comfortable without being anything special, though its proximity to decent restaurants, a bar, swimming pool, bike rental, grocery shops and evening entertainment makes it perhaps the most convenient all-around accommodation in the Valley. Rooms fall into two categories; all have private bathroom and phone but no TV or a/c. The cheaper are the standard or cottage rooms, some fairly spacious with two double or king size beds. The lodge rooms mostly have ceiling fans, a separate dressing area and often a small patio or balcony with a couple of chairs. Children under 12 stay free. ❻–❼

THE REST OF THE PARK

The Redwoods Vacation Home Rentals

Map 8, F1. Open all year, Chilnualna Fall Rd, Wawona, ⓣ209/375-6666, Ⓕ375-6400, ⓦwww.redwoodsinyosemite .com.

The only private accommodation in the Park, the *Redwoods* brings together 130 fully furnished private homes around Wawona, each let for a minimum of two nights (three in summer). Some are rustic log cabins, others plush modern homes, and almost all have a TV, spacious deck with barbecue, and firewood for your stove or open fire. Bedding, towels and kitchen utensils are all provided but you'll need to supply all your own food. Rates for a one- or two-bedroom cottage range from $90 to $150 a night; well-appointed full-size homes are mostly around $250. ❺

Tuolumne Meadows Lodge

Map 6, J3. Open early/mid-June to Sept; reserve with YCS.

Though in Tuolumne Meadows – and perfect as a base for high-country hikes – this isn't really a lodge at all but a large grouping of seventy wooden-floored tent cabins, each with four beds (bedding supplied) and a wood-burning stove but no electricity. This was one of the original High Sierra Camps (see box p.164) and it maintains much the same spirit, with hikers still using it as an overnight stop on the full High Sierra Camp Loop. The lodge is over a mile from the remainder of the Tuolumne Meadows facilities, but there's a restaurant (see p.196) and showers (free for guests). ❸

Wawona Hotel

Map 8, C3. Open year round; reserve with YCS; front desk ⓣ209/375-6556.

Second in elegance only to the *Ahwahnee*, the New England-style *Wawona Hotel* (see p.74 for historic detail and other services) dates in part back to 1879. Its various buildings are all painted white, with wide wraparound verandahs scattered with cane loungers and Adirondack chairs. The cheapest rooms – all in the main building – are smallish, and they're supplied with robes for late-night dashes to the shared bathrooms. It is a significant step up to the majority of rooms, located in various buildings around the grounds. These more expensive en suite rooms have been restored gracefully, all with old-style furniture, Victorian patterned wallpaper and ceiling fans. None of the rooms has a phone, TV or a/c. Ask to look at a few rooms, as they differ greatly. Meals are served in the *Wawona Hotel Dining Room* (see p.196), and you can bookend your meal with drinks in the lounge. It pays to check web specials for deals such as the Wawona Winter B&B package, which includes a lift ticket for Badger Pass. En suite rooms ❽, rooms ❻

White Wolf Lodge

Map 5, F7. Mid-June-early Sept; reserve with YCS.

White Wolf Lodge is the only Park lodging that's away from the main human honeypots of the Valley, Tuolumne and Wawona. Though only a mile down a side road off Tioga Road, *White Wolf* feels quite isolated, surrounded by lodgepole pines and perfect for easy hikes to Lukens Lake (see Hike 15), Harden Lake (see Hike 18) and longer forays down into the Grand Canyon of the Tuolumne River (see p.142). The 24 spacious canvas tent cabins sleep four, have a wood-burning stove and a candle for light but have no electricity. Bedding is supplied, though there is no daily maid service. The four hard-walled cabins are like regular motel rooms with double beds, chairs on the small porch, propane heating, electricity when the generator is running, bed linen and a daily maid service. Communal showers are free to guests and there's a restaurant on site (see p.197). Cabins ❺, tent cabins ❸

YOSEMITE WEST

- -

Yosemite Falls B&B

Map 2, C11. 7210 Yosemite Park Way, Yosemite West ⓣ 209/375-1414, ⓦ www.yosemitefalls.com. An extravagant B&B whose rooms all have private bath, satellite TV, VCR and a complimentary bottle of bubbly. Spend the evening around the bar's pool table then fortify yourself for another day's sightseeing with a huge breakfast. Located in a small enclave fourteen miles from the Valley, just outside the National Park but only accessible from Wawona Rd. ❼

Yosemite Peregrine

Map 2, C11. 7509 Henness Circle, Yosemite West ⓣ 1-800/396-3639 or 209/372-8517, ⓕ 209/372-4241, ⓦ www .yosemitewest.com/falcons. Well-appointed B&B a few blocks from the *Yosemite Falls B&B* (see above), tastefully decorated in Southwestern and woodsy themes, and with a hot tub. Home cooked breakfast is served on the deck if the weather cooperates. The adjacent *Falcon's Nest* (same contact details) has a couple of more budget-oriented rooms and a two-night minimum (❹). ❻

HWY-120 WEST: GROVELAND, COULTERVILLE AND AROUND

- -

The following are listed in order of distance from Yosemite Valley.

Yosemite Lakes

31191 Hwy-120, eighteen miles east of Groveland, and seven miles from the Big Oak Flat Entrance ⓣ 1-800/533-1001 or 209/962-0100, ⓕ 209/962-0106. Scattered family-oriented resort that's not especially appealing, but benefits from being close to the Park. Tent sites are well spaced ($22; full hookup $30), there are rustic shared-bath bunkhouse cabins (❶), and conical canvas-walled yurts with polished wood floors, a deck, cooking facilities, shower and toilet, which sleep four in considerable comfort. **❻**

Yosemite Westgate Buck Meadows Lodge,

7633 Hwy-120, eleven miles east of Groveland, and fifteen miles from the Big Oak Flat Entrance
ⓣ1-800/253-9673 or 209/962-5281, ⓕ209/962-5285, ⓦwww.tales.com/ca/yosemite westgatemotel.

The closest standard motel to the Park on Hwy-120 W, the *Lodge* is comfortable and has all the expected amenities including cable TV, phone, pool and spa. Some deluxe rooms have limited cooking facilities, and there's decent diner-style eating next door at *Buck Meadow's Restaurant*. Two kids under twelve stay free with two adults; rates drop greatly in winter. **❻**

Groveland Motel & TeePee Village

18933 Hwy-120, Groveland
ⓣ1-888/849-3529 or 209/962-7865, ⓕ209/62-0664,
ⓦwww.grovelandmotel.com.

A wide array of accommodation options scattered about pleasant wooded grounds. Choices include fairly basic air-conditioned cabins with cable TV (**❹**), an assortment of mobile homes – mostly with small kitchens (**❹**), and a three-bedroom house that sleeps six (**❽**). There are also concrete-floor tepees (**❶**) clustered around a campfire: it's like camping only with a double bed and somewhere to plug in your hair dryer. **❶**–**❽**

Hotel Charlotte

18959 Hwy-120, Groveland
ⓣ1-800/961-7799 or 209/962-6455.

Basic but full of character, this warm and no-nonsense eleven-room hotel dates back to 1921. Rooms are mostly small and without phone or TV, and some share beautiful old-fashioned bathrooms. There's a common TV room, and rates include a good continental breakfast. **❹**

Groveland Hotel

18767 Hwy-120, Groveland
ⓣ1-800/273-3314 or 209/962-

4000, ⓕ 209/962-6674,
ⓦ www.groveland.com.
Built for VIP guests during
the damming of Hetch
Hetchy, this historic 1914
hotel is now run as a B&B
with luxurious antique-filled
rooms, most containing high,
quilted beds and deep baths.
Best are the three suites,
complete with fireplace and
spa tub. Wicker chairs on the
verandah are perfect for
catching the early evening
sun before dining in the
Victorian Room (see p.197),
which is also used for the
buffet breakfast. Suites ❾,
rooms ❼.

All Seasons Groveland Inn

18656 Main St, Groveland
ⓣ 209/962-0232, ⓕ 962-0250,
ⓦ www.allseasonsgrovelandinn
.com.
Very comfortable lodging in
an 1897 house boasting a

MERCED

- -

Happy Inn

740 Motor Drive
ⓣ 209/722-6291.

decor of bold colors and
designs, each room designed
with a "dramatic feature," be
it a small waterfall,
extravagant hand-painted
mural, steam room, or private
deck with telescope.
Breakfast is not served, but all
rooms have a fridge and
private bathroom. ❼

Hotel Jeffery

Cnr Hwy-49 and Hwy-132,
Coulterville
ⓣ 1-800/464-3471 or 209/878-
3471, ⓕ 209/878-3473, ⓦ www
.yosemitegold.com/jefferyhotel.
Classic gold-era hotel used by
original Yosemite sightseers as
well as John Muir and
Theodore Roosevelt. Rooms
are mostly old-fashioned and
rather small, but there are also
some two- and three-room
suites. All have access to a
communal lounge and sunny
deck. Suites ❻, en-suite
rooms ❺, rooms ❹

The best motel deal in town,
right by the Mariposa/
Yosemite exit of Hwy-99

(20–30min walk from the bus and train stations) with a pool and continental breakfast included in the rates. ❶

HI-Merced Home Hostel

Call for pick-up or directions once in Merced.
ⓣ 209/725-0407,
ⓔ merced-hostel@juno.com.
The best place to stay in Merced if you are relying on public transportation, this reservations-only establishment is a hospitable private home with just two single-sex, four-bunk dorms ($14.30; nonmembers $17.60). Check-in is between 5pm and 10pm only, and you must be out of the house by 9am. Still, this is a small inconvenience for the benefits of a free ride to and from the train and bus stations, an enthusiastic welcome, loads of Yosemite information and free dessert nightly. The hostel also rents sleeping bags ($3 a night) and two-person tents ($5).

Holiday Inn Express

730 Motel Drive
ⓣ 1-800/465-4329 or 209/383-0333, ⓕ 383-0643.
High-standard motel with all the expected facilities, including cable TV and a pool. Located right beside the *Happy Inn.* ❹

Slumber Motel

1315 W 16th St
ⓣ 209/722-5783.
The pick of a string of basic, budget motels half-a-mile west of the Transpo Center, with a small pool and cable TV. ❷

HWY-140: MARIPOSA, MIDPINES AND EL PORTAL

- -

The following are listed in order of distance from Yosemite Valley.

Yosemite View Lodge

11136 Hwy-140, El Portal, two miles west of the Arch Rock Entrance
ⓣ 1-888/742-4371 or 209/379-2681, ⓕ 209/379-2704,
ⓦ www.yosemite-motels.com.
Vast and luxurious – though

slightly soulless – complex with rooms, suites, moderately priced restaurant, convenience store, and several swimming and spa pools, located just on the Park boundary beside the tumbling Merced River. The modern rooms all have a/c, phone, cable TV and either one king or two queen beds (and most have a balcony of some sort), but you pay a premium to get a river view, fireplace, in-room spa and kitchenette. The entire place is often booked well in advance, but it may be worth trying for no-shows; winter prices start under $100. Premium rooms ❼, basic rooms ❻

Yosemite Redbud Lodge

Hwy-140, eleven miles west of the Arch Rock Entrance ☎209/379-2301.
Road- and riverside lodge right by Savage's Trading Post with just eight rooms, each styled with a good deal of character. Rooms all come with a/c, fridge, barbecue, fresh fruit and coffee, and the suites have fireplaces,

kitchenette and a small deck overlooking the river. They'll even loan you a lunch cooler for your day in the Park. Suites ❺, rooms ❹

Yosemite Bug Hostel & Lodge

6979 Hwy-140, Midpines, ten miles east of Mariposa, 23 miles west of the Arch Rock Entrance. Office open 6.30am–11pm.
☎209/966-6666, 🖷966-6667, 🌐www.YosemiteBug.com.
Set in twenty acres of woodland, this lodge, HI-AYH hostel, and campground is the handiest budget lodging near Yosemite. Self-catering facilities exist for those staying in dorms, but there's also the excellent *Recovery Bistro* (see p.199) on site. Mixed- and single-sex dorms ($14.30; nonmembers $17.60) are clean and comfortable; those wanting a little privacy might prefer the tent cabins (❶) or shared-bath private rooms (❷). If looking to splurge, there are also comfortable en-suite rooms with decks but no phone or TV (❻). Pitching

your own tent costs $17 per site. Other facilities include laundry and internet, a lounge, access to a good summer swimming hole, and mountain bike ($15 a day, guests $12) and snowshoe ($8) rentals. *VIA* and *YARTS* (see p.10) buses run into the Park from the stop right outside. Reservations essential May–Oct. ❶–❻

Bear Creek Cabins

6993 Hwy-140, Midpines, ten miles east of Mariposa, 23 miles west of the Arch Rock Entrance
Ⓣ1-888/303-6993 or 209/966-5253, Ⓦwww.yosemitecabins.com.
Well-maintained series of cabins including a basic option with full kitchen, sleeping up to four (❹), larger standard cabins (❺) with polished log finish, kitchenette, tub and shower, and very spacious suites (❻) with a separate living room, gas fireplace and a full kitchen. All have access to a deck and barbecue area. ❹–❻

EC Yosemite Motel

5180 Jones St, Mariposa
Ⓣ209/742-6800, Ⓕ742-6719.
Pleasant, reasonably priced motel with some new, large a/c rooms mostly with two beds; all rooms have shower/tub combos and cable TV. There's a heated pool and spa, and rates may drop to as little as $55 a night in winter. ❹

Sierra View Motel

4993 Seventh St, Mariposa
Ⓣ1-800/627-8439 or 209/966-5793, Ⓕ209/742-5669.
Peaceful, friendly and good-value budget motel just off Mariposa's main drag, offering continental breakfast with smallish rooms and larger suites, all equipped with a/c. ❸

Mariposa Hotel Inn,

5029 Hwy-140, Mariposa
Ⓣ1-800/317-3244 or 209/966-4676, Ⓕ209/742-5963,
Ⓦwww.yosemitehotel.com.
A very welcoming B&B in a historic home decorated in a homey floral style and loaded with heavy wood and antique

furniture. The rooms all have a/c and private bathrooms (many with tubs), cable TV and access to verdant sunny communal decks away from the street. Room rates include vouchers for breakfast at the *Meadows Ranch Café* across the street (see p.200). ⑤

Best Western Yosemite Way Station

4999 Hwy-140, Mariposa
Ⓣ 1-800/528-1234 or 209/966-7545, Ⓕ 209/966-6353,
Ⓦ www.yosemite-motels.com.
Comfortable chain motel whose fairly large, modern rooms all come with shower/tubs and cable TV, and have access to a heated outdoor pool overlooking a small stream. Continental breakfast is included. Rates down to $55 in winter. ⑤

Sierra House B&B

4981 Indian Peak Rd, Mariposa
Ⓣ 1-800/496-3515 or Ⓣ &
Ⓕ 209/966-3515,

Ⓦ www.sierrahousebnb.com.
Welcoming rural B&B right beside Hwy-49, four miles southeast of Mariposa. The three rooms all have private facilities, though you'll need to snag the Middle East Room (⑤) to get a clawfoot bath. A full breakfast is served, and you can plan your day in the lounge or out on the sunny porch. ④

Highland House B&B

3125 Wild Dove Lane, Mariposa
Ⓣ 1-888/477-5089 or 209/966-3737, Ⓕ 209/966-7277 Ⓦ www
.highlandhousebandb.com.
Tucked away amid ponderosa pines over six miles off Hwy-140, this superb B&B is worth the effort to reach. Its three elegantly furnished rooms all have private bath with tub and shower, and the suite (⑦) has a four-poster bed, fireplace and TV/VCR. The breakfasts are wonderful, and the common area even has a pool table. ⑤

HOTELS, MOTELS, LODGES AND B&BS

HWY-41: OAKHURST AND FISH CAMP

The following are listed in order of distance from the Park's South Entrance.

Owl's Nest Lodging

1235 Hwy-41, Fish Camp
Ⓣ559/683-3484, Ⓕ683-3486,
Ⓔowlsnest@sierratel.com.
Perhaps the best deal south of the Park, the *Owl's Nest* has large guest rooms for two (❹) and self-contained chalets that sleep up to six (❻). Nicely decorated, friendly, and right by a stream. Closed Nov–March. ❹–❻

White Chief Mountain Lodge

7776 White Chief Mountain Rd, Fish Camp
Ⓣ559/683-5444, Ⓕ/683-2615,
Ⓔwhitechiefmtnlodge@sierratel .com.
Located just 300 yards off of Hwy-41, the *White Chief* offers clean, basic motel units (❸) and nicer cabins for up to four (❻), along with a very good on-site restaurant (see p.201). Closed Nov–March. ❸–❻

Tenaya Lodge

1122 Hwy-41, Fish Camp
Ⓣ1-800/635-5807 or 559/683-6555, Ⓕ559/683-6147,
Ⓦwww.tenayalodge.com.
Attractive four-star complex with a Southwestern motif and over 200 modern comfortable rooms, three on-site restaurants, indoor and outdoor pools, sauna, hot tubs, a gym and a host of outdoor activities like mountain biking and horseback riding. Midweek winter rates can drop by almost half; in summer it pays to reserve well in advance. ❾

Narrow Gauge Inn

48571 Hwy-41, Fish Camp
Ⓣ1-888/644-9050 or 559/683-7720, Ⓕ559/683-2139,
Ⓦwww.narrowgaugeinn.com.
Attractive lodge with a wide selection of rooms, many with a balcony and views over the forest. All come with phone, TV, and include continental breakfast. There's also a pool

and spa, and a fine on-site restaurant (see p.201). Closed Jan–March. ⑥

Snowline Lodge

42150 Hwy-41, 3 miles north of Oakhurst

ⓣ & ⓕ 559/683-5854.
Slightly run-down motel offering small cabins with bathrooms and TV, plus an outdoor pool. ③

Hounds Tooth Inn

42071 Hwy-41, three miles north of Oakhurst

ⓣ 1-888/642-6610 or 559/642-6600, ⓕ 559/658-2946;
ⓦ www.houndstoothinn.com.
Modern B&B with a dozen individually decorated a/c

rooms, most with either a fireplace or spa bath. Complimentary wine served each evening, and the buffet breakfasts are delicious. ⑥

The Homestead

41110 Road 600, 2.5 miles off Hwy-49 in Ahwahnee, near Oakhurst

ⓣ 559/683-0495, ⓕ 683-8165, ⓦ www.homesteadcottages .com.
A handful of very attractive and beautifully outfitted adobe cottages – a/c, TV, gas grill – each with full self-catering facilities, comfortable lounge area and a nice deck. Two-night minimum stay at weekends. ⑧

HWY-120 EAST AND LEE VINING

The following are listed in order heading east from Tioga Pass.

Tioga Pass Resort

Two miles east of Tioga Pass. No phone reservations, ⓦ www.tiogapassresort.com.
Streamside, woodsy mini-resort geared mostly toward anglers comprising self-contained cabins rented by the week and motel units

with a two-night minimum, along with a grocery store and diner. For advance reservations (essential in July and Aug) write to PO Box 307, Lee Vining, CA 93541. Open late May to mid-Oct. Cabins $840–1015 per week, motel units ④

El Mono Motel
US-395, Lee Vining
℡ 760/647-6310.
Basic motel that's the place to go if you're looking for the cheapest roof over your head around Lee Vining. ❸

Murphey's Motel
US-395, Lee Vining
℡ 1-800/334-6316 or 760/647-6316, ⓦ www.murpheys yosemite.com.
Very clean and well presented motel in the center of town, with satellite TV and a large hot tub. Some units have a kitchen at no extra cost, and there are bathrooms with both shower and tub. ❹

CAMPGROUNDS AND RV PARKS

As with any national park, **camping** is the best way to really feel part of your surroundings in Yosemite, though this is perhaps less true in the Valley, where the large campgrounds are crowded, especially from May to September. Around 700,000 people camp in the Valley annually; rules here are strictly imposed and camping outside of recognized sites is forbidden. In other parts of the Park, things improve dramatically with a number of delightful road-accessible campgrounds.

Park campgrounds vary in altitude from 4000 feet in Yosemite Valley to 8600 feet at Tuolumne Meadows. Take note of the altitude listed under each campground: a balmy summer evening in the Valley could easily be decidedly chilly in Tuolumne. Wherever they are, Park campgrounds are all set amid pines and are eternally dusty affairs. Typically costing $18 per site, they offer toilets with plumbing, potable water, and space for up to six people (including children) and two vehicles. Several have more limited facilities and charge less. In addition, there is the *Camp 4* walk-in site in the Valley, and a couple of tent-only sites outside.

Outside of the Park there are a number of commercial campgrounds along the access roads. Most have some tent sites, but generally cater to RVs and offer all manner of facilities and charge accordingly. Since Yosemite is surrounded by national forests, there is also a wide selection of simple USFS campgrounds that supplement the Park's sites when filled.

Reservations

Campgrounds in the Park remain busy for most of the year, even winter weekends. If headed for one of the first-come, first-served campgrounds, you'll usually get a place if you arrive before noon, though chances are better midweek. At bookable campgrounds, **reserve** beforehand through the National Park Reservation System (NPRS), which accepts mail reservations at NPRS, PO Box 1600, Cumberland, MD 21502, and takes phone bookings daily from 7am to 7pm. Within the US and Canada call ☏1-800/436-7275, from outside the US or Canada ☏301/722-1257, or book through the website at ⓦreservations.nps.gov. Reservations open up in one-month chunks, **four to five months in advance**. To book for the period between July 15 and August 14, for example, you should call or check the site from March 15, or, if booking by mail, ensure your letter arrives up to two weeks before the opening date for your desired dates (not more, otherwise your request will be returned). Include the desired campground and dates, number of people and pets, use of tent or RV (including length of vehicle), method of payment, and any eligible discounts such as Golden Age passports (see box p.12). Up to two campsites can be booked at one time; for busy periods it may pay to suggest alternate dates or campgrounds. After booking, any changes or **cancellations** incur a cost of $13.25 per reservation.

Those **without reservations** will need to show up very early in the morning and hope for cancellations at one of the reservations offices: either the Curry Village Reservations Office (Map 4, J4; daily: May to mid-Oct 8am–5pm; mid-Oct to April 8.30am–4.30pm) or its equivalent in Tuolumne Meadows (Map 6, I3; same hours) or Wawona (Map 8, C2; same hours).

Campground practicalities

Camping in Yosemite is restricted to one month per person in any calendar year, but between May and mid-September fourteen days is the **maximum stay**, of which only seven can be spent in the Valley and seven more at Wawona. Check-in and **check-out times** are 10am in Yosemite Valley and noon outside the Valley.

All campgrounds in Yosemite have **tent sites**, often well away from the **RV sites**, which exist at all but three campgrounds – *Camp 4*, *Tamarack* and *Yosemite Creek*. **RVs** over forty feet are not permitted in Valley campgrounds and 35 feet is the maximum in campgrounds outside the Valley. Currently there are **no hookups** of any sort in Yosemite, and sparing generator use is only permitted between 7am and 7pm: **quiet hours** are from 10pm to 6am.

Free **dump stations** exist in Yosemite Valley by the entrance to the *Upper Pines* campground (Map 4, K5; open all year); Wawona (Map 8, C3; open all year) and Tuolumne Meadows (Map 6, H3; June to early Sept). **Pets** are not encouraged in Yosemite campgrounds but are allowed in most (see "Directory" on p.215).

None of the Valley campgrounds have **showers**. To get clean, visit the 24-hour facilities at Curry Village, which cost $2 and include the use of a towel (though outside peak times in summer there is often no one in attendance to either take your money or provide a towel). There are also showers at *Housekeeping Camp* (mid-April to late Oct daily 7am–2pm & 3.30–10pm; $2 with towel), and you can always pay to use the swimming pools at Yosemite Lodge and Curry Village. Outside the Valley, campers can shower at *Tuolumne Meadows Lodge* (daily noon–3.30pm; $2). *Housekeeping Camp* offers public coin-op **laundry** facilities (mid-April to late Oct daily 7am–10pm).

Though no limitations apply in winter, from May to mid-October air quality restrictions in Yosemite Valley allow **campground fires only** between 5pm and 10pm. Neither firewood nor kindling (including pine cones and needles) can be gathered in the Valley, so you'll need to either bring wood with you from outside or buy supplies (around $7 a box) from the stores in Yosemite Village and Curry Village. Campfires are permitted at all times in other areas, but only dead and downed wood may be collected, and not in the giant sequoia groves or above 9600ft. Outside the Valley you can buy firewood at the Wawona and Tuolumne Meadows stores.

IN THE VALLEY

Camp 4 Walk-In

Map 4, A4. Open all year; space for 210 people; 4000ft; $5 per person; shuttle stop 7. First-come, first-served site west of (and away from) the other Valley campgrounds, popular with rock climbers. It is a fairly bohemian place with six-person sites just a few yards from the dusty parking lot. The campground is often full by 9am, especially in spring and fall, so join the line early. There's piped water and flush toilets, but no showers, and inadequate washing facilities. No pets.

Lower Pines

Map 4, I4. March–Oct; 60 tent and RV sites; 4000ft; $18; shuttle stop 19. One of three almost identical Valley campgrounds surrounded by evergreens (along with North Pines and Upper Pines), with the Merced River running along one side, and Stoneman Meadow on the other. The only Valley campground specifically designed with wheelchair-accessible sites, it also has RV and tent sites with tap water, flush toilets, picnic tables and fire pits. The Curry Village showers are close by, and there's an amphitheater for ranger programs.

North Pines

Map 4, J4. April to mid-Oct; 81 tent and RV sites; 4000ft; $18; shuttle stop 18.
Similar to Lower Pines (p.183) but slightly more isolated from Curry Village and a touch quieter.

Upper Pines

Map 4, K5. Open all year; 238 tent and RV sites; 4000ft; $18; shuttle stop 15.
Easily the biggest of the Valley campgrounds with pine-shrouded sites, toilets, water, and fire rings; especially popular with RVers. It has the Valley's only RV dump station, which can also be used by guests staying at other campgrounds.

THE REST OF THE PARK

Bridalveil Creek

Map 3, H7. July to early Sept; 110 tent and RV sites; 7200ft; $12.
A high-country first-come, first-served site just off Glacier Point Rd, and a cooler midsummer alternative to the Valley campgrounds. Set beside Bridalveil Creek, its access to wilderness trails is excellent. Snow can stick around here well into June.

Crane Flat

Map 5, B12. June–Sept; 166 tent and RV sites; 6200ft; $18.
Northwest of the Valley, at

the beginning of Tioga Rd, this large but appealing reservation-only campground is particularly handy for the Tuolumne and Merced groves of giant sequoias. There's piped water, flush toilets, fire rings, picnic tables, and an evening ranger program.

Hodgdon Meadow

Map 5, A10. Open all year; 105 tent and RV sites; 4900ft; $12–18.
Relatively quiet creekside campground with flush toilets, right on the Park's western boundary, just off

Hwy-120 W. Reservations are required from May to Sept when the cost is $18, but for the rest of the year, when the piped water is turned off, it becomes a $12 first-come, first-served campground.

Porcupine Flat

Map 5, H10. July to mid-Sept; 52 tent and RV sites; 8100ft; $8. Beautifully sited primitive campground along Tioga Rd, nearly forty miles from the Valley but close to Tuolumne Meadows and some important trailheads. Though small, it is often one of the last to fill at busy times, partly because facilities are limited to pit toilets and stream water that should be treated.

Tamarack Flat

Map 5, D12. June to early Sept; 52 tent sites; 6300ft; $8. Small first-come, first-served site two miles down a rough road off Tioga Rd, 23 miles from the Valley and with limited RV access. Pit toilets and stream water only.

Tuolumne Meadows

Map 6, I3. July to late Sept; 304 tent and RV sites; 8600ft; $18. Yosemite's largest campground, but still an attractive affair beside a sub-alpine meadow right by the Tuolumne River. Popular with both car campers and backpackers, it is effectively three campgrounds in one, with half the sites available by advance booking and half by same-day reservation at the office near the entrance. A further 25 sites are only available to backpackers who hold a wilderness permit for the previous or following night ($5 per person). There are flush toilets, piped water and a dump station; showers are available at *Tuolumne Meadows Lodge* for $2 (see p.169).

Wawona

Map 7, A4. Open all year; 93 tent and RV sites; 4000ft; $12–18. The only site in the southern sector of the Park, approximately a mile north of the *Wawona Hotel*, this campground is located right by the south fork of the Merced River, less secluded and shaded than many Park campgrounds, it is nonetheless handy for the Merced Grove of sequoias and the Pioneer Yosemite History Center. Reservations required from May to Sept ($18), but for the rest of the year, when piped water is turned off, it becomes a $12 first-come, first-served campground.

White Wolf

Map 5, F7. July to early Sept; 74 tent and RV sites; 8000ft; $12.

Forest-shrouded first-come, first-served tent and RV campground a mile north of Tioga Rd, midway between the Valley and Tuolumne Meadows. It is a particularly pleasant site with good hiking all around (see Hike 15 and Hike 18), but can be plagued by mosquitoes in June and July. You can buy meals and limited groceries at nearby *White Wolf Lodge* (see p.170).

Yosemite Creek

Map 5, H9. July to early Sept; 75 tent sites; 7700ft; $8.

First-come, first-served tent-only site five miles down a rough road that discourages all except those keen on a bit of solitude. It is often one of the last places to fill up but can still be packed on summer weekends. Basic amenities include pit toilets and stream water that must be treated.

HWY-120 WEST: STANISLAUS NATIONAL FOREST AND GROVELAND

The following are listed in order of distance from Yosemite Valley.

Dimond O

Map 5, A7. Stanislaus National Forest. Evergreen Rd, 25 miles east of Groveland and one mile west of the Big Oak Flat Entrance. April–Nov; 38 sites; 4400ft; $13.

The nearest forested campground to the Valley, located six miles north of Hwy-120, with tent and RV sites, pit toilets, piped water and fishing on the middle fork of the Tuolumne River. Reservable from mid-May to mid-Sept (contact NRRS Ⓣ 1-877/444-6777, Ⓦ www .reserveusa.com); otherwise it's first-come, first-served.

The Pines

Stanislaus National Forest. Hwy-120, nine miles east of Groveland and seventeen miles west of the Big Oak Flat Entrance.

May–Nov; 12 sites; 3200ft; $10.

Standard first-come, first-served Forest Service campground amid the pines, near the Groveland Ranger Station. It has RV and tent sites, toilets and piped water. For kids there's the Little Golden Trail running through the so-called Children's Forest.

Yosemite Pines RV Resort

Half a mile off Hwy-120, one mile east of Groveland and 25 miles west of the Big Oak Flat Entrance Ⓣ 1-800/368-5368 or 209/962-5042, Ⓕ 209/962-5269, Ⓦ www.yosemitepines.com.

Open all year; 160 sites; 3000ft; $17–32.

Major RV park with plenty of activities – pony rides, gold panning, bike rentals, etc – and its own shuttle bus into the Park. Tents can be rented ($8) for tent sites ($17), full hookups ($32) are available, and there's also an array of cabins and units where just about everyone should find something to suit. Units $75, trailers $68, cabins with kitchen and bath $75, basic cabins $49.

HWY-140: MARIPOSA, MIDPINES AND EL PORTAL

- -

The following are listed in order of distance from Yosemite Valley.

Indian Flat RV Park

Hwy-140, eight miles west of the Arch Rock Entrance Ⓣ 209/379-2339.

Open all year; 40 sites; 1400ft;

$25–29.

The nearest hookups to the Valley are at this simple RV park that also has a separate, reasonably shaded tent area, fire rings, picnic tables, and a clean shower block ($5 for nonguests). Rates start at $25 for two people (tent or RV), going up to $27 for power and water and $29 for waste hookup.

McCabe Flat

Turn off Hwy-140 near the Briceburg Information Center, 21 miles west of the Arch Rock Entrance.

Open all year; 1000ft; $10. The handiest of three first-come–first, first-served $10-a-night campgrounds situated along the Merced River each with pit toilets and river water which must be treated. It's 2.3 miles along a fairly rough road on a former trackbed of the Yosemite Railroad.

KOA Yosemite/Mariposa

6323 Hwy-140, Midpines, six miles east of Mariposa, 27 miles west of the Arch Rock Entrance ☎1-800/562-9391 or 209/966-2201, ✉koa@yosemite.net. Open all year; 46 sites; 2600ft; $27–38.

Full-facility RV-oriented site with a separate woodland tent area, laundry, outdoor swimming pool, on-site catch and release lake fishing, TV lounge, and convenience store. Basic tent sites are $27, full hookups cost $38, and there are log cabins ($48), some with decks overlooking the fishing pond.

HWY-41: OAKHURST AND FISH CAMP

The following are listed in order of distance from the Park's South Entrance.

Summerdale

Map 7, D8. Sierra National Forest, 1.5 miles south of the South Entrance and half a mile north of Fish Camp ☎1-877/444-6777; ⓦwww.r5.fs.fed.us/sierra.

May–Oct; 30 sites; 5000ft; $14. Primarily wooded site that takes the overflow when the Wawona site is full; consequently, it's packed most summer weekends.

Nelder Grove

Sierra National Forest, off Sky Ranch Rd, 8 miles east of Hwy-41 ⓣ 1-877/444-6777, ⓦ www.r5.fs.fed.us/sierra. Open all year; 7 sites; 5500ft; free. Primitive, waterless campground inconveniently sited along winding roads some distance from the Park, but it is free and is close to a grove of sequoias threaded by a nature trail.

High Sierra RV & Mobile Park

40389 Hwy-41, Oakhurst ⓣ 559/683-7662, ⓦ www.highsierrarv.com. Open all year; 126 sites; 2000ft; tents $18, hookups $23. Small RV park in the heart of Oakhurst with electricity and water hookups and clean facilities.

HWY-120 EAST: INYO NATIONAL FOREST AND LEE VINING

The following are listed in order heading east from Tioga Pass.

Tioga Lake

Inyo National Forest, one mile east of Tioga Pass Entrance. June to mid-Oct. 13 sites; 9700ft; $12. Located lakeside with a real alpine feel, this is the best of the highway-side Inyo National Forest campgrounds. It is a first-come, first-served RV-dominated site that's popular when Tuolumne Meadows is full. There are flush toilets, pump water, fire rings and picnic tables.

Junction

Inyo National Forest, 2.2 miles east of Tioga Pass Entrance ⓣ 760/872-4240. June to mid-Oct; 13 sites; 9600ft; $7. First-come, first-served tent and RV site arranged around a meadow, popular with anglers. Less appealing than *Tioga Lake* but half the price and with the pleasant Nunatak Nature Trail just nearby. Pit toilets, and stream water that must be treated.

CAMPGROUNDS AND RV PARKS

Sawmill Walk-in

Mile 1.5 Saddlebag Lake Rd,
3.7 miles from the Tioga Pass
Entrance.
June to mid-Oct; 12 sites;
9800ft; $7.

Primitive walk-in
campground approximately
four hundred yards from its
parking lot, superbly sited
amid jagged peaks that feel a
world away from the glaciated
domes around Tuolumne. No
reservations.

Ellery Lake

Inyo National Forest, 2.5 miles
east of Tioga Pass Entrance
℡ 760/872-4240.
June to mid-Oct; 15 sites;
9500ft; $12.

Small campground among
pines and rocks with a high-
mountain feel, but contrary
to the name, it's not next to a
lake. Piped water.

Lee Vining Creek

Poole Power Plant Rd, roughly
3.5 miles east of Lee Vining and
9 miles west of the Tioga Pass
Entrance.
Late April to end Oct; 7800ft; $7.

A collection of near-identical
streamside campgrounds, all
surrounded by trees and each
with a campground host in
summer. Choose from *Boulder*,
Aspen, *Big Bend*, *Moraine*,
Cattleguard and, the largest of
them, *Lower Lee Vining*.

Campers can take **showers** ($2) and do laundry
at the northern end of Lee Vining at the *Mono Vista
RV Park*, on US-395 (daily 9am–noon & 1–6pm).

Eating and drinking

With the notable exceptions of the *Ahwahnee Dining Room* and the *Mountain Room Restaurant*, **eating** in Yosemite is more a function than a pleasure. Dishes at the better places can be tasty and even, on occasion, decent value (relatively speaking), but food, whether in restaurants or in the grocery stores, is around twenty percent more expensive inside the Park than out.

The cheapest option is to make your own meals, buying **groceries** either outside the Park – Mariposa (see p.85) has the closest large supermarket – or in some of Yosemite's stores. The biggest and most varied is at Yosemite Village, and there are narrower selections at Curry Village, Wawona, Crane Flat and Tuolumne Meadows (summer only). All of these places are fine for putting together a picnic lunch, but you can also order **box lunches** from most of the Park hotels by calling the front desk the night before.

There are enough restaurants and snack bars in Yosemite Valley to satisfy most needs, and many of the more upscale restaurants have alcohol licenses. Most of the Valley's real **drinking** action, though, takes place in the *Mountain Room Lounge* at Yosemite Lodge, with outdoor possibilities at the *Pizza Deck and Terrace Bar* in Curry Village, and more refined imbibing at the bar in the *Ahwahnee Hotel*.

Outside the Valley, Yosemite's restaurant and bar

choices are very limited, and you may be tempted to stray **beyond the Park**. In the gateway towns of Groveland, Merced, Mariposa, Oakhurst, Lee Vining, and around you'll find plenty of good eating establishments charging reasonable prices, as well as a smattering of bars.

We've listed all eating options within the Park and a selection of the best places in the surrounding area, **Normal summer opening hours** are given; expect shorter hours in fall and spring, and occasional winter closures.

IN THE VALLEY

Ahwahnee Bar
Map 4, H3. *Ahwahnee Hotel*; shuttle stop 3.
Mon–Fri noon–11pm, Sat & Sun 11am–11pm. **Food served until 10pm.**
Recently refurbished, this intimate piano bar has a deck and a cozy nook perfect for indulging in a "wine flight" with four half-glasses for $17, a "bourbon flight" of four small shots for $18, or something from their selection of Armagnacs, ports, classic martinis and other cocktails. You can also get light food such as chicken salad ($10), an antipasto plate ($20) and a daily dessert.

Ahwahnee Dining Room
Map 4, H3. *Ahwahnee Hotel*; shuttle stop 3.
Breakfast 7–10.30am; lunch 11.30am–3pm; dinner 5.30–10pm. Sunday brunch 7am–3pm. **Reservations (℡209/372-1489) are essential for dinner and suggested for breakfast and lunch.**
One of the most beautiful restaurants in the US, built in baronial style with 34-foot-high ceilings of exposed pine beams, rustic iron chandeliers, and floor-to-ceiling leaded windows. The food served is by far the best in Yosemite, and the prices are the highest; main courses

range from $25 to $30 and starters are over $10. Dinner might consist of a salmon terrine or an endive and watercress salad followed by seared tuna with shoyu butter and wasabi. Dishes are simpler earlier in the day with items like a three-egg frittata ($13) or an apple crepe ($14) for breakfast, then a portobello mushroom and sundried tomato roll ($11) or a smoked duck Caesar salad ($14.50) for lunch. The Sunday brunch ($32) is particularly sumptuous. Casual dress is permitted during the day, but at dinner formal wear is expected (sports coats are available free of charge).

Coffee Corner & Ice Cream Corner
Map 4, I5. Curry Village; shuttle stops 14 and 20. Coffee 6am–10pm, ice cream noon–10pm.
Simple coffee bar serving light breakfasts, moderately palatable espresso coffees, pastries, muffins and ice cream starting from around $1.30.

Curry Taqueria
Map 4, I5. Curry Village; shuttle stops 14 and 20. Daily 11am–5pm.
Hole-in-the-wall takeout joint with deck seating and simple menu of tasty Tex-Mex concoctions. Choose from a basic taco ($2.40), beef and bean burrito ($4), or taco salad ($5.75).

Curry Village Pavilion
Map 4, I5. Curry Village; shuttle stops 14 and 20. Mid-April to mid-Oct: breakfast 7–10am, dinner 5.30–8pm.
Attractive wood-paneled cafeteria serving all-you-can-eat breakfasts and dinners. Breakfast ($10) is especially good value with plenty of fresh fruit, juices, eggs, bacon, hash browns, waffles, yogurt and the like. Dinner ($12) suffers a little from overcooked vegetables and sloppy preparation but you can still fill up on salads, build-your-own tacos, chicken-fried steak, pasta, and cakes. No alcohol.

IN THE VALLEY

Degnan's Café
Map 4, F2. Yosemite Village; shuttle stop 4.

Daily 7am–3pm.

Reasonable espresso coffees and specialty teas plus a selection of Danishes, cinnamon rolls (both around $2), and lunchtime wraps ($3–6). Good spot for a light bite, and outside seating is available.

Degnan's Deli
Map 4, F2. Yosemite Village; shuttle stop 4.

Daily 7am–7pm.

Some of the best takeout in the Valley with bowls of soup ($2.50–3.25) and chili ($4–5), and massive sandwiches, burritos and salads at under $6 – try Yosemite Sam's, a pastrami sandwich big enough for two small appetites. There's also a small selection of snacks and drinks.

Degnan's Loft
Map 4, F2. Yosemite Village; shuttle stop 4.

Mid-April to Oct daily noon–9pm.

Though lacking the atmosphere of the *Pizza Patio* in Curry Village (see opposite), this is *the* place for gourmet pizzas ($17–22 for a large) such as chicken pesto or "The Mountain," laden with pepperoni, sausage, ham, tomato, olives, etc. You can also select from soups, salads, draft beers and bottled wines.

Mountain Room Lounge
Map 4, C3. *Yosemite Lodge*; shuttle stop 8.

Mon–Fri 4–10pm, Sat & Sun noon–10pm.

The Valley's only straightforward drinking bar, particularly convivial in cold or inclement weather when everyone huddles around the huge circular central fireplace heated by a big brazier. There's a full bar service, and outdoor seats to escape the continual sports TV inside. Light snacks are available.

Mountain Room Restaurant
Map 4, C3. *Yosemite Lodge*; shuttle stop 8.

Daily 5.30–9pm; reserve through YCS on ☎ 559/252-4848.

Second only to the *Ahwahnee Dining Room* (see p.192) in the culinary hierarchy, the *Mountain Room* offers formal dining in a more modern setting, with huge picture windows facing Yosemite Falls. The short menu includes soup ($3), then perhaps an appetizer of lamb shank ravioli with candied shallots ($10) followed by Moroccan-style pork rib roast with couscous and red onion and apple relish ($23), topped off with a raisin bread pudding smothered in caramelized banana rum sauce ($7).

Pizza Patio and Terrace Bar

Map 4, I5. Curry Village; Shuttle stops 14 and 20.
Pizza noon–9pm, drinks 4.30–9.30pm.

The place to go on balmy evenings after a hard day of hiking. Fight for an outdoor table while you wait for a pretty decent create-your-own pizza (from $12 for twelve slices), and a pint of good draft beer ($4) or a frosty margarita ($4.50).

Village Grill

Map 4, F3. Yosemite Village; shuttle stops 2 and 10.
April–Oct daily 11am–5pm.

Fast food Yosemite-style with the likes of double cheeseburgers ($5.25), fish sandwiches ($4.25), and burger-fries-and-a-drink combos ($7–9) to eat out on the deck.

Yosemite Lodge Food Court

Map 4, C3. *Yosemite Lodge*; shuttle stop 8.
Coffee and baked goods 6.30am–8pm; breakfast 6.30am–10am; lunch 11.30am–2.30pm; dinner 4.30–8pm.

Bright and cheerful self-serve café/restaurant offering a full range of cold and cooked breakfasts ($4–7), muffins and coffee, plus lunches and dinners that range from a grilled chicken sandwich ($5) or tuna salad ($5) to pasta and meatballs ($9) or chicken with vegetables and rice ($8). Some outdoor seating.

IN THE VALLEY

THE REST OF THE PARK

Tuolumne Meadows Grill
Map 6, H3. Tuolumne Meadows.
Mid-June to late Sept Sun–Thurs 8.30am–6pm Fri & Sat 8am–7pm.
Basically a canvas-roofed shed harboring a takeout fast-food counter with outside seating; poor value, but always popular with hungry hikers. Eggs, bacon, hash browns and biscuits ($6) are served until 11.30am, then it is cheeseburgers ($4), sandwiches ($4.50) and chili dogs ($3.50) until closing.

Tuolumne Meadows Lodge
Map 6, J3.
Mid-June to Sept. Breakfast 7–9am (no reservation necessary); dinner 6pm and 8pm (reserve on ☎209/372-8413).
Family-style tent dining room that mainly caters to lodge guests but also serves non-guests hearty breakfasts ($5–10) and equally filling dinners ($10–17) ranging

from burgers to steak, chicken or trout. Beer and wine are served, and they'll also prepare box lunches ($6.25) if requested before 8pm the night before.

Wawona Hotel Dining Room
Map 8, C3. Dinner reservations for large parties ☎209/375-1425.
Easter–Oct daily, rest of year generally weekends only and holidays. Breakfast 7.30–10am, lunch 11.30am–1.30pm, dinner 5.30–8.30pm, cocktails 5–9.30pm.
White linen tablecloths and uniformed wait staff in a grand century-old room lend this dining room a semi-formal atmosphere, though the food is neither very expensive nor particularly special. Still, you can dine well during the day on items like chicken alfredo, ratatouille or a club sandwich ($8). Dress smart for dinner, which might feature pan-fried trout ($16) and a

raspberry nut cake ($4). In summer you can eat on the broad verandah. Look out, too, for the wonderful Sunday brunch buffet (Easter–Thanksgiving 7.30am–1.30pm), which costs $10.35 before 10.30am, $16.60 afterwards when extra meat dishes are added. The hotel also has a Lawn Barbecue on summer Saturdays (late May to early Sept 5–8pm).

White Wolf Lodge
Map 5, F7.
Mid-June to early Sept.

Breakfast 7.30–9.30am, dinner 6–8pm. **Dinner reservations required on** ☎ 559/252-4848. A simple lodge serving typical American food at wooden tables on the broad verandah or, on chilly evenings, inside by a roaring fire. Standard breakfasts are available, and for dinner expect the likes of chicken, fish of the day or steak ($13–17). There's always a vegetarian dish ($10–12) and a children's menu ($6). Guests can order box lunches ($6.25) and the adjacent store has ready-made sandwiches.

HWY-120 WEST: GROVELAND AND COULTERVILLE

Cocina Michoacana
13955 Hwy-120, Groveland.
Daily 8am–9pm. Closed Sun Jan–March.
Low-priced authentic Mexican spot; six bucks will get you a great breakfast of scrambled eggs with strips of steak, and later they serve a full range of favorites including great fajitas ($16–18 for two) and melt-

in-your-mouth breaded shrimp.

Iron Door
18761 Main St, Groveland
☎ 209/962-6244.
Lunch daily 11am–5pm, dinner Mon–Wed 5–9pm, Thurs–Sun 5–10pm; bar nightly to 2am.
With its grill and soda fountain, the *Iron Door* is a fine place to eat, with

excellent garlic soup, tasty New York steak ($18), buffalo and black bean burgers, and a host of other beautifully prepared dishes. But what makes it special is the atmospheric bar, claimed to be the oldest saloon in California. It comes with pool table and all manner of paraphernalia on the walls, and features a live band most weekends.

Magnolia Saloon & Grill

Hotel Jeffery (see p.173), cnr Hwy-49 and Hwy-132, Coulterville ☎ 1-800/464-3471 or 209/878-3471.
Daily 11am–9pm. Meals Wed–Sun only.
Authentic Old West watering hole, around since 1851 and laden with character. The food is pretty good – burgers, steak sandwiches, ribs, etc – but principally it is a place to drink. You might even catch someone plunking away at the piano in the corner.

The Round Up Barbecue

18745 Back St, Groveland ☎ 209/962-0806.
May–Oct Wed & Thurs

noon–9pm, Fri & Sat noon–10pm, Sun noon–8pm. Lively outdoor barbecue joint with meats pit-grilled over almond wood. Sink your teeth into half-racks of ribs ($8–17), half a chicken ($9) or an equally juicy burger or sandwich ($5–8). Fill up on salad and corn-on-the-cob, and wash it all down with a cold beer.

Victorian Room

Groveland Hotel (see p.172), 18767 Hwy-120, Groveland ☎ 209/962-4000.
Daily 6–9.30pm.
The best restaurant in town with a seasonally changing menu and nightly chef's specials like crab cakes with cilantro and caper sauce, and honey-glazed baby back pork ribs. Expect to pay $40–50 for three courses including a glass or two from their extensive wine list. Reservations suggested in summer.

MERCED

- -

La Nita's

1327 18th St at T ⊺ 209/723-
2291.

Tues–Sat 9am–9.30pm, Sun
8am–9.30pm.

Affordable, authentic
Mexican dining about ten
blocks from the bus station
offering all the expected
staples along with *menudo*
(tripe and hominy soup) and
albondigas (meatballs), both
for $5.

Paul's Place

2991 G St at Alexander
⊺ 209/723-1339.

Daily 6am–midnight.

Very popular diner offering a
broad range of ethnic and
American dishes at very
reasonable prices; try the
Portuguese *linguica* sausage
omelette.

Wired

450 W 18th St at Canal
⊺ 209/386-0206.

Mon & Tues 6am–8pm, Wed–Fri
6am–10pm, Sat 8am–10pm,
Sun 8am–8pm.

Downtown internet café
close to the Transpo Center,
with good coffee, muffins,
bagels and fast web access for
$5 an hour.

HWY-140: MARIPOSA, MIDPINES AND EL PORTAL

- -

The following are listed in order of distance from Yosemite Valley.

Recovery Bistro

Yosemite Bug Hostel & Lodge
(see p.175), Midpines.

Breakfast 7–9.30am, lunch
noon–3pm, dinner 6–9pm.

Excellent-value licensed café
with tasty food at good
prices. Wholesome breakfasts

($4–6), packed lunches
($5.50) and dinners ($7–13)
are served to all-comers. If
you don't mind the slightly
frenetic hostel atmosphere, it's
definitely worth the drive out
for dishes like slow-roasted
Cajun pork or baked trout

199

filet with butter pecan sauce. Good microbrews on tap as well.

High Country Café

Cnr Hwy-140 and Hwy-49, Mariposa.

Mon–Sat 9am–3pm.

Health food café with sandwiches ($5), salads, enchiladas, and carrot cake for dessert. The health food shop next door (Mon–Sat 9am–5pm) offers good bread, organic fruit, and goodies in bulk bins that are perfect for making trail mix.

Java Joe's

Cnr Jesse and 12th sts, Mariposa.

Coffee cart selling the town's best takeout espresso, usually found in the Mariposa Museum parking lot from 10am to 4.30pm.

Charles Street Dinner House

5043 Hwy-140, Mariposa
℡ 209/966-2366.

Wed–Sun 5pm–midnight. Closed Jan.

Mariposa's premier fine dining establishment. Discerning diners might kick off with a Portobello ravioli parmesan ($12) and follow with scallop and abalone served with toasted almonds and lemon butter ($13), making sure to leave space for the mocha ice cream pie ($5). There's a full wine list, and all dishes are cooked to order.

Meadows Ranch Café

5024 Hwy-140, Mariposa
℡ 209/966-4242.

Mon–Sat 7.30am–11pm, Sun 8am–2pm.

An 1896 former general store that's now an excellent family restaurant with attached juice counter, espresso café and bar. Regulars arrive early for tasty baked goods or a hearty breakfast ($5–8), and return throughout the day for sandwiches, burgers, pasta dishes and tacos, mostly under $10.

HWY-41: OAKHURST AND FISH CAMP

The following are listed in order of distance from the Park's South Entrance.

White Chief Mountain Lodge

Hwy-41, Fish Camp ⓣ 559/683-5444. May–Sept 6–9pm.
Simple surroundings, but great value for steaks, fish and sandwiches.

Jackalopes Bar & Grill

Tenaya Lodge (see p.176), 1122 Hwy-41, Fish Camp ⓣ 559/683-6555. Daily 7am–11pm.
The pick of the restaurants at *Tenaya Lodge*, where you can sit outside and order soups, salads, burgers, pizza and pasta, all well prepared and for only a little more than typical diner prices. The *Sierra Restaurant* next door is pricier and more formal.

The Narrow Gauge Inn

48571 Hwy-41, Fish Camp ⓣ 559/683-6446.
May–Oct 5.30–9pm.
Fine dining in an Old World setting with candlelight and a warming fire. Start by dipping sourdough into a rich fondue and continue with charbroiled swordfish or filet mignon. Expect to pay $40 per person, more with wine.

Mountain House

Junction of Hwy-41 and Bass Lake Road, five miles north of Oakhurst ⓣ 559/683-5191.
Daily 6am–9pm
The best of the local diner-style restaurants with burgers, sandwiches, and pasta dishes along with New York steak ($17) and charbroiled trout ($12).

Yosemite Coffee Roasting Company

40879 Hwy-41, a mile north of Oakhurst ⓣ 559/683-8815.
Sun–Thurs 6.30am–7pm, Fri & Sat 6.30am–11pm.
This local java joint with mismatched chairs and modest prices provides a relaxed setting for reading the paper while digging into breakfast burritos, scrumptious muffins,

HWY-41: OAKHURST AND FISH CAMP

sandwiches, cakes and good espresso.

Three Sisters Café
39993 Hwy-41 near junction with Hwy-49, Oakhurst
☎559/642-2253. Breakfast and lunch Wed–Sun 8am–1.15pm; dinner Fri & Sat 5–7.15pm.

Worth planning around their limited opening hours, for breakfasts like chicken-fried pork cutlet with eggs ($7) or eggs forestiere with wild mushroom sauce ($8), and eclectic dinner specials ($15) ranging from lamb scaloppini to Navajo buffalo stew.

HWY-120 EAST: LEE VINING

Mono Inn Restaurant
55620 US-395, almost five miles north of Lee Vining
☎760-647-6581,
ⓦwww.anseladams.com.
May–Sept daily except Tues: lunch noon–2.30pm, dinner 6.30–9.30pm.

Classy but relaxed lakeside restaurant run by Ansel Adams' granddaughter, featuring lovingly prepared meals ($30–40 for the works) on the patio or inside. There's a strong south-of-the-border flavor, with dishes such as medallions of lamb in tomatillo mint sauce accompanied by homemade jalapeño bread. The inn also houses a gallery presenting exhibits by photographers

and an art/gift shop stocking Ansel Adams books and prints.

Nicely's
On US-395 in Lee Vining
☎760/647-6477.
Daily 6am–9pm.

Great 1950s vinyl palace serving up reliable diner food to tourists and dedicated locals. All the standards are offered including three-egg omelettes ($7), burger and fries ($7), breaded steak ($10) and the obligatory slice of one of their many fruit pies ($2.50).

Whoa Nellie Deli
Inside the Tioga Gas Mart at cnr of Hwy-120 and US-395

☏ 760/647-1088.

Daily 8am–5pm.

The best quick food for miles around is served in this less than inspiring location. Menu items include barbecue chicken sandwiches ($7.50), veggie burgers ($7.50) and their celebrated fish tacos ($9). There's also pizza by the slice and pitchers of margaritas and microbrews. Carry-out is available.

HWY-120 EAST: LEE VINING

Entertainment and family activities

With boundless opportunities for sightseeing, hiking, and other outdoor pursuits, most of Yosemite's visitors have little trouble keeping busy, but your experience here can be greatly enhanced by taking advantage of some of the Park's organized activities and entertainment, the majority of which are in the form of **ranger programs** and include walks, talks and campfires. Put on by the Park Service in conjunction with Yosemite Concession Services and occasionally other parties, most are free, informative, and fun, and though the Valley hosts the majority of events, they take place all over the Park. Activities vary with the seasons, with most happening from April or May until the end of September. There are also **films**, **slide presentations**, and **musical acts**, which generally take place at night. Not surprisingly, many of the programs are family oriented, and a number of them are aimed specifically at **kids**.

See the latest *Yosemite Today* for full listings and schedules of the following programs.

DAYTIME PROGRAMS AND WALKS

Various ranger-led walks fan out around the Valley during the day. The program is constantly changing, but typical topics include animals and their tracks, Yosemite's first people, and how to catch a fish. Valley-based **photo walks** (also known as camera walks; see box p.147) set off around 8am or 9am and usually last an hour, with an experienced photographer advising on how to capture Yosemite at its best. Though perfect for keen novices, the level they're pitched at depends largely on the group; the walks run by the Ansel Adams Gallery tend to be more technical.

Elsewhere in the Park, Tuolumne and Wawona have more modest ranger programs. Glacier Point frequently has sunset talks and an occasional sunset photo shoot, and Tuolumne Meadows sometimes has star viewing walks.

TALKS, FILMS, SHOWS AND CAMPFIRES

Few come to Yosemite expecting more from their **evening entertainment** than a few yarns and a beer or two around the campfire, but once the sun goes down, much of the action in the Valley concentrates around the amphitheaters at Curry Village and Yosemite Lodge, where a full **evening program** of talks, films (including one on the Firefall – see p.44), and slide shows take place. Look out also for the *Yosemite Theater* program which presents two ninety-minute one-man shows featuring the talents of actor **Lee Stetson**, who has been impersonating John Muir since 1982. The admirable "Conversations with a Tramp" (Tues, Thurs & Sat 8pm; $7) focuses on Muir's two-year battle to save Hetch Hetchy, while "The Spirit of John Muir" (Wed & Fri 8pm; $7) evokes the spirit of Yosemite's foremost conservationist and his encounters with nature in the American wilderness. Both shows take place in the East Auditorium behind the main visitor center.

A sporadic event to catch if you can is one of the talks or film shows introduced by paraplegic **Mark Wellman**, who made history in 1989 by climbing El Capitan and followed this feat by an ascent of Half Dome in 1991 and a second El Cap assault in 1999. His book *Climbing Back* (Mark Wellman and John Flinn; Globe Pequot Press; $15) tells of his return to climbing, and the inspirational video *No Barriers* also features the skiing and kayaking adventures of other disabled athletes.

The eternal mainstay outside the Valley is the **Ranger Campfire**, an hour-long talk around a roaring campfire on most nights in summer (and weekends in spring and fall) at the campgrounds in Tuolumne Meadows and Wawona, and occasionally at other campgrounds.

If you're interested in a little vaudeville music and Yosemite history, check out pianist **Tom Bopp**'s entertaining (if somewhat cheesy) act at the *Wawona Hotel* lounge. He usually performs one of his two shows, "Vintage Songs of Yosemite" or "History of Wawona" (8.30pm; free) a couple of times a week in summer, which include an interesting slide show along with the music (see p.76).

KIDS' YOSEMITE

Yosemite can be a great place for **kids**, what with all the adventuring, camping, and swimming to be done – just don't expect them to thank you for dragging them on long treks. Taking advantage of a few of the organized activities targeted at children will supplement the above nicely.

One of the best ways to prepare kids for exploring Yosemite is to visit the **Nature Center at Happy Isles** (see p.44), which is specifically set up to introduce children and their parents to what's out there alongside the trails.

Here you can borrow (with $50 deposit) an Explorer Pack of guidebooks designed to help identify flowers, trees, animals and geologic features.

The Nature Center is also the place for kids aged 7–13 to join up for the summertime **Junior Ranger Program**, to spend time with a ranger and bring the sheer scale of Yosemite down to something tangible to the young mind; younger kids (aged 3–6) can become **Little Cubs**. Both programs require the purchase of an activity booklet ($3–4), and Junior Rangers receive a certificate upon completion, while the little ones get a Little Cubs button.

Most of the standard ranger programs are suitable for kids – star gazing, learning about bears, etc – but there are also programs designed especially for kids and families such as campfire sing-alongs, stories, and even a children's photo walk.

Another favorite is the **Art Activity Center** (mid-April to early Oct and Thanksgiving week daily 9.30am–5pm), in Yosemite Village, which has free art classes for children (generally ten years and over). Kids might also enjoy the hands-on section of the **Yosemite Museum** (see p.35) as well as demonstrations of **basket weaving**.

In winter, the Badger Pass Ski Area is a great place for families, with an extensive kids program (see box p.156).

Groceries, gear and gifts

W hen you find yourself looking for that perfect Yosemite souvenir, there are several places to avail yourself of a "Go Climb a Rock!" T-shirt or a Half Dome paperweight. Other **shopping** needs are likely to be more practical – groceries, film, books and, for hikers and climbers, whatever equipment was left at home.

The vast majority of shops are in Yosemite Valley, with only the bare minimum found elsewhere, principally Crane Flat, Tuolumne Meadows, and Wawona. **Prices** for groceries and incidentals are around twenty percent higher than outside the Park, and souvenirs range from cheap trinkets to elegant and expensive Native crafts.

ALL-PURPOSE SHOPS: FILM, FOOD, ETC . . .

The Yosemite Village Store (Map 4, F2; shuttle stop 2; daily 8am–8pm or later) is easily the biggest shop, with a huge gift department, a book corner, and a small supermarket stocking the Park's best selection of groceries, beer and wine, and even **fresh fruit and vegetables** (virtually unheard of elsewhere in the Valley). Nearby, there's a smaller selection of snacks at *Degnan's Deli* (see "Eating," p.194).

We've quoted normal summer opening hours for the following stores; expect shorter hours in the spring and fall, and occasional winter closures.

The Curry Village Store (Map 4, I5; shuttle stops 14 and 20; daily 8am–10pm) is strong on souvenirs, film, beer, ice and firewood, and also has groceries, though the emphasis is on ready-to-eat snack food rather than raw materials for cooking. Much the same can be said for both the Yosemite Lodge Store (Map 4, C3; shuttle stop 8; daily 8am–8pm) and the Housekeeping Camp Store (Map 4, G4; shuttle stop 12; May–Sept daily 8am–8pm).

Outside the Valley, shops are scarce. The best bets are the stores at Crane Flat (Map 5, B12; daily 8am–8pm), Tuolumne Meadows (Map 6, H3; June–Oct daily 8am–7pm) and Wawona (Map 8, B3; daily 9am–6pm), all of which have film, postcards, books, snacks and a modest grocery selection including ice, beer and wine, and firewood. Elsewhere there is just a very small store at White Wolf (Map 5, F7; mid-June to early Sept 9am–5pm) and the Glacier Point Snack Stand and Gift Shop (Map 4, I7; June–Sept daily: snacks 9am–4pm, gifts 9am–7pm).

BOOKS, PRINTS AND NEWSPAPERS

All the stores mentioned above sell postcards, magazines and Yosemite-related guides and videos, but a couple of places offer a more specialized selection of **books**. First stop should be the Yosemite Valley Visitor Center (see p.34), which has a wide range of maps and books on the Park's flora and fauna, Native legends and social history.

Anyone interested in **photography** should devote some

time to the **Ansel Adams Gallery** (Map 4, F2, shuttle stops 4 and 5; daily 9am–5pm; ⓦwww.anseladams.com), which specializes in work by the world-renowned photographer (see box p.42), from postcards, calendars and photographic books to posters and high-grade prints. Adams' successors are also represented, and there is usually a display of images by a photographer currently working in the field. The gallery also has a healthy selection of outdoors- and ecology-based books on the Sierra and the greater American West, as well as a reasonable choice of novels.

Fine art books and painting materials can be obtained from the Art Activity Center (Map 4, E2; mid-April to early Oct daily 9.30am–5pm), and The Curry Village Mountain Shop (see below) stocks **climbing and hiking guides. Newspapers** – the *New York Times*, *LA Times*, *San Francisco Chronicle*, *USA Today*, *Fresno Bee* and others – are available from boxes outside Degnan's in Yosemite Village, in front of the Curry Village Mountain Shop, near the front desk at *Yosemite Lodge*, and from the Ahwahnee Sweet Shop (daily 7am–10pm) inside the *Ahwahnee Hotel*.

OUTDOOR EQUIPMENT

While cost-conscious hikers and campers should bring their **gear** with them, almost all the **backpacking supplies** you're likely to need can be bought within the Park at high but not unreasonable prices. The best stocked shop for serious outdoor gear is the Curry Village Mountain Shop (Map 4, I5; daily 8.30am–6pm or later), which sells tents, sleeping bags, thermal and waterproof clothing, cooking gear and fuel, dried meals, and a full range of **climbing equipment**. A more modest range of gear is available at the Village Sport Shop (Map 4, E2; daily 9am–5pm), which also stocks **fishing** essentials.

Outside the Valley, make for the Tuolumne Meadows

Sport Shop (Map 6, H3; June–Sept daily 9am–6pm), a smaller cousin of the Curry Village Mountain Shop located at the gas station close to the *Tuolumne Meadows Grill*. More specialized sports stores include the Wawona Golf Shop (Map 8, C3; May–Sept Mon–Fri 8am–6pm Sat & Sun 7am–6pm), and the winter-only Badger Pass Sport Shop (Map 3, F7; daily 9am–5pm), which sells **ski clothing**, sunglasses, waxes and other incidentals.

SOUVENIRS AND SPECIALTY GIFT SHOPS

The **gift shops** at grocery stores in Yosemite Village and Curry Village, and at *Yosemite Lodge* (see "All-purpose shops" p.208) mostly have uninspired souvenirs such as stuffed bears and Yosemite baseball caps. For something a little more imaginative, try Yosemite Village's Habitat Yosemite (Map 4, F2; shuttle stop 4; daily 9am–6pm) and *Yosemite Lodge*'s Nature Shop (Map 4, C3; shuttle stop 8; daily 9am–6pm), both of which sell Yosemite-branded clothing and Native artwork along with postcards, videos and the like. For Native pieces, an even better bet is the Museum Store (Map 4, E2; daily 9am–5pm, closed for lunch), with its appealing displays of beadwork and silver jewelry, soaproot baskets, Miwok charmstones and Native books, much of it quite affordable. Price and quality go up appreciably at the Ahwahnee Gift Shop (Map 4, H3; shuttle stop 3; daily 8am–9pm) at the *Ahwahnee Hotel*, which also specializes in authentic Native American jewelry along with handicrafts, rugs, leather goods, works by local artists, Ansel Adams prints and more.

Outside the Valley, the Big Tree Gift Shop (Map 7, F7; May–Sept daily 9am–6pm) in Mariposa Grove, features all things sequoia.

Directory

BABYSITTING There is no formal system, but staff at the *Yosemite Lodge* and *Ahwahnee Hotel* can often arrange something for their guests.

BANKING AND ATMS There are no banks in the Park, but the surrounding towns have full banking facilities and Yosemite Concession Services has a check cashing service (Mon–Thurs 8am–4pm, Fri 8am–6pm, Sat 8am–2pm, Sun 8am–noon) in Yosemite Village in the lobby of the Art Activity Center ($5 fee for each check). In addition, there are 24hr ATMs in the Yosemite Village Store, outside the Art Activity Center, in the lobby of Yosemite Lodge, inside the Curry Village Store, inside the Wawona Store and just outside the Park at the *Yosemite View Lodge* in El Portal. Most retail outlets accept cash, US$ traveler's checks and credit cards.

BEAR-RESISTANT FOOD CANISTERS These can be rented for $3 with a $75 deposit per trip (no matter how long) from the Yosemite Village Sports Shop, the Yosemite Valley wilderness center, the Curry Village Mountain Shop, Tuolumne Meadows Mountaineering School, Tuolumne Meadows Store, Crane Flat Store, Big Oak Flat Information Station, Wawona Store, and Wawona Information Station. You can also buy canisters ($75) from sports shops in the Valley.

BINOCULARS These can be rented from the tour desk at *Yosemite Lodge* for $3 a day.

CAMPFIRES For information on campfires and firewood see p.183; for backcountry campfire regulations see p.136.

CAMPING EQUIPMENT Camping gear can be rented from the Yosemite Mountaineering School at Curry Village – expect to pay $10 for a sleeping bag, $8 for a pack, and comparable rates for tents, snowshoes, etc – and bought from the Village Sport Shop in Yosemite Village or the Mountain Shop in Curry Village. The store in Tuolumne Meadows also stocks camping equipment and climbing gear.

CAR RENTAL The best car rental deals (around $150 a week for a subcompact) are usually at the international airports which serve Yosemite. All the major rental agencies are represented at San Francisco International and Los Angeles' LAX, and Avis, Dollar, Enterprise, Hertz and National handle rental at Fresno Yosemite International. Closer to Yosemite, the best bets are in Merced, where Aide Rent-a-Car, 1530 W 16th St (☎209/722-8085), have vehicles from around $30 a day, and Hertz, 1710 W Hwy-140 at X St (☎1-800/654-3131 or 209/722-4200), charges closer to $40 a day for more recent models and less than $80 a day for 4x4s.

EMERGENCIES ☎911; Yosemite Medical Clinic ☎209/372-4637; Yosemite Dental Clinic ☎209/372-4200; emergency road service ☎209/372-8320.

FILM Virtually every store in the Park sells film. For more specialized needs, visit the Ansel Adams Gallery (see box p.147).

GAS Available at good prices in Oakhurst, and moderate prices in Mariposa and Groveland. Midpines Country Store has some of the best prices around and is reasonably close to Yosemite. In the Park, gas is fairly expensive, but is available year-round at Wawona and Crane Flat, and at Tuolumne Meadows whenever Tioga Pass is open. Hours are printed in the *Yosemite Guide* and most places have 24hr operation with credit and debit cards. The nearest gas to the Valley is Crane Flat, fifteen miles away.

INTERNET ACCESS The Yosemite Village public library (see below) has a couple of machines with free internet access. Demand is high so book in advance (in person); you can only reserve one session a week. There is also free access at the library in Wawona and in the gateway towns (see Chapter 5). Those carrying a laptop will have difficulty finding a dataport in the Park, unless you are staying at the *Ahwahnee Hotel* or *Yosemite Lodge*, the only hotels with phones in rooms.

LAUNDRY FACILITIES See p.182.

LEFT LUGGAGE Yosemite Lodge has a "bellman room" with limited space where nonguests can leave a backpack at no charge. There are a few small lockers (big enough for a medium-sized backpack) close to the tour desk in Curry Village (75¢). The Wilderness Center, visitor centers, and information stations will not store food or equipment. For longer-term storage, some hikers commandeer the bear-proof lockers at the Curry Village parking area or elsewhere.

LIBRARY A public research library (usually Tues–Fri 8am–noon & 1–5pm) is situated upstairs from the museum entrance in Yosemite Village and contains all manner of materials including recent magazines and daily papers. There is also a public library (Mon 11am–2pm, Tues 10am–2pm, Wed 11am–3pm & Thurs 3–6pm) located just west of the Yosemite Museum in a building signed "Girls Club." Outside the Valley you'll find a library at Wawona (see p.76), and more in the gateway towns.

LOST AND FOUND For lost and found in hotels, restaurants, shuttle buses and on tours call YCS at ☏ 209/372-4357; anywhere else, call the Park Service at ☏ 209/379-1001.

MEDICAL ASSISTANCE Yosemite Medical Clinic (Map 4, F2; ☏ 209/372-4637) has 24-hour emergency care and accepts appointments (Mon–Fri 8am–5pm). Consultations cost $120; medication is extra. Dental treatment (Mon–Thurs 8am–4.30pm plus emergency care; ☏ 209/372-4200) is also available. The nearest pharmacies to the Park are in Mariposa and Oakhurst. Serious emergencies are medivaced to Modesto.

PETS The best advice is to leave your dog at home. The Park Service discourages pets by limiting where you can take them. Hiking trails, shuttle buses and accommodation are all off-limits, and dogs cannot be left unattended in vehicles, tents or tied up anywhere. They are, however, allowed in all campgrounds except *Camp 4*, *Tamarack Flat*, and *Porcupine Flat*. Gentle, properly immunized dogs weighing more than ten pounds can be boarded at the kennels at the stables by North Pines (April–Oct; ☏ 209/372-8348, ⓔ vstables@dncinc.com). Don't forget to scoop your dog's poop.

POST OFFICES The main post office is in Yosemite Village (Mon–Fri 8.30am–5pm, Sat 10am–noon) and offers general delivery (Mon–Fri 8.30am–9.30am & 11.30am–5pm); other year-round services exist at Yosemite Lodge (Mon–Fri 9am–1pm & 2–4.30pm) and Wawona (Mon–Fri 9am–5pm, Sat 9am–noon), with summer-only service at Curry Village (June to early Sept Mon–Fri 11.30am–2.30pm) and Tuolumne Meadows (mid-June to mid-Sept Mon–Fri 9am–5pm, Sat 9am–1pm). The latter has general delivery for hikers on the John Muir and Pacific Crest trails. The zip code for the whole of Yosemite National Park is 95389.

RECYCLING Just about anything can be recycled at the Yosemite Village Store Recycling Center (Tues, Thurs, Sat & Sun noon–4pm) and at Curry Village (summer-only); locally bought beverage containers may be returned for a 5¢ deposit at all retail outlets.

RVs RV campers can use all the main campgrounds but there are currently no hook-ups in Yosemite. Dump stations are in Yosemite Valley (*Upper Pines* campground), Wawona and Tuolumne Meadows (summer only).

SHOWERS See p.182.

TAXES Within Yosemite National Park anything federally run is not subject to state tax, but you'll still have 7.5 percent tax added to meals and most items bought in Park shops. The prices quoted for accommodation, tours and activities are all inclusive of tax.

TELEPHONES AND FAX SERVICES Phones are located pretty much everywhere people congregate – including some of the more popular trailheads. Faxes can be received (free of charge) and sent (for a small fee) at the *Ahwahnee Hotel*, Curry Village, Yosemite Lodge and the *Wawona Hotel*: see the hotel secretary or concierge.

TIME Yosemite is on Pacific Standard Time – three hours behind the East Coast, and eight hours behind Greenwich Mean Time.

WEATHER Current conditions and forecasts (including road conditions) are available on the web at ⓦ www.nps.gov/yose or by calling ⓣ 209/372-0200.

WHEELCHAIRS These are available ($5.50 per hour; $21 per day) from the *Yosemite Lodge* and Curry Village bike stands.

DIRECTORY

CONTEXTS

A brief history of Yosemite

Yosemite's written history dates back barely 150 years, to 1851, when gold rush pioneers chased the native Ahwahneechee from their home in what is now Yosemite Valley. Since then its scenic splendor has drawn ever more people: John Muir for its wild beauty, Ansel Adams for its picture-perfect rocks and trees, and millions more to hike, climb the magnificent granite monoliths, or stroll along the meadows.

Early sightings

Native Americans have been visiting Yosemite for over seven thousand years, and the **Ahwahneechee** (see box p.36) have been living here on a more or less permanent basis for the last three thousand. Despite hundreds of years of exploration along the California coast, no non-natives had bothered to penetrate inland far enough to set eyes on Yosemite. The region was still loosely under Spanish rule in 1827 when American fur trappers started arriving in the

Sierra Nevada from Wyoming. Hearing tales of bounty, one Joseph Walker led what is now known as the **Walker Party** over the mountains from Nevada in late 1833. Deep snows claimed the lives of many horses and the party members were in a sorry state as they became the first whites to enter the region. They recorded seeing giant sequoias (probably the Tuolumne Grove) and may have been the first to sight Yosemite Valley from one of the surrounding ridges, though their accounts are too vague to be sure.

The 49ers and the Mariposa Battalion

Non-natives started flooding into the surrounding hills in the immediate aftermath of the 1849 **gold rush**. While the gateway towns of Groveland and Mariposa were important gold settlements, the 49ers left Yosemite alone as there was little to indicate the source of the gold that lay in that direction. But traders and pastoralists followed the gold diggers, and whites were soon encroaching on native territory, threatening their supply of game, stealing land and using their superior firepower to remove anyone who stood in their way. To protect Ahwahneechee interests, raiding parties were dispatched to nearby encampments, and by 1851 the whites in the surrounding towns were losing patience. An initial punitive foray in January 1851 was led by **James Savage**, a trading post owner at the settlement of Big Oak Flat on the Tuolumne River. It met with little success and a month later the fledgling state of California sanctioned the formation of a vigilante group, subsequently dubbed the **Mariposa Battalion**. With Savage installed as "Major" and chief scout, they followed the south fork of the Merced River to present-day Wawona where some Ahwahneechee were captured and others surrendered. The battalion pursued the rest to their villages and became the first non-native Americans to set foot in Yosemite Valley.

While camping in the Valley, the battalion agreed to call the place **Yosemite**, wrongly believing it to be the native name for the area. It turned out, however, that the Ahwahneechee word *yohemite* or *yohometuk* means "some of them are killers," a reference to grizzly bears and possibly their name for the Mariposa Battalion.

White settlement and early tourism

A second expedition by the Mariposa Battalion tracked down the rest of the Ahwahneechee, capturing their chief, **Tenaya**, on the shores of what is now called Tenaya Lake. Defeated, most of the remaining population was relocated to other areas in California's Central Valley, where large numbers succumbed to European diseases. White foresters and farmers now established themselves in Yosemite Valley using the high-country grasslands, particularly Tuolumne Meadows, for summer grazing. Lured by tales of great waterfalls, and tempted by the early paintings of Thomas Ayers, the first 48 **tourists** arrived in the summer of 1855. Word spread rapidly and despite the lack of anything more than a horse trail, numbers of visitors increased. Meanwhile, many of the remaining Ahwahneechee had filtered back to the Valley, the men adopting European dress and working as guides, wranglers and wood-cutters. The women maintained more traditional ways, adapting their basket making to the demands of souvenir hunters.

One of the earliest tourists was mining company employee **Galen Clark**, who, in 1856, quit his job for health reasons and homesteaded 160 acres at what is now Wawona. As the nearby **giant sequoias** of Mariposa Grove became an essential tourist sight, the first stagecoach road was routed this way and visitors spent the night here before continuing to Yosemite Valley. When the focus shifted towards the Valley and hotels began to spring up there, new and more direct roads were pioneered, most of them being cut in the early 1870s.

The Whitney Survey and John Muir

As academic interest in California grew, the **Whitney Survey**, or, more correctly, the California State Geological Survey, was sent, under Josiah D. Whitney, to explore the Sierra Nevada. In the early 1860s they named Mount Whitney along with numerous mountains and features in Yosemite, and developed theories on how glaciers helped shape much of the landscape. They were adamant, though, that Yosemite Valley could only have been caused by some great cataclysm or devastating earthquake. Into this framework strode **John Muir** (see box p.29) who arrived in 1868 and spent much of the next ten years living in or frequently visiting Yosemite, soaking up everything it had to offer and expanding on his theory of the Valley's glacial formation. Muir also became a vociferous advocate for the protection and preservation of the land he had come to love.

Protection and administration

Back in the early 1860s, hoteliers were converting meadows into hay fields and planting orchards. This didn't sit well with public-spirited men of influence, and in 1864 (right in the middle of the Civil War) senator John Conness convinced Congress to establish the **Yosemite Land Grant**, with Yosemite Valley and Mariposa Grove being transferred from federal to state ownership under the guardianship of Galen Clark. As the first public park expressly set aside to protect wilderness, it became the template for the first national park, Yellowstone, which was established in 1872.

Though the Yosemite Grant afforded some protection, Muir wasn't happy with the logging taking place and described the sheep grazing in the meadows as "hoofed locusts." In 1889 he met Robert Underwood Johnson, the editor of the influential *Century* magazine, who convinced Muir to write a couple of articles stating his case. These, and Underwood's machinations in Washington, helped the creation of **Yosemite National Park**, which in 1890 became the nation's third national park (after Yellowstone, in Wyoming, and Sequoia, not too far south of Yosemite). The original Yosemite Grant sections were initially administered separately, but these were incorporated into the national park in 1906 after Muir convinced President Teddy Roosevelt of the benefits of such a move during a camping trip to Yosemite.

Here comes the cavalry

With the creation of the new park, the **cavalry** came to Yosemite to drive out illegal homesteaders, poachers and hopeful prospectors. They stayed in Yosemite until 1914, then after a short unregulated period were replaced in 1916 by rangers from the newly formed **National Park Service**. The Park's protection was also high on the agenda for the **Sierra Club**, the environmental campaigning organization jointly founded by Muir, who became its first president, a position he filled for 22 years until his death.

Yosemite had initially been visited by the relatively well-to-do, but with its designation as a national park, and the existence of several coach roads, numbers increased rapidly and included tourists of varying social classes. In 1899 David and Jennie Curry established **Camp Curry**, the forerunner of today's Curry Village (see box p.41), to cater to these new arrivals in modest fashion, and their business grew quickly. With the arrival of the railroad at El Portal in 1907 and the Park's legalization of automobile traffic in 1913, Yosemite became truly accessible to the public.

When the National Park Service came into being in 1916, the Curry Company earned the main concession to run services in Yosemite for the annual influx of 35,000 visitors.

Modern Yosemite

Throughout the 1920s and 1930s the Park Service sought to further increase visitor numbers with an aggressive policy of Park **development**, which saw the introduction of bear feeding and native dances for the edification of tourists. Facilities that are today considered out of keeping with national park values were keenly promoted with the building of the *Ahwahnee Hotel* in 1927, and the subsequent development of a golf course at Wawona, the ice rink at Curry Village, and the Badger Pass ski area. There was even a failed attempt to bring the 1932 winter Olympics to Yosemite.

By 1930, half a million people a year were visiting Yosemite, and the Park Service was forced to impose controls. Camping in and driving through meadows was banned, and there were greater efforts to manage development. Nonetheless, numbers continued to grow steadily – though the group that initially laid claim to the lands was on its way out. By the late 1960s, the last of the Ahwahneechee residents were effectively forced out of the Valley and their village razed (see p.36).

Meanwhile, the Park's image was growing exponentially thanks largely to the efforts of **Ansel Adams** (see p.42), who had begun photographing the Park to matchless effect as far back as the late 1920s. He also campaigned to maintain Yosemite's ecological values, mainly through his role as a director of the Sierra Club, which he held throughout the mid-century; he even campaigned (unsuccessfully) on his own behalf when he objected to plans to reroute Tioga

Road along the shores of Tenaya Lake.

It was in the 1960s, near the end of Adams' tenure, that climber bums began arriving in droves to scale the great rocks of Yosemite; the decade lives on as the golden age of Yosemite climbing. The counterculture ethic espoused by many climbers flowed through to the next decade when **hippies** started arriving in Yosemite Valley, camping in the meadows, hanging out and generally getting up the noses of uptight rangers. Things came to a head leading up to Independence Day in 1970 with the **Stoneman Meadow Riots**, when mounted rangers fought a pitched battle with the hippies to clear them out of the meadows. A few dozen were jailed for a short time but both sides compromised and peace returned to the Valley.

The decades since have been marked by an increasing tension between visitor numbers and environmental concerns. Recognizing that Yosemite was unable to cope with the strain of so many tourists, in 1980 the Park Service released the **General Management Plan**, a document that engendered much talk but little action. Following several rockfalls close to Valley accommodation and some devastating floods in January 1997 which caused the Park to close for ten weeks, the Park Service came up with the **Final Yosemite Valley Plan** (see p.23), which looks set to dictate the Park's development over the next couple of decades. It's doubtful that the tide of sightseers will be stemmed – estimated at one point in the 1990s to be some four million per year – but perhaps some of the damage to the remaining wilderness will be.

Landscapes and wildlife

Yosemite's landscapes stretch from semi-arid foothills in the west to the alpine summits of the Sierra Nevada in the east, with much of the intervening country covered by mature evergreen forests that John Muir felt were the "grandest and most beautiful in the world." Along with the meadows, streams and lakes, the forests provide habitats for some eighty species of mammals, hundreds of varieties of plants and wildflowers, over two hundred bird species, and dozens of types of reptiles and amphibians.

Land formation

Yosemite National Park is defined by its distinctive granite architecture of domes, spires and waterfall-strung cliffs, much of which was shaped by deep rivers of ice over the last million years. But the formation of the rock itself dates back some 500 million years to a time when what is now Central California was under some primordial sea. Over eons, marine sediments were deposited on the sea floor to form **sedimentary rocks**. Around 200 million years ago,

plate tectonics came into play as the Pacific plate started to slide under the North American plate. As it was subducted, the rock melted then welled up, then cooled underground into dome-shaped blocks of granite. By 50 million years ago, the sea had receded, leaving a gentle landscape of rolling hills with the Merced River winding through hardwood forests on a bed of sedimentary rock with no granite in sight. Over the next forty million years or so the river gradually cut a V-shaped valley three thousand feet deep.

The redwood forests and much of the vegetation familiar today was already established when the Ice Ages began around a million years back. The first wave of glaciation lasted until 250,000 years ago and covered the entire Yosemite area with glaciers forging down the V-shaped river valleys, scouring away the weaker rock to form the classic glacial **U-shaped valley** form. Most of the overlying sedimentary rock was ground away, leaving the awe-inspiring granite features we now know as Half Dome and El Capitan. Thirty thousand years ago, the most recent Ice Age brought the Yosemite Glacier into Yosemite Valley to add the finishing touches.

Glacial effects

Rock carried along by glaciers was deposited at its furthest extent as a **terminal moraine**, which often held back a lake that, over the millennia, filled with sediment to form the characteristic **flat floor** of glaciated valleys. Tributary glaciers carved shallower channels to create **hanging valleys**: Upper Yosemite Fall, Bridalveil Fall and Ribbon Fall all tumble from such features.

The very highest peaks - Cathedral Peak and Unicorn Peak in Tuolumne, for example - always stood above the ice sheet as unglaciated **nunataks** (the name for rocks protruding through the ice), though their lower flanks were carved into deep rock bowls known as **cirques** by infant glaciers. Rocks embedded in the base of glaciers scraped across the bedrock, leaving tell-tale parallel scarring known as **striations**. Around Tuolumne Meadows in particular the grinding effect is so pronounced that large patches of rock were rubbed smooth to form what's known as **glacial polish**, which gleams in the sunlight.

As the world warmed up and the glaciers melted, rocks carried along with the ice were randomly deposited as **erratics**, and large hunks of ice left behind by retreating glaciers melted to form **kettle lakes** in the deep impressions they created. Dana Meadows, east of Tuolumne, contains numerous classic examples.

Flora, fauna and ecosystems

When the last glacier retreated from Yosemite Valley, it left behind a terminal moraine at the foot of El Capitan, and behind that the prehistoric five-mile-long Lake Yosemite. This gradually filled in to form the extensive **meadows** of the Valley floor. As the ground dried out it was colonized by forests of **black oak**, still an important tree in the Valley today and useful as a source of acorns for squirrels and mule deer. When white Americans arrived in the Valley, black oaks predominated. Things began to change when the Park's first guardian, Galen Clark, tried to reduce periodic flooding by dynamiting part of the El Cap moraine, and succeeded in drying out the meadows. Evergreen species such as **ponderosa pine**, **incense cedar** and **Douglas fir** then began to take hold, their saplings shading the young oaks and quickly outgrowing them. Normally, lightning-strike fires would give the oaks a chance, but a century of **fire suppression** until the 1970s gave the evergreens a head start. This is now being redressed with active planting and oak management, something especially visible around

Yosemite Village where the deer are prevented from browsing on the young shoots. Elsewhere in the Valley, **dogwoods** line the riverbanks and bloom profusely in May with a burst of white flowers, and several oak species and **big-leaf maples** populate the talus slopes at the foot of the Valley cliffs.

As well as protecting the black oaks, **environmental management** seeks to bring the Valley ecosystems closer to their natural state by widening bridge abutments so that natural flooding can occur, moving buildings out of flood zones, restricting access to delicate riparian ecosystems and directing swimmers to less vulnerable beaches. Also, meadows have been fenced, boardwalks installed and non-native plants removed.

The most visible mammals in Yosemite are the **mule deer**, which graze the meadows and are virtually oblivious to human activity. **Black bears** are present too, but are usually only seen around campgrounds and parking lots when they're after a free meal. The last Yosemite grizzly bear was killed in 1895. **Chipmunks** show up everywhere in the Valley, especially around campgrounds, where you might also see Douglas and Western Gray **squirrels**, and occasionally **raccoons**.

Of all campground foragers, the boldest and most raucous is the **Steller's jay**, a western cousin of the blue jay, with its bright blue sides and black topknot. **Woodpeckers** can be heard among the trees, especially the pilated, acorn, downey and white-headed varieties, and soaring high on the cliffs you might even spot the **peregrine falcons** which have returned to Yosemite in recent years in small numbers.

The foothills and giant sequoias

As altitude increases, precipitation (both snow and rainfall) increases and temperature decreases, so the low altitude western fringes of the Park are relatively warm and dry. These areas support **chaparral**, made up of low thickets of **canyon oak**, smooth red-barked **manzanita** and scrubby ceanothus, and are the only places in Yosemite where **rattlesnakes** are commonly found.

Higher up, you're into the sort of forest found in Yosemite Valley and around Wawona. Known as **transition forest**, it ranges up to around 8000 feet, and towards the top of the range is where the **giant sequoias** (see box p.79) are found. There are only three groves of these magnificent trees in the Park, and they are usually mixed with **white fir**, characterized by its upright cones, and **Jeffrey pine**, which is similar to the ponderosa but with larger cones. Deer and black bears roam the forests, and there may be very rare sightings of **mountain lions**, which prey on deer both here and up in the high country. Other possible but unlikely sightings include **bobcats** and **coyotes**.

Wildflowers exist throughout the Park, but it is at these middle altitudes where they really stand out. Shooting stars, California cornflower, rein orchid, hellebore, fireweed and many more cover the meadows as the snow melts, the blooming season getting later as you increase in height up to the alpine meadows around Tuolumne.

High country and alpine Yosemite

Between 8000 and 10,000 feet you're in Yosemite's high country, most easily seen from Tioga Road. The forest here is dominated by **lodgepole pine**, which grows in nearly pure stands and can be identified by only having two needles in a cluster (or "bract"). **Red fir**, with its cinnamon-colored bark, is also common, and you'll see the deciduous **aspen** growing in wet meadows.

A few small mammals have adapted themselves to life in the high country where snow covers the ground for seven months of the year; some even remain active under the snow for much of the winter. One such is the **pika**, a guinea pig-like creature that can often be heard making its distinctive "enk" warning whistle when danger is near. Lodgepole chipmunks are very visible, but you'll have to be more vigilant to catch the **Belding's ground squirrel**, often known as the "picket pin" for its habit of standing bolt upright on its hind legs in the meadows.

Up above 10,000 feet, you'll have a chance of spotting the yellow-bellied **marmot**, a large rodent that loves to hide among rock piles high on the Sierra crest.

Rock climbing in Yosemite

Rock climbers the world over flock to Yosemite, drawn by the challenge of inching up three-thousand-foot walls of sheer granite which soar skyward under the California sun. Quite simply, the Valley is seen as the pinnacle of climbing aspiration, thanks to its acres of superb, clean rock, easily accessible world-class routes, and reliable summer weather.

The best place to marvel at climbers' antics is **El Cap Meadows**, always dotted with tourists craning their necks and training binoculars on the biggest slab of granite of them all, El Capitan. The apparently featureless face of El Cap hides hairline crack systems a thousand feet long, seemingly insurmountable overhangs and gargantuan towers topped off with narrow ledges for which only the flea-like figures of climbers give any sense of scale. Look for climbers' brightly colored haul sacks, or come after dark when their glowing headlamps and faint, distant chatter give the game away. Be sure to stick to the roadside when watching, as the meadow is getting trampled from overuse.

The most famous climb in the world, **The Nose** route of El Capitan, traces a line up the prow of the cliff and passes the relative luxury of El Cap Tower. This twenty-foot by six-foot patio, over 1500 feet above the Valley floor, is used as a bivvy spot by climbers who typically spend three to five nights on the route. "In-a-day" attempts usually involve 24 hours of continuous climbing, though the current record (set in late 2001) stands at an astounding three hours and twenty-four minutes.

Bathooks and bugaboos

Many of the most celebrated routes in Yosemite are what's known as "Big Wall" routes, tackled by **aid climbing**, where bits of metal are hammered into cracks and hauled on to achieve upward movement. The demands of ever harder climbs have pushed the development of an extensive armory that's totally baffling to the uninitiated: bathooks, birdbeaks, bongs, bugaboos, circleheads, fifi hooks, a funk-ness device, lost arrows and RURPs are all employed either to grapple a ledge or wedge into cracks of different sizes. The scale of Yosemite's walls is such that few cracks can be followed from bottom to top. To get from one crack to another, climbers employ death-defying **pendulums**, and repeatedly sweep across the face gaining momentum until they can lunge out at a tiny flake or fingertip hold. All this "nailing" and swinging takes time and most Big Wallers are forced to spend nights slung in a kind of lightweight camp bed known as a **portaledge**. Food, gallons of water, sleep-ing bags, warm clothing and wet-weather gear must all be lugged up in haul sacks, along with the seemingly requisite boombox and a rack of cassettes deviously strapped and arranged so they can't be dropped – after all it can get a bit tedious hammering away up there for hours on end.

Some climbing history

Technical rock climbing didn't kick off in the Park until 1933, when four Bay Area climbers used meager equipment to reach what is now known as the **Lunch Ledge**, 1000 feet up Washington Column – the tower opposite Half Dome. With the aid of heavy steel **pitons** for driving into cracks, and equally weighty **carabiners** for attaching the ropes to the pitons, climbers began to knock off climbs such as the fifteen-pitch **Royal Arches** route that weaves its way up the ledges and slabs behind the *Ahwahnee Hotel*.

After World War II, climbers employed newly developed, tough nylon ropes and lightweight safety equipment to raise standards, and pipe dreams became realistic propositions. An early conquest, in 1947, was **Lost Arrow Spire**, which rises to the right of Upper Yosemite Fall. This was the first route intentionally approached as a multiday ascent, much of the groundwork being laid by Swiss-born blacksmith **John Salathé**. He was at the cutting edge of climbing, putting up technically demanding aid routes through the late 1940s and early 1950s, and even fashioning his own carbon-steel pitons from the axles of a Model A Ford.

For the next twenty years Salathé's mantle was assumed by classical purist **Royal Robbins** and by **Warren Harding**, who was prepared to bang in a piton just about anywhere if it would help him get up something new. Little love was lost between them, but when Robbins' team first scaled the face of **Half Dome** Harding was on the summit to congratulate them. It was a magnificent effort and ranked as the hardest climb in North America at the time.

Now even mighty El Cap seemed possible. **The Nose** was the most obvious line but remained stubborn, even after Harding used four massive pitons that had been made from stove legs scavenged from the Berkeley city dump and drove them into what are still known as the Stoveleg

Cracks. Harding and two colleagues finally topped out in 1958 after a single thirteen-day push, the culmination of 47 days work on the route.

With these critical ascents completed, aspirations broadened, and the 1960s heralded a **golden age** of climbing in the Valley, when it drew a motley collection of dropouts and misfits, many among the world's finest climbers. Almost all the major walls and hundreds of minor routes were completed at this time. Purists at the top of their sport became disenchanted with the artificiality of aid ascents and began to favor **free climbing**, using only their body and the rock to ascend, but still employing ropes and assorted hardware for protection in case of a fall. This culminated with **Lynn Hill** doing months of route-specific training before making her groundbreaking free ascent of The Nose in 1993. It was admired by all, if ruefully by some in the traditionally macho climbers' community.

Practicalities

To follow in the paths of these forebears, read Chapter 8, "Summer activities," which has practicalities on climbing and contains information for the Yosemite Mountaineering School and its organized introduction to the sport. The **bulletin board** at **Camp 4**, near *Yosemite Lodge*, a noisy, trampled and dusty site, where pretty much every climber stays, is a useful source as well. Whatever type of climbing you do, follow the guidelines for "**minimum impact climbing**" – never chip holds or add bolts to existing routes, and remove all litter, including human waste.

See also "Books", p.239 for reviews of guides to climbing in Yosemite.

Books

ost of the following books are widely available in stores in Yosemite National Park and the surrounding towns, but may be harder to find further afield and are virtually unseen outside North America. All are available through the major internet booksellers, but try first the Yosemite Store section of the Yosemite Association's website (Ⓦwww.yosemitestore.com), which has all worthwhile Yosemite-related books.

Travel and impressions

John Muir *The Yosemite* (Yosemite Association). There are various paperback versions of this Muir classic, but it is worth splurging on this large-format version, which includes a hundred excellent color photos by Galen Rowell. It contains the full text, a wonderful introduction to the Park, its history, flora, fauna and plenty of full-blooded tales of Muir's adventures.

John Muir *The Wild Muir: 22 of John Muir's Greatest Adventures* (Yosemite Association). Some readers get caught up in Muir's detailed descriptions; this boils it all down to 22 thrilling and often death-defying adventure stories: riding an avalanche from the Valley Rim, scaling Mount Ritter, experiencing a windstorm from atop a tree, and playing chicken with the wind-swayed Yosemite Fall.

John Muir *John Muir, the Eight Wilderness Discovery Books* (Diadem). The Muir completist's bible.

Steve Roper *Camp 4: Recollections of a Yosemite Rockclimber* (Mountaineers Books). The Yosemite veteran tells an entertaining and engag-

ing tale about Yosemite's golden age of climbing during the 1960s. Catches the spirit of the times.

Galen Rowell *Vertical World of Yosemite* (Wilderness Press). Well written and nicely photographed book covering the epic drama of many of the classic Yosemite climbs, often described by those who made the first ascents.

History, people and society

Ansel Adams *An Autobiography* (Little, Brown & Co). Written in his final years, this is a fascinating insight into the man and his work (both photographic and environmental); liberally illustrated with Adams' own photos.

Martha Lee and Stan Johnson *Guide to the Yosemite Cemetery* (Yosemite Association). Pretty self-explanatory, this guide is available from the Valley visitor center for $3.50.

Margaret Sanborn *Yosemite* (Yosemite Association). Probably the best all-around Yosemite history, which avoids

a sequential timeline and focuses instead on specific events and the lives of key players in the Park's development.

Shirley Sargent *Yosemite's Innkeepers* (Ponderosa Press). Sargent, a prolific historian, profiles life in Yosemite's many early inns; an interesting if somewhat specialist read.

Jonathan Spaulding *Ansel Adams and the American Landscape: A Biography* (University of California Press). An important biography of Adams, fully documented and researched, but lacking any of the great man's photos.

BOOKS

Dwight Willard *A Guide to the Sequoia Groves of California* (Yosemite Association). Yosemite's three sequoia groves and the 61 others along a narrow band of the Sierra Nevada are covered. Includes color photos, full details of each grove and the historical framework of their exploitation and preservation.

Native life and legend

S.A. Barrett and E.W. Gifford *Indian Life of the Yosemite Region: Miwok Material Culture* (Yosemite Association). An academic but readable depiction of Miwok life after European contact, researched in the early 1900s and published in 1933. Learn about herbal medicines, basket-making, food production and much more.

Craig D. Bates and Martha J. Lee *Tradition and Innovation: A Basket History of the Indians of the Yosemite-Mono Lake Region* (Yosemite Association). A pricey large-format book with thorough coverage of the history, styles, and techniques of Miwok and Paiute basketry from the Yosemite region.

Frank LaPena, Craig D. Bates, and Steven P. Medley *Legends of the Yosemite Miwok* (Yosemite Association). Contains what are thought to be the most authentic versions of Miwok legends about Park geology and environment. Nicely illustrated, too.

Landscapes: geology, flora and fauna

Gary Brown *The Great Bear Almanac* (Lyons & Burford). Exhaustive tome, full of photos and facts, providing everything you always wanted to know about all types of bears, not just the black variety found in Yosemite.

Richard Ditton and Donald McHenry *Yosemite Road Guide* (Yosemite Association). Just about every wayside point of interest (and many of little interest) along all of Yosemite's roads; reads a bit dated.

David Gaines and Keith Hansen *Birds of Yosemite and the East Slope* (Artemisia Press). The best guide to the birds of Yosemite and the Mono Lake region, fully illustrated with location and occurrence maps, drawings and photos, plus full coverage of all species found in the area.

N. King Huber *The Geologic Story of Yosemite National Park* (Yosemite Association). The most current and authoritative description of how Yosemite was formed, with a minimum of pointy-headedness.

Lynn Wilson, Jim Wilson and Jeff Nicholas *Wildflowers of Yosemite* (Sierra Press). Handy and easy to use guide to identifying Yosemite's wildflowers, with lots of color photos, comprehensible text, and maps to illustrate the range of many species.

Outdoor activity guides

Michael Frye *Photographer's Guide to Yosemite* (Yosemite Association). Color guide to photographing the Park, with numerous technical tips, suggestions for different seasons and times of day, and recommended locations.

John Moynier *Backcountry Skiing California's High Sierra* (Falcon Guides). A collection of day and overnight cross-country skiing and snowboarding routes, including multiday classics and most of the important descents.

Don Reid *Yosemite: Free Climbs* (Falcon Guides). General route descriptions for a huge number of free climbs in the Valley and nearby. *Yosemite: Big Walls* and *Tuolumne Meadows* round out the series.

Jeffrey P. Scheffer *Yosemite National Park: A National History Guide to Yosemite and its Trails* (Wilderness Press). True to its subtitle, with detailed flora, fauna and geology notes for a hundred hikes throughout the Park, plus a supplementary topographic map.

Supertopo (Ⓦwww.supertopo.com) A series of guides giving highly detailed route descriptions for selected climbs. Titles include *Yosemite Ultra Classics*, *Tuolumne Ultra Classics*, *Yosemite Big Walls*, and *The Road to The Nose*.

Michael C. White *Snowshoe Trails of Yosemite* (Wilderness Press). Meticulous details of over forty of the Park's most scenic trails for a range of abilities.

Thomas Winnett and Kathy Morey *Guide to the John Muir Trail* (Wilderness Press). Comprehensive guide to the JMT described in both directions. Includes additional access routes, ascent profiles, numerous maps and full trip-planning details.

INDEX

INDEX

around the world

Alaska ★ Algarve ★ Amsterdam ★ Andalucía ★ Antigua & Barbuda ★ Argentina ★ Auckland Restaurants ★ Australia ★ Austria ★ Bahamas ★ Bali & Lombok ★ Bangkok ★ Barbados ★ Barcelona ★ Beijing ★ Belgium & Luxembourg ★ Belize ★ Berlin ★ Big Island of Hawaii ★ Bolivia ★ Boston ★ Brazil ★ Britain ★ Brittany & Normandy ★ Bruges & Ghent ★ Brussels ★ Budapest ★ Bulgaria ★ California ★ Cambodia ★ Canada ★ Cape Town ★ The Caribbean ★ Central America ★ Chile ★ China ★ Copenhagen ★ Corsica ★ Costa Brava ★ Costa Rica ★ Crete ★ Croatia ★ Cuba ★ Cyprus ★ Czech & Slovak Republics ★ Devon & Cornwall ★ Dodecanese & East Aegean ★ Dominican Republic ★ The Dordogne & the Lot ★ Dublin ★ Ecuador ★ Edinburgh ★ Egypt ★ England ★ Europe ★ First-time Asia ★ First-time Europe ★ Florence ★ Florida ★ France ★ French Hotels & Restaurants ★ Gay & Lesbian Australia ★ Germany ★ Goa ★ Greece ★ Greek Islands ★ Guatemala ★ Hawaii ★ Holland ★ Hong Kong & Macau ★ Honolulu ★ Hungary ★ Ibiza & Formentera ★ Iceland ★ India ★ Indonesia ★ Ionian Islands ★ Ireland ★ Israel & the Palestinian Territories ★ Italy ★ Jamaica ★ Japan ★ Jerusalem ★ Jordan ★ Kenya ★ The Lake District ★ Languedoc & Roussillon ★ Laos ★ Las Vegas ★ Lisbon ★ London ★

in twenty years

London Mini Guide ★ London Restaurants ★ Los Angeles ★ Madeira ★
Madrid ★ Malaysia, Singapore & Brunei ★ Mallorca ★ Malta & Gozo ★ Maui
★ Maya World ★ Melbourne ★ Menorca ★ Mexico ★ Miami & the Florida
Keys ★ Montréal ★ Morocco ★ Moscow ★ Nepal ★ New England ★ New
Orleans ★ New York City ★ New York Mini Guide ★ New York Restaurants
★ New Zealand ★ Norway ★ Pacific Northwest ★ Paris ★ Paris Mini Guide
★ Peru ★ Poland ★ Portugal ★ Prague ★ Provence & the Côte d'Azur ★
Pyrenees ★ The Rocky Mountains ★ Romania ★ Rome ★ San Francisco ★
San Francisco Restaurants ★ Sardinia ★ Scandinavia ★ Scotland ★
Scottish Highlands & Islands ★ Seattle ★ Sicily ★ Singapore ★ South Africa,
Lesotho & Swaziland ★ South India ★ Southeast Asia ★ Southwest USA ★
Spain ★ St Lucia ★ St Petersburg ★ Sweden ★ Switzerland ★ Sydney ★
Syria ★ Tanzania ★ Tenerife and La Gomera ★ Thailand ★ Thailand's
Beaches & Islands ★ Tokyo ★ Toronto ★ Travel Health ★ Trinidad &
Tobago ★ Tunisia ★ Turkey ★ Tuscany & Umbria ★ USA ★ Vancouver ★
Venice & the Veneto ★ Vienna ★ Vietnam ★ Wales ★ Washington DC ★
West Africa ★ Women Travel ★ Yosemite ★ Zanzibar ★ Zimbabwe

also look out for our maps, phrasebooks, music guides and reference books

ROUGH GUIDES | TWENTY YEARS

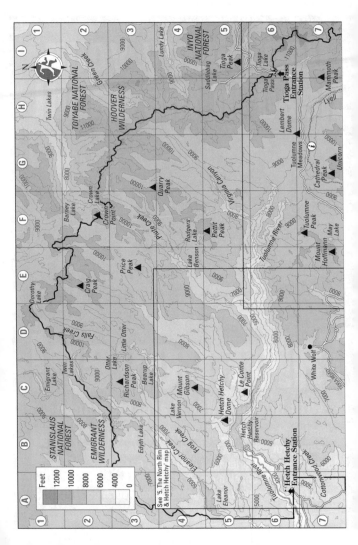

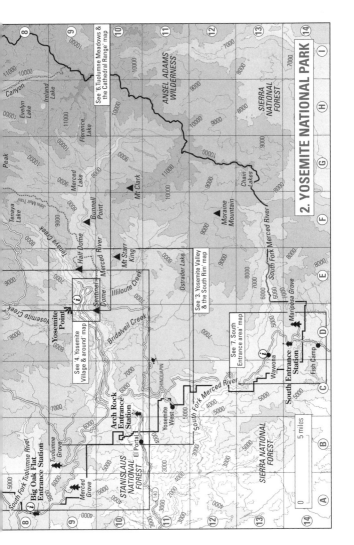

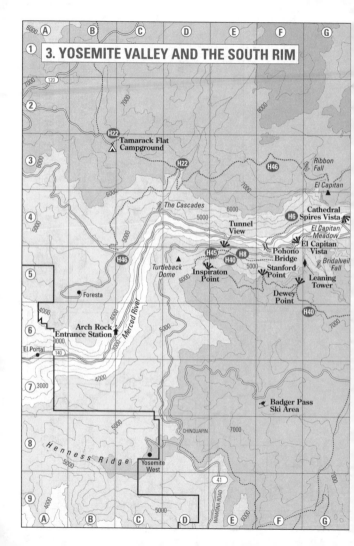

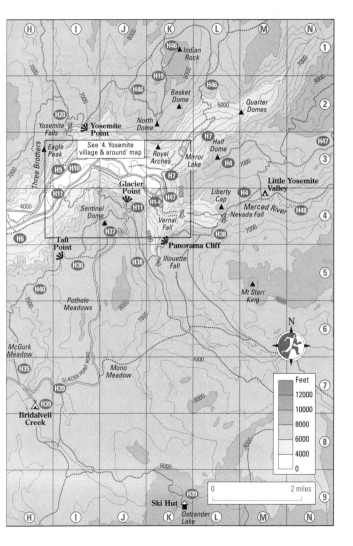

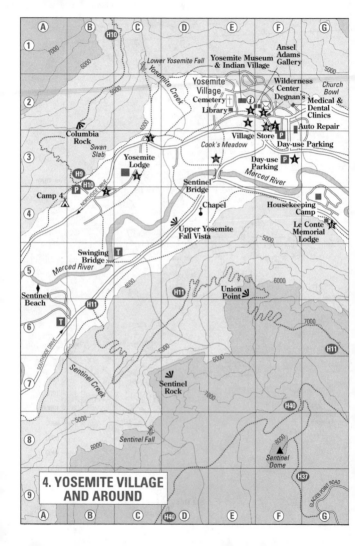

4. YOSEMITE VILLAGE AND AROUND

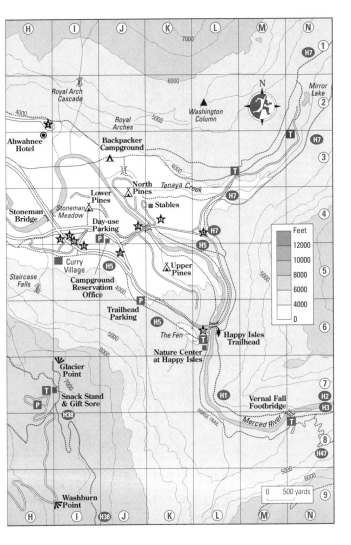

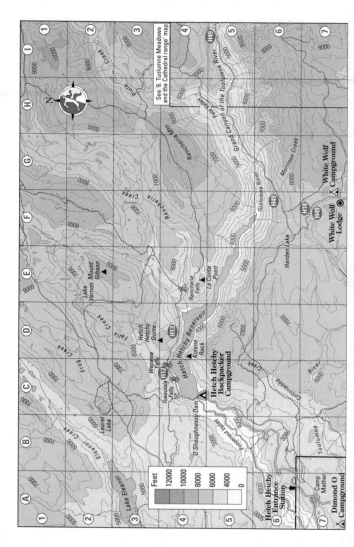

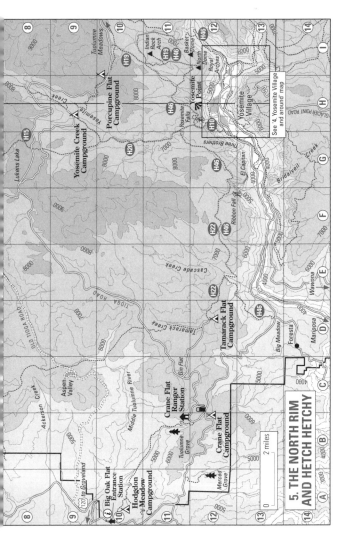

5. THE NORTH RIM AND HETCH HETCHY

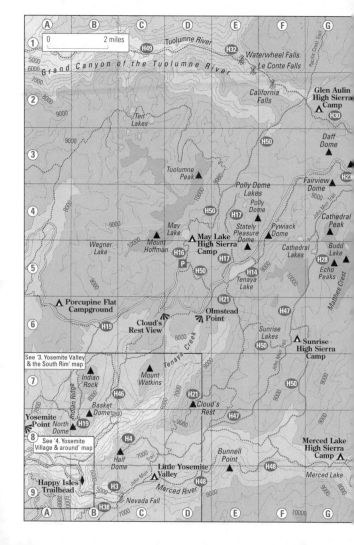

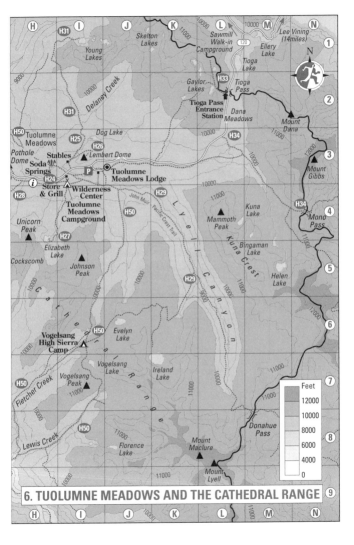

6. TUOLUMNE MEADOWS AND THE CATHEDRAL RANGE

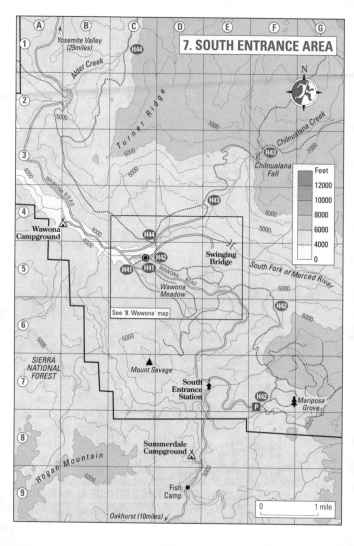

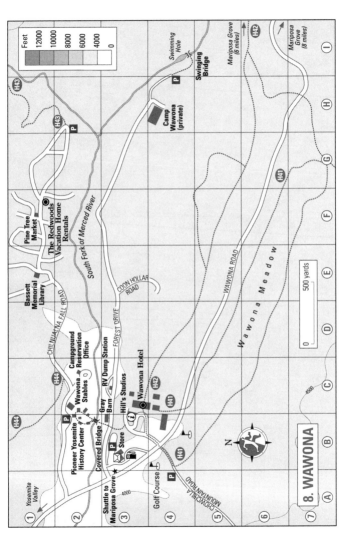

8. WAWONA